IMAGES
of America

MATUNUCK

On the Cover: This photograph was taken in front of the store at Roy Carpenter's Beach in the 1940s. J. Francis Gallogly is just to the left of the chowder sign, wearing a white hat. He has his hand on the shoulder of his brother Felix Gallogly Jr. Directly to J. Francis Gallogly's right is Eleanor Ahearn Gallogly, Felix's wife. (Courtesy of Eleanor Gallogly Mullaney and Margaret Gallogly Navin.)

IMAGES
of America

MATUNUCK

Marilyn Bellemore

ARCADIA
PUBLISHING

ISBN 978-1-4671-2141-5

Published by Arcadia Publishing
Charleston, South Carolina

Printed in the United States of America

Library of Congress Control Number: 2013949191

For all general information, please contact Arcadia Publishing:
Telephone 843-853-2070
Fax 843-853-0044
E-mail sales@arcadiapublishing.com
For customer service and orders:
Toll-Free 1-888-313-2665

Visit us on the Internet at www.arcadiapublishing.com

This book is dedicated to the locals, the tourists, and everyone who has ever enjoyed this place we call Matunuck.

CONTENTS

ACKNOWLEDGMENTS

To the numerous people who contributed to this book, your love of Matunuck is what made it a reality. Thank you for taking the time to share and explain the history of each and every photograph. The stories you told and the help you provided made this project all the more enjoyable. Most importantly, I hope that you refer to this book often as a keepsake and reminder of your connections to Matunuck. Thank you Ann Terry, Timothy J. Riordan, Albert T. Klyberg, David Yale, David Gallogly, Eleanor Gallogly Mullaney, Margaret Gallogly Navin, Regina Russell Goodwin, John Goodwin, Susan Rivera Russo, Jeanne McHenry Helma, Michael McKenna and Peggy Amatore, Mary Ann Gallogly Scott, Thomas James Tetzner, John LaCroix, John and Carol Szymanski, Henry and Rachel Craven, Levon Kasparian, Pat Saber and Seaview Market, Bob Stockley, Bill Ainsworth, Kim Patterson, Cody Carpenter, Bill and Roberta Browning, Jennifer Hopkins Manzo, Raymond Beausejour, Bill Arcand, Dennis McAllister, Tom McVey, Bob McKenna, Bill Leddy, Caitrin Cunningham (editor at Arcadia Publishing), Narragansett Salt Water Fishing Club, University of Rhode Island Special Collections, and Robert Beverly Hale Library.

INTRODUCTION

The village of Matunuck, on the south coast of Rhode Island in the town of South Kingstown, was first inhabited by Native Americans followed by the early Pettaquamscutt settlers. The village takes its name from a Native American word meaning "look out."

South Kingstown grew out of the pioneering settlements in the 17th century known as the Pettaquamscutt Purchase. The early Pettaquamscutt settlers were Samuel Wilbor, John Hull, John Porter, Samuel Wilson, and Thomas Mumford. Later additions were Benedict Arnold and William Brenton.

The scattered farms benefitted from the open expanse of coastal plain, but they did not really flourish until the Native American claims and litigious strife of competing colonial land companies of Massachusetts, Connecticut, and Rhode Island were extinguished in the early 1700s.

Unlike other English settlements in New England, which were carved out of forests, the agricultural pursuits of the Rhode Island farmers were focused on pasturing flock and herd animals as opposed to crop fields. With the establishment of stock raising on the coastal plain came the era of the Narragansett Planters and the Narragansett Pacers horse breed. By the time of the American Revolution, the age of the planters was over. The great farms had been divided and subdivided by the later generations. Focus shifted away from the farms to the streams of South County and the emergence of mills and mill villages between 1800 and 1850.

The earliest attention to tourism potential began at Narragansett Pier before the Civil War. After the Civil War, the pier developed as both a steamboat stop and a railhead, with wealthy people from as far away as St. Louis, Missouri, coming with their own railroad parlor cars to spend the summer at the Casino and grand hotels. Within a five-year period from 1871 to 1875, some 10 hotels were built at the pier.

At the other end of the Atlantic coast, Watch Hill in Westerly had a similar experience at the same time. However, between the pier and Watch Hill, something else was happening. A middle-class clientele was looking at Matunuck, Green Hill, and places in Charlestown.

The idea of play and idleness had been contrary to the Puritan and Dissenting theologies of the early settlers. But, by the 19th century, the positive psychological and physical health values of recreation became acceptable to New England society. Puritan attitudes about leisure and play receded, and it was okay to have fun and relaxation.

First, this took the form of tent colonies on the beach; then local farmers took in boarders. Isolated beach hotels and some cottages sprang up. This would have been at the end of the Civil War, in 1865. It was not easy to get to these spots.

There were some locations that catered to artists and writers, in particular along and near Post Road and the Matunuck Hills. Author Edward Everett Hale was a summer resident. He appreciated the isolated area with its seashore and hilly terrain.

Post Road (Route 1), established in 1702, was the main artery to get into the area. But, real roads into the area had to await the early years of the 20th century. The first highway legislation in Rhode Island for paved roads did not come about until 1904. It was a response to the bicycle craze as much as the automobile interests.

With the beauty of many seaside villages comes the risk of flooding and erosion along the coast. Since the early 1950s, Matunuck's mile-long stretch of waterfront has migrated roughly 300 feet inland. Since 2010, it has accelerated even faster, in part because of a string of storms.

The popular Ocean Mist Beach Bar sits between the ocean and a wall of stone and sod. At high tide, customers who go out to the back deck to enjoy their drinks, the sunset, or a cigarette can see the water run under the wood pilings that support the building. Kevin Finnegan, the bar's owner, recently installed wooden planks under the building to reinforce its foundation. The town of South Kingstown intends to install a wall to protect Matunuck Beach Road, which provides access to residences and businesses.

For more than two decades, parts of the town beach have been destroyed by waves and flooding. Storms took out a row of protective sand dunes and a boardwalk. Hurricane Sandy destroyed a large seating area at the front of the pavilion. Construction of a leaching field is underway to manage wastewater. The pavilion will be moved 300 feet inland as the sea level rises and continues to threaten the entire structure.

For the first time since 1976, the Fourth of July fireworks display at Roy Carpenter's beach community on Cards Pond Road were cancelled. Since the beach is no longer wide enough to provide a safe distance from the cottages, a permit was denied by the fire marshal.

About 377 cottages that make up the community are spaced close together, and many are on cinderblocks. Hurricane Sandy washed away three homes from the front row of cottages. Several others were demolished because of structural damage. Thankfully, there is farmland behind the rows of homes that is available to relocate structures that are too close to the beach.

At nearby Browning Beach stands a home that has piqued the interest of many people because of the structural damage it has endured. It was built hundreds of feet from the beach in 1900 as part of a beach colony of five large Queen Anne shingle-style summer homes. The hurricane of 1938 and Hurricane Carol in 1954 wiped out several of the larger structures. The buildings were moved 50 feet inland because of the continued and increased beach erosion since the 1970s. Finally, damage from Hurricane Sandy led to the demolition of two of the remaining cottages.

It is estimated that two feet of beach is now being washed away each year. The bottom line is that coastal erosion is a natural effect of Matunuck's exposure to the elements in an area prone to nor'easters.

This book focuses on the happier times, as we walk through the community, beaches, and the village of long ago.

One

The Community

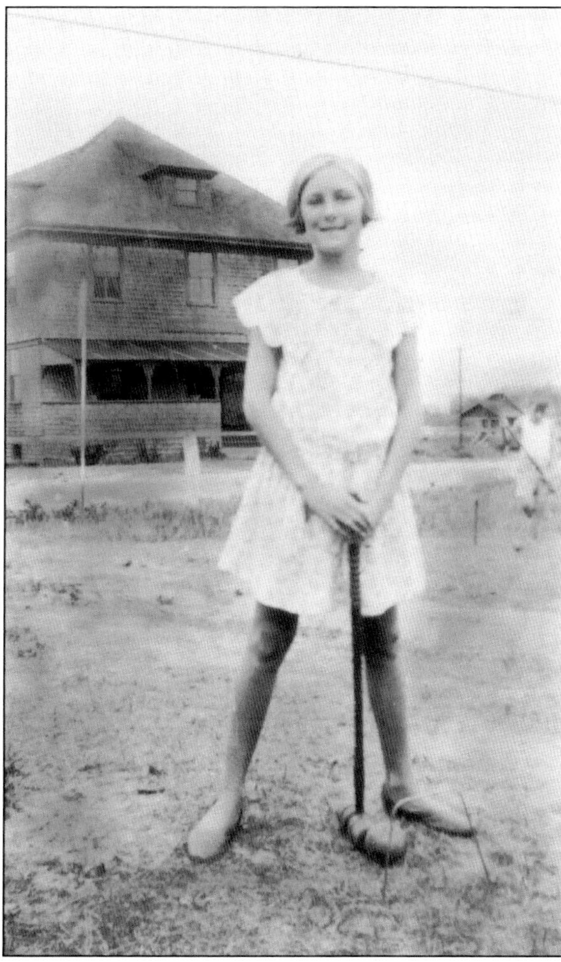

Margaret Gallogly Terry plays a game of croquet in the late 1920s at her family's home, the Lund Cottage, on Matunuck Beach Road. She was the only daughter of Felix Sr. and Margaret Harrington Gallogly, who first came to Matunuck in 1909. (Courtesy of Ann Terry.)

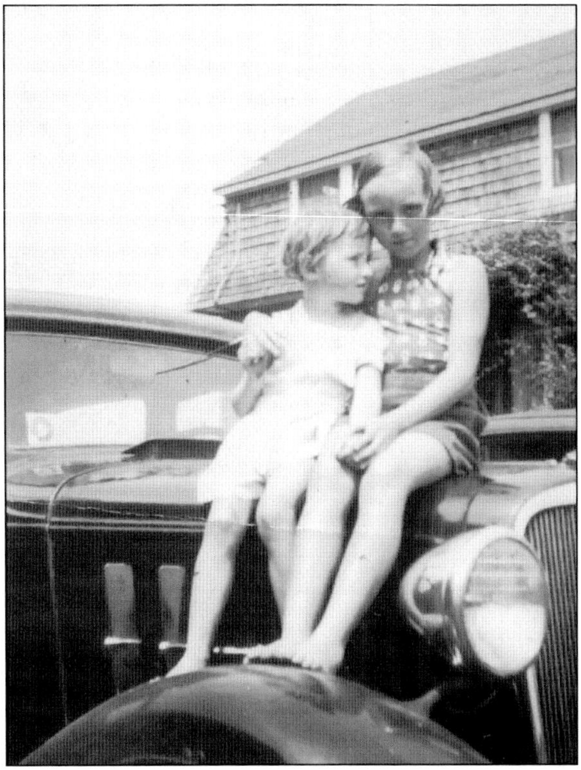

Sisters Helen Russell Henley and Regina Russell Goodwin are at their home on Atlantic Avenue in the 1930s. The girls' parents, Henry and Helen Grady Russell of Providence, bought the property in 1933. The original house was said to have been a store run by Sadie Carpenter, according to John Goodwin, son of Regina Russell Goodwin. (Courtesy of Regina Russell Goodwin.)

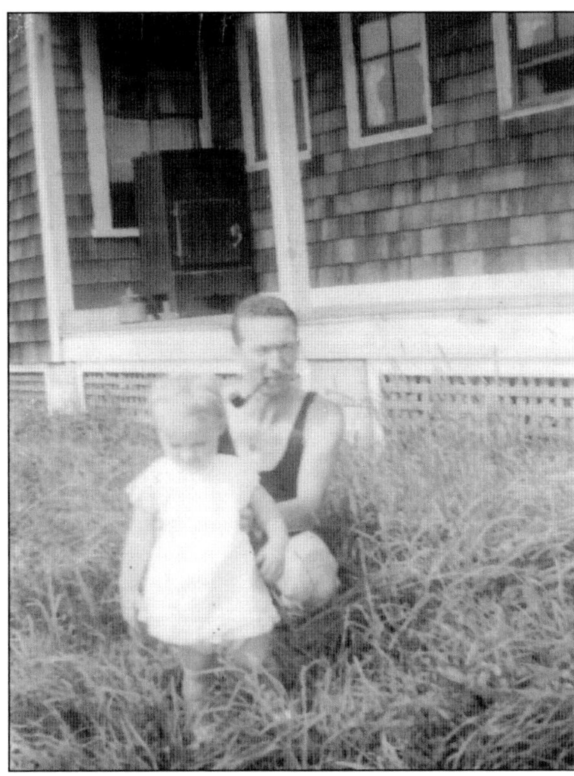

Helen Russell Henley is pictured here with her uncle George Grady in the mid- to late 1930s at her home on Atlantic Avenue. (Courtesy of Regina Russell Goodwin.)

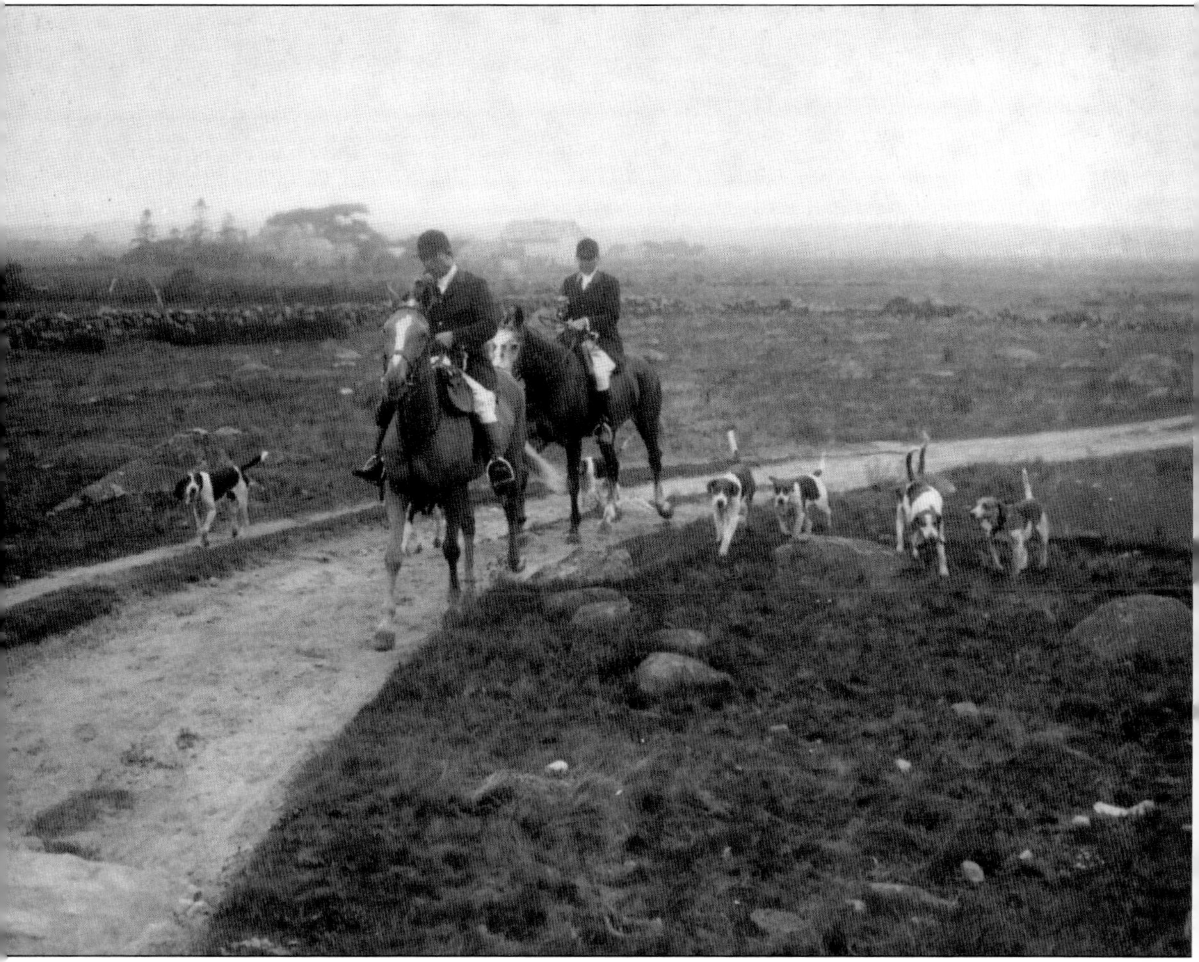

A foxhunt begins at the entrance of today's Browning Homestead Farm on Matunuck School House Road. It was the oldest working dairy farm in Rhode Island until 2009, when dairy was phased out. Bill Browning is the 11th generation of his family to run the farm, which now offers grass-fed beef, pork, and lamb. (Courtesy of Bill and Roberta Browning.)

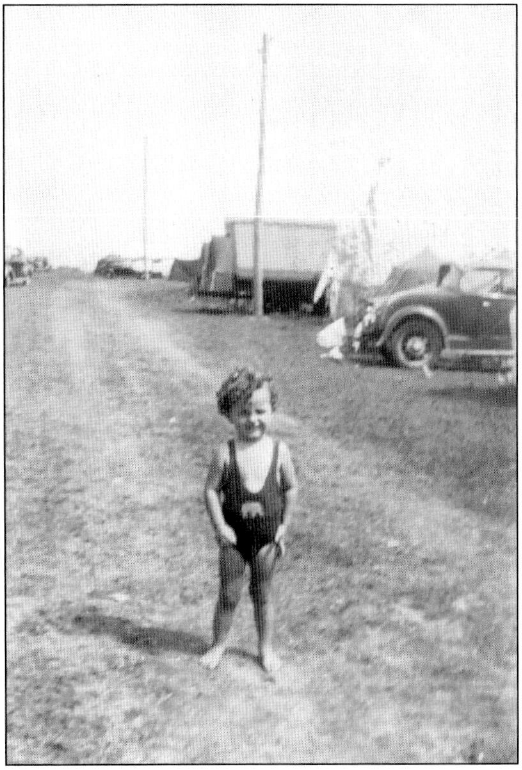

Russell Patterson enjoys the day at his family's home at Carpenter's Beach in August 1937. Nearly 80 years later, his daughters Kim Patterson and Tracey Patterson Siravo continue the family tradition of summering at Roy's, each owning her own beach cottage. (Courtesy of Kim Patterson.)

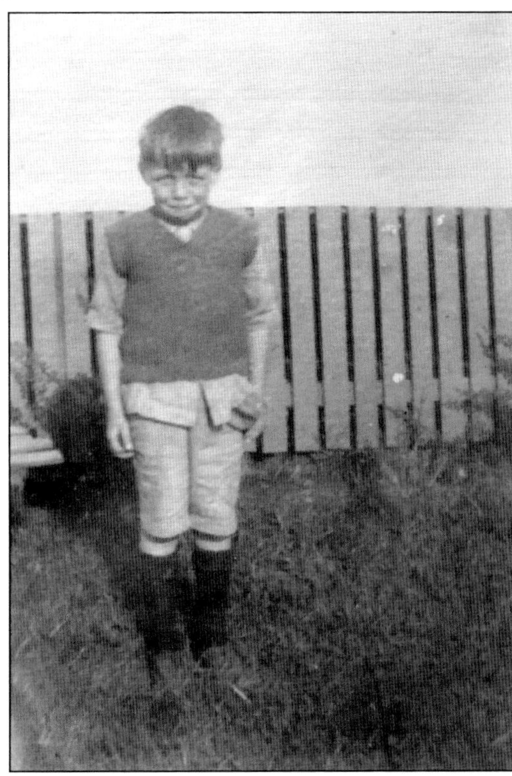

John Lane Yale Jr. is in his yard on Prospect Road in the 1930s. His mother, Virginia Broome Yale, lived in Matunuck since childhood. She married John Lane Yale Sr. at Kingston Congregational Church in Kingston, Rhode Island, in 1929. John Jr. was their first child. (Courtesy of David Yale.)

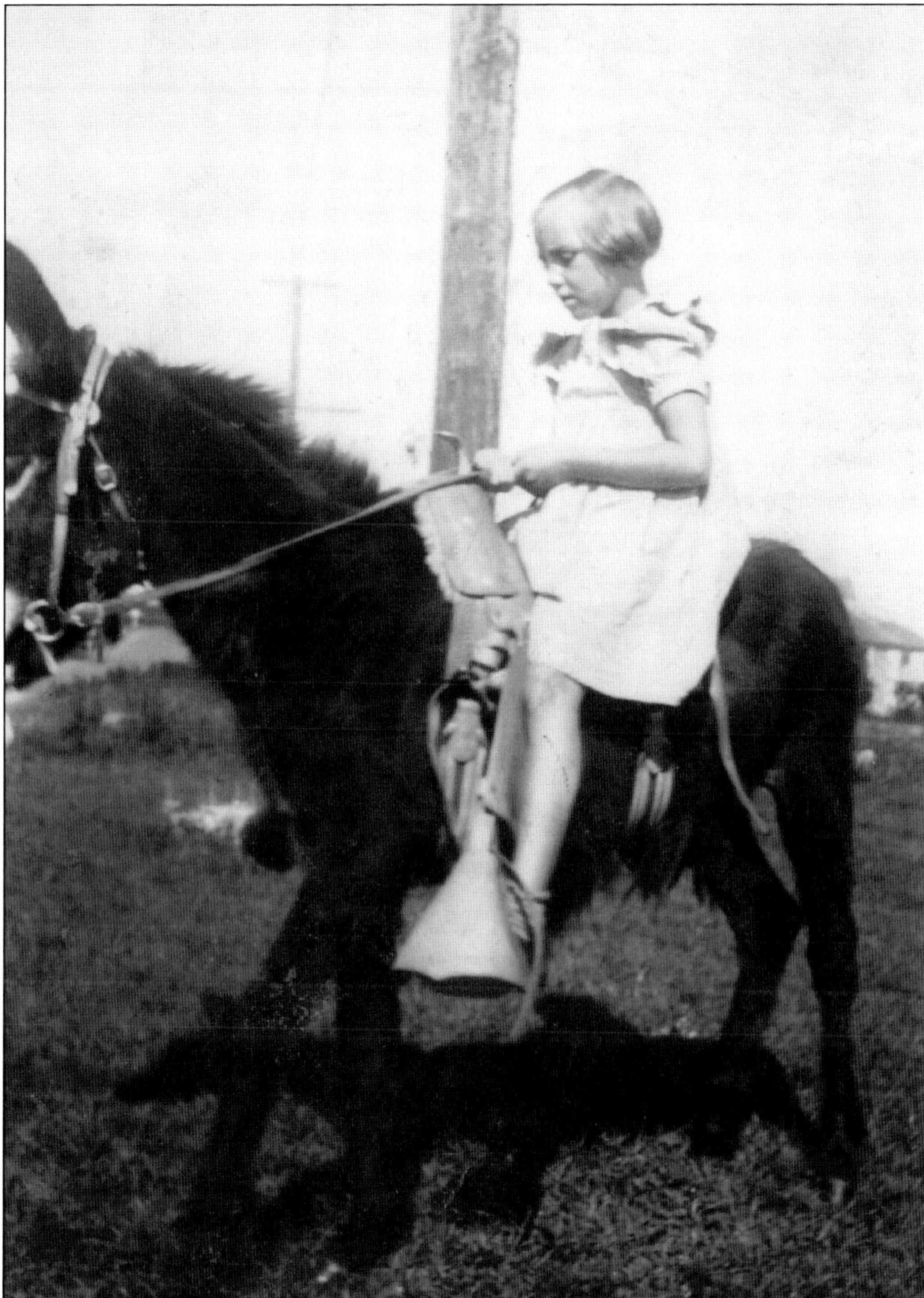

Regina Russell Goodwin rides her neighbor's pet donkey on Atlantic Avenue in July 1936. Goodwin, now in her 80s, is still a summer resident of Matunuck. (Courtesy of Regina Russell Goodwin.)

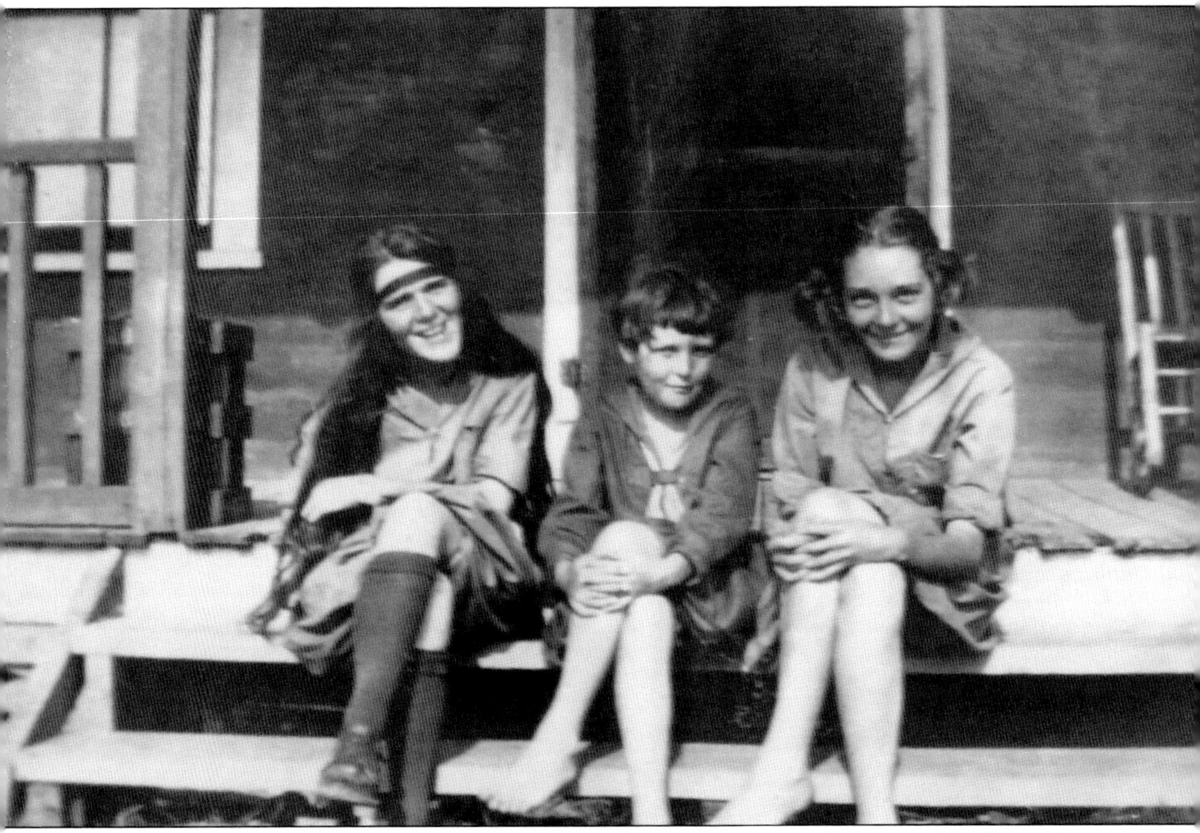

Three unidentified girls pose on the porch of a house on Prospect Street in the 1930s. (Courtesy of David Yale.)

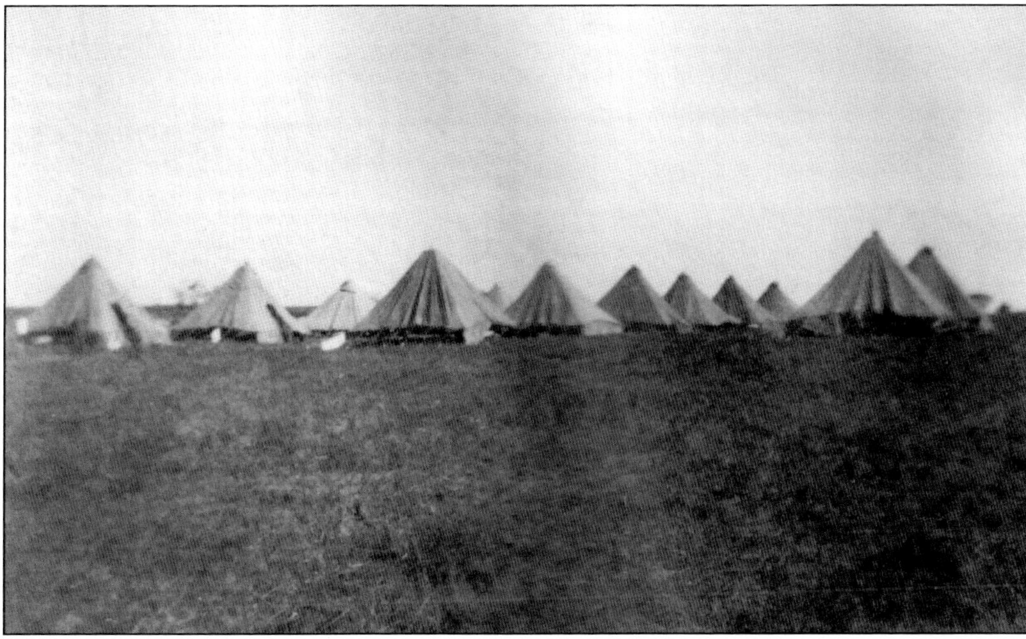

This collection of tents is believed to be Carpenter's Beach Meadow in the 1920s. Today, locals refer to the site of about 290 cottages and trailers as Mary Carpenter's. As a 17-year-old in 1935, Mary began working at the family business and still made daily visits there until her death in September 2012. (Courtesy of David Yale.)

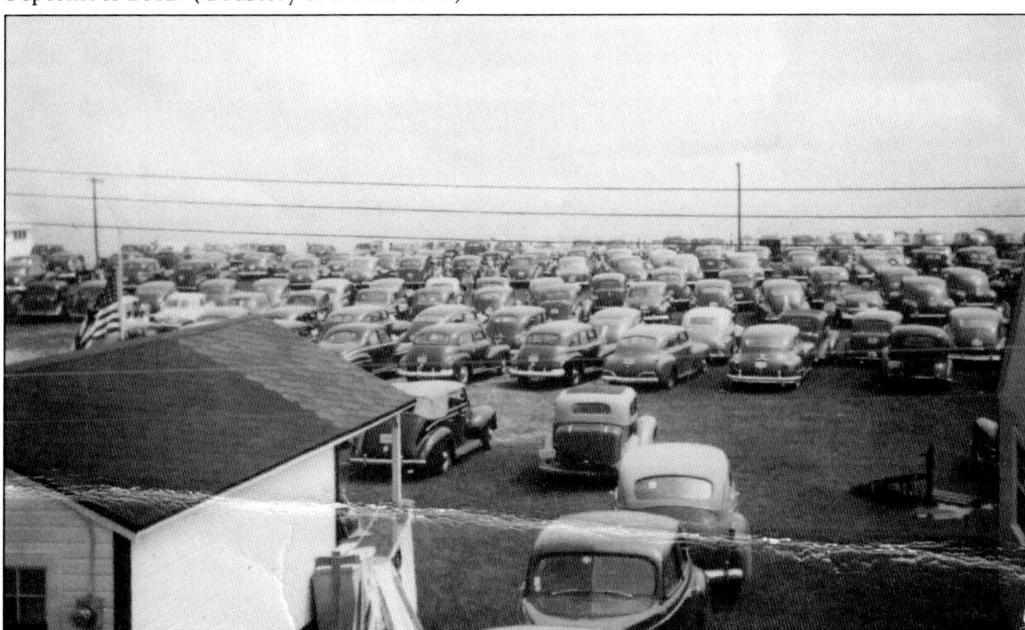

Cars are parked at Roy Carpenter's Beach, Cards Pond Road, in the 1930s. The late Roy Carpenter started renting the land for daily parking and gradually included overnight stays for people with trailers and tents. The cottages were built after the hurricane of 1938. There are about 377 cottages there today. Many were passed down within families, from one generation to the next. (Courtesy of Kim Patterson.)

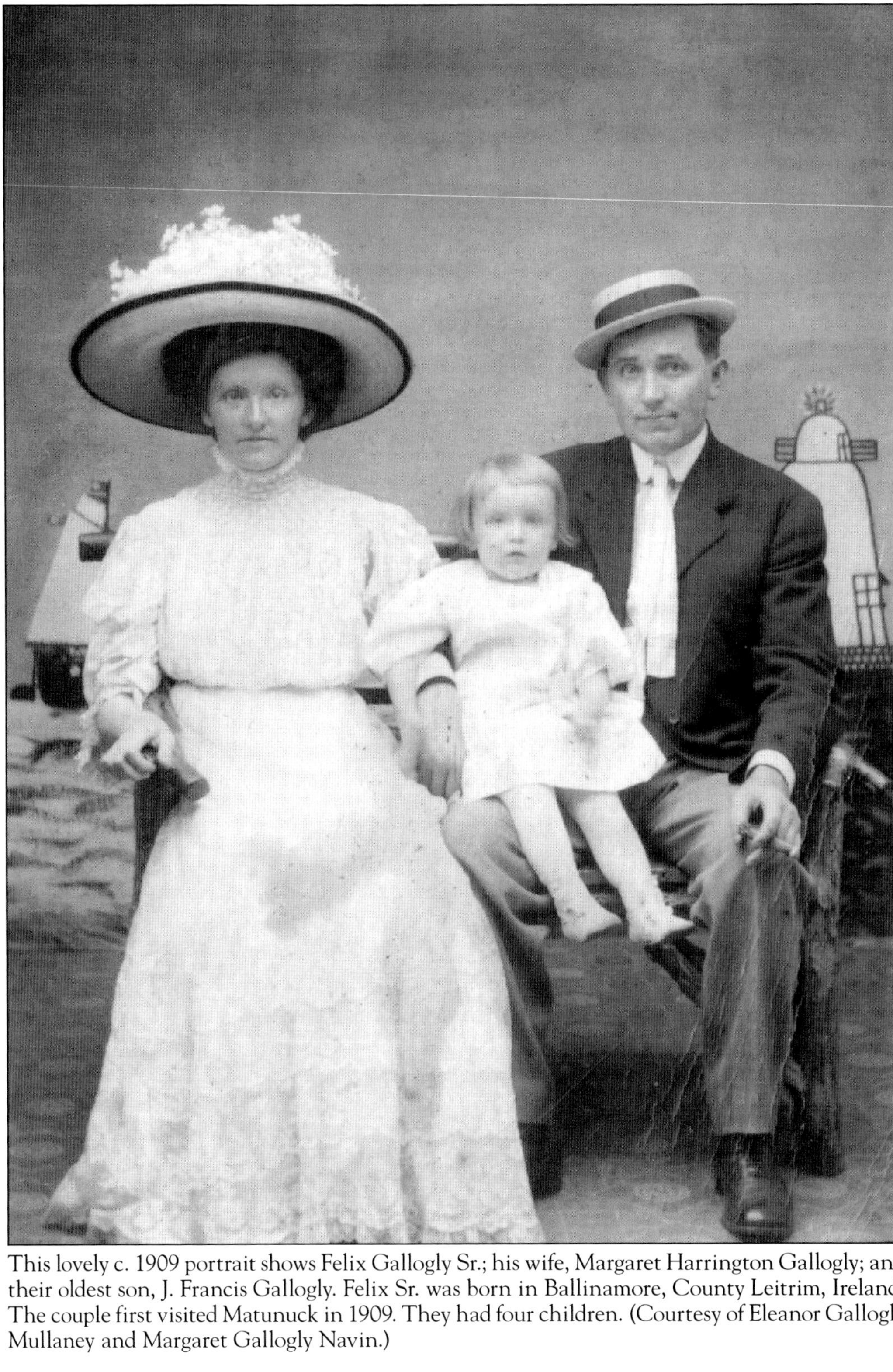

This lovely c. 1909 portrait shows Felix Gallogly Sr.; his wife, Margaret Harrington Gallogly; and their oldest son, J. Francis Gallogly. Felix Sr. was born in Ballinamore, County Leitrim, Ireland. The couple first visited Matunuck in 1909. They had four children. (Courtesy of Eleanor Gallogly Mullaney and Margaret Gallogly Navin.)

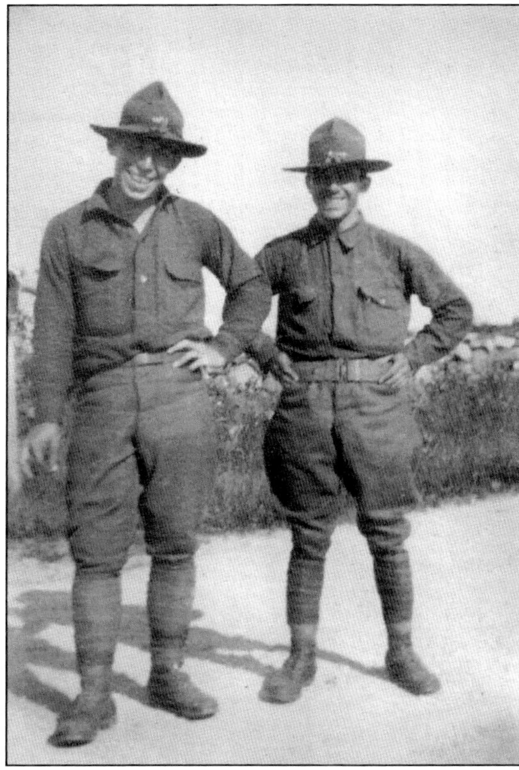

World War I soldiers have a laugh along a road in Matunuck. (Both, courtesy of David Yale.)

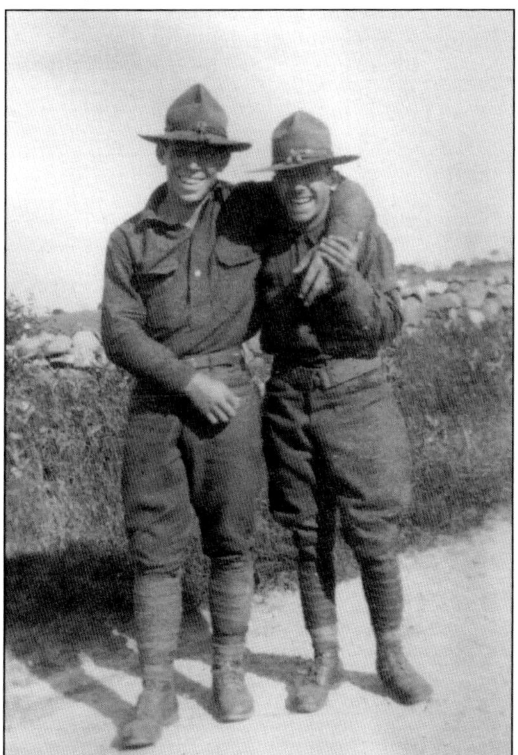

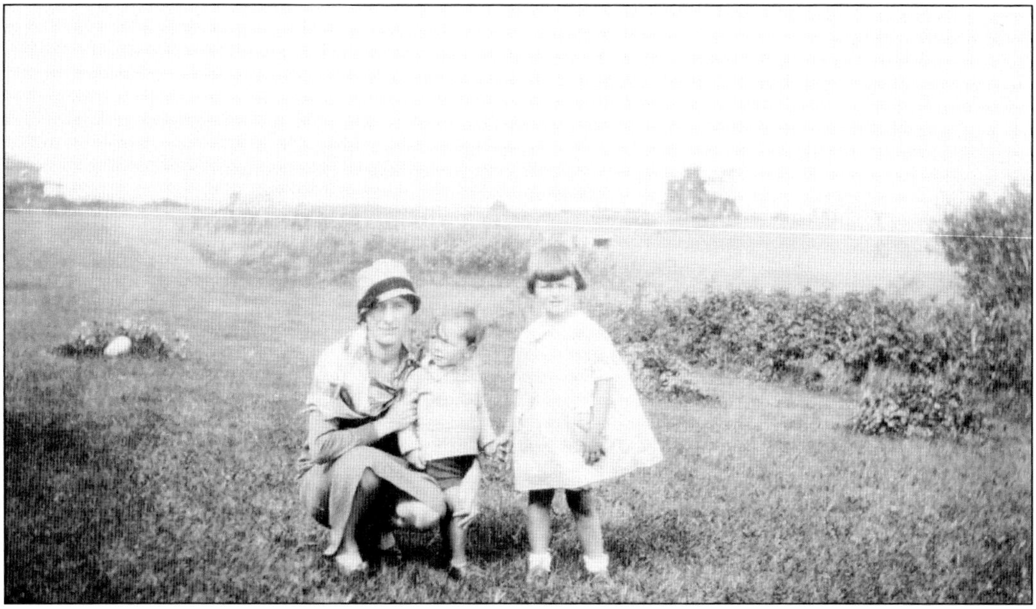

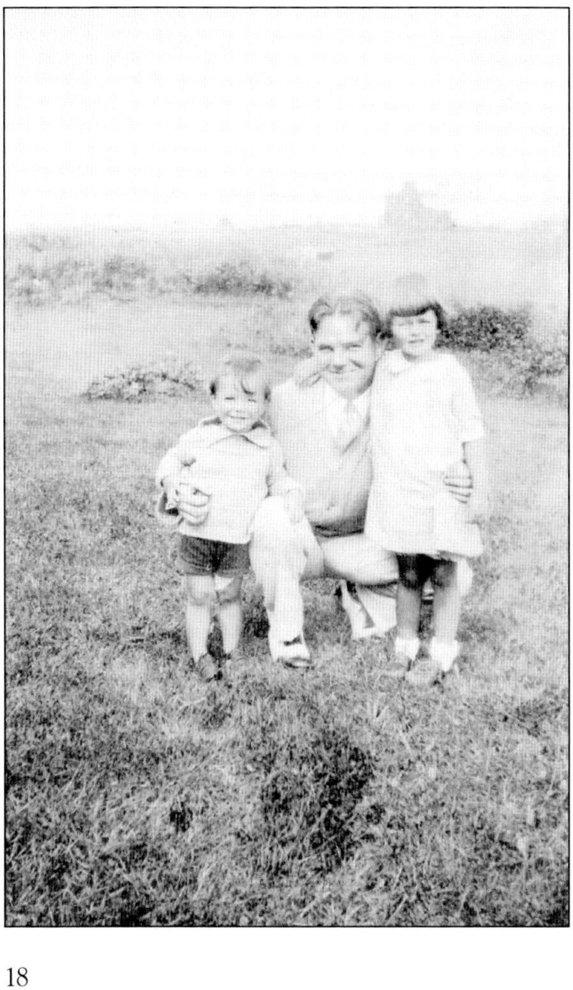

Margaret Cummings McHenry is pictured here with her son John L. McHenry Jr. and niece Jane Cummings around 1929. Margaret married John L. McHenry Sr. in 1927, the year they purchased a house on Park Avenue. Margaret grew up right next door on Atlantic Avenue. (Courtesy of Jeanne McHenry Helma.)

John L. McHenry Sr. poses with his son John L. McHenry Jr. and niece Jane Cummings around 1929. John Sr. purchased his house on Park Avenue in 1927. Although his granddaughter Jeanne McHenry Helma said she heard he won it in a card game, she thinks it was just folklore. John Sr. passed away in 1961 and his wife, Margaret, in 1971. (Courtesy of Jeanne McHenry Helma.)

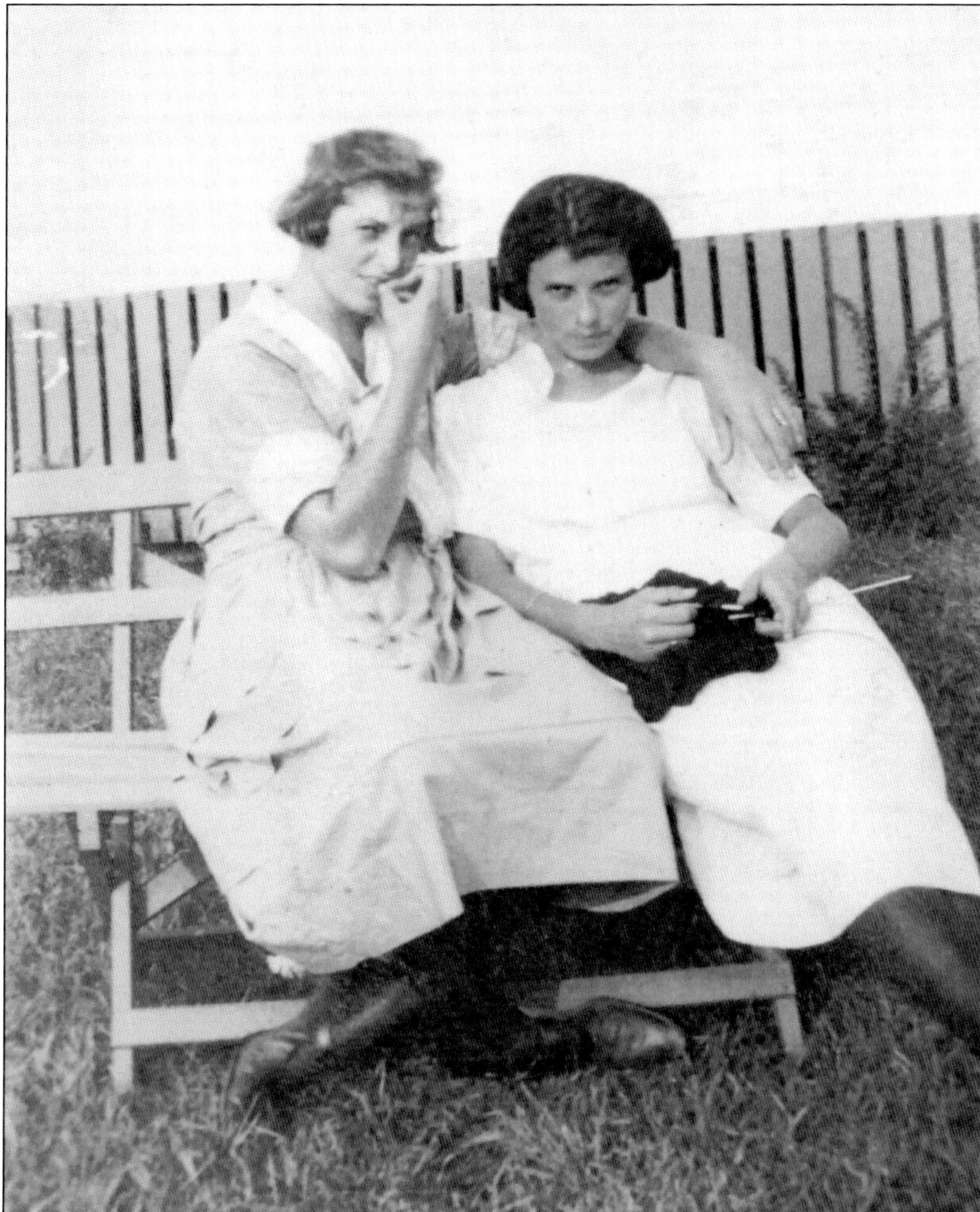

Virginia Broome Yale (right) appears to be knitting alongside her friend at a picnic table in the 1920s. Virginia's parents, Charles and Esther Rebecca Weeden Broome, built their house on Prospect Road in 1917. (Courtesy of David Yale.)

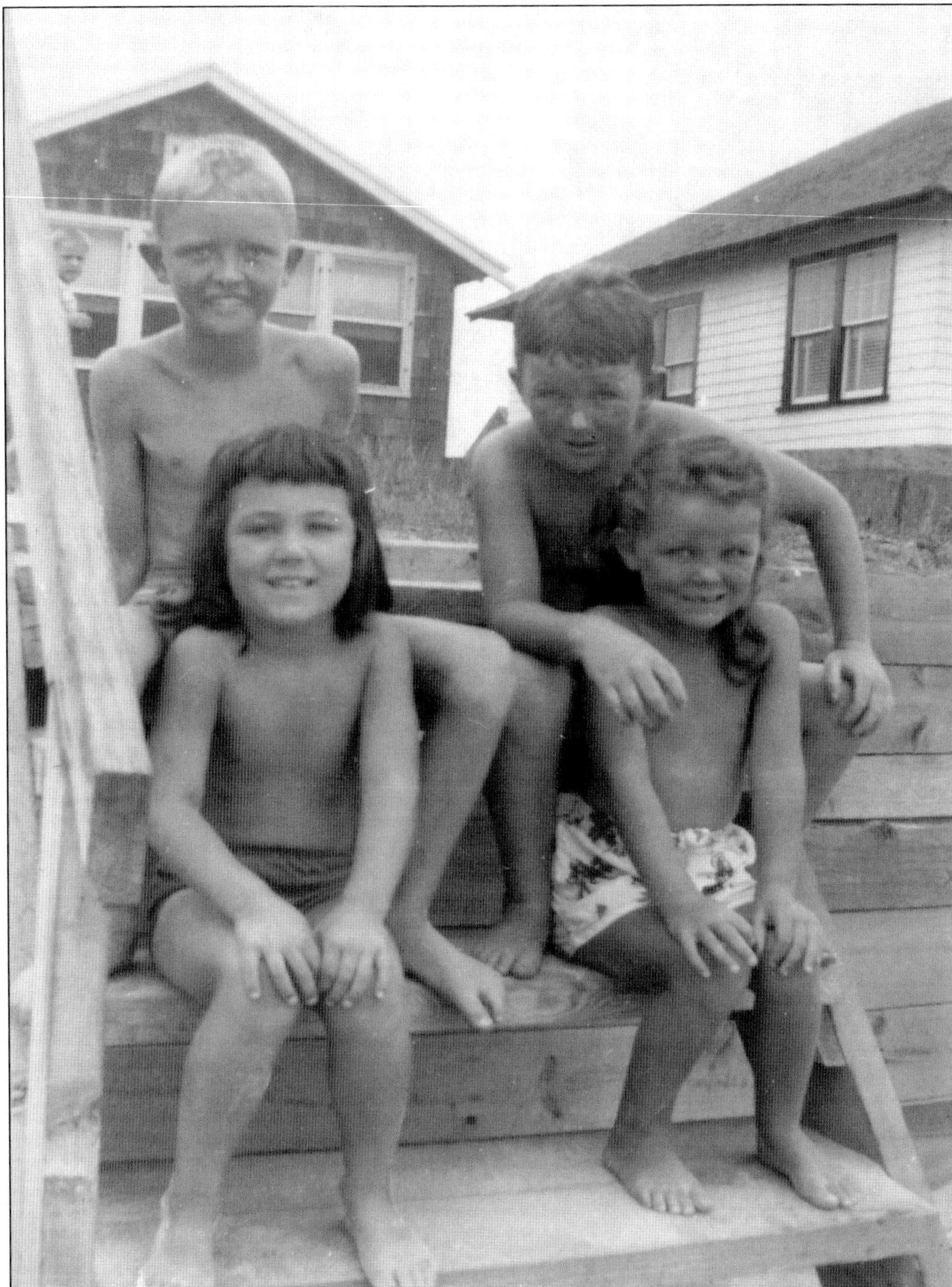

A group of children sit on steps at the Ahearn Cottages in 1949. The cottages were owned by James and Mary Callahan Ahearn. Their only child, Eleanor Ahearn Gallogly, and her family summered in one of them, and the other two were available for rent. The cottages remained in the family until they were sold in 1985. From left to right are (first row) Joyce Jadosz and Jane Gallogly McLaughlin; (second row) Donald Gallogly and David Gallogly. (Courtesy of David Gallogly.)

Margaret Gallogly Terry poses in her bathing costume in front of her family's Lund Cottage on Matunuck Beach Road around 1929. The cottage was damaged in the hurricane of 1938, and her parents sold it later that year. (Courtesy of Ann Terry.)

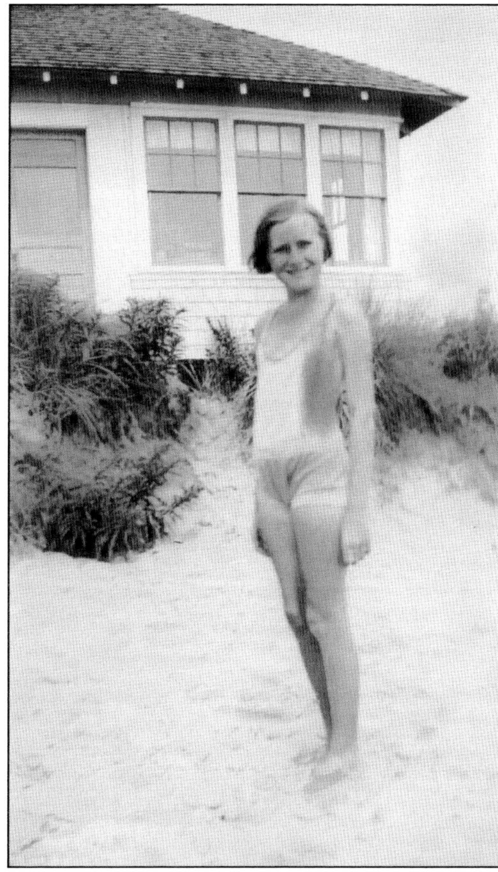

David Yale (sitting) is at his family's home on Prospect Road with a friend in 1940. David, the second son of John Lane Yale Sr. and his wife, Virginia Broome Yale, is now in his 80s and lives across the street from that very home. (Courtesy of David Yale.)

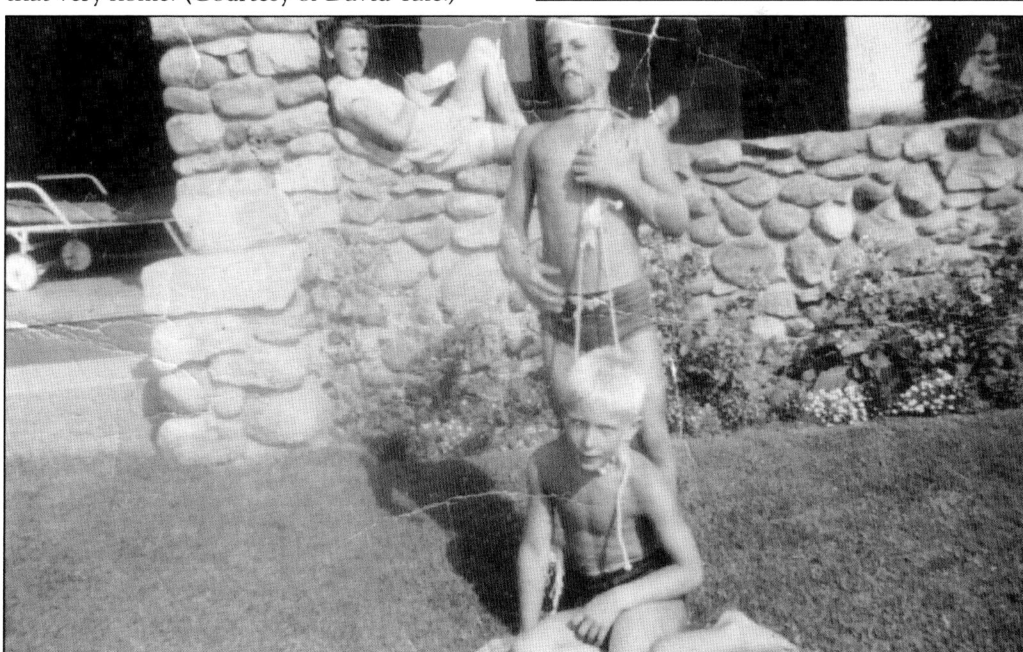

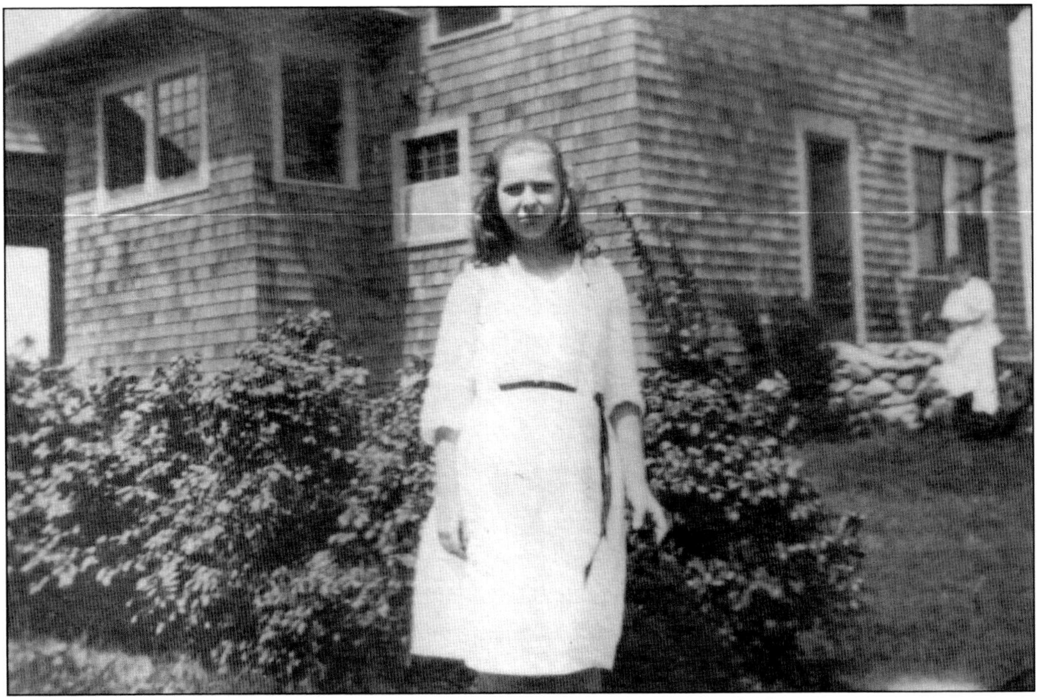

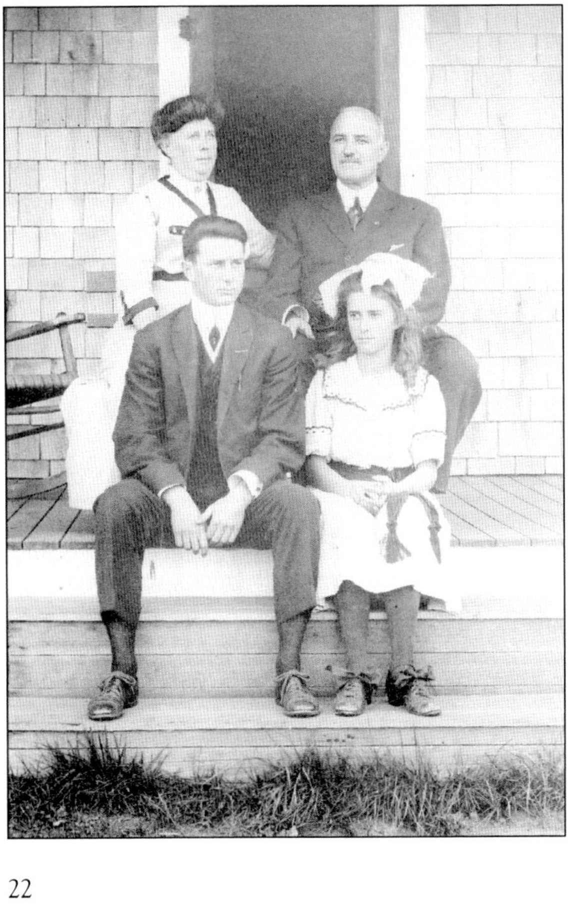

An unidentified young woman poses in a yard on Prospect Road. (Courtesy of David Yale.)

The family of Matthew Joseph Cummings Sr. is on the porch of their summer home on Atlantic Avenue in 1914. Cummings, who was from Providence's East Side, purchased the home in 1895. He was the overseer of the poor for the State of Rhode Island and died in 1929. His wife, Mary, passed away in 1941. Their children, pictured here, owned homes in Matunuck as adults. Matthew Joseph Cummings Jr. lived by the pond at the end of Lake Avenue, and Margaret Cummings McHenry lived on Park Avenue. From left to right are (first row) Matthew Joseph Cummings Jr. and Margaret Cummings McHenry; (second row) Mary Cummings and Matthew Joseph Cummings Sr. (Courtesy of Jeanne McHenry Helma.)

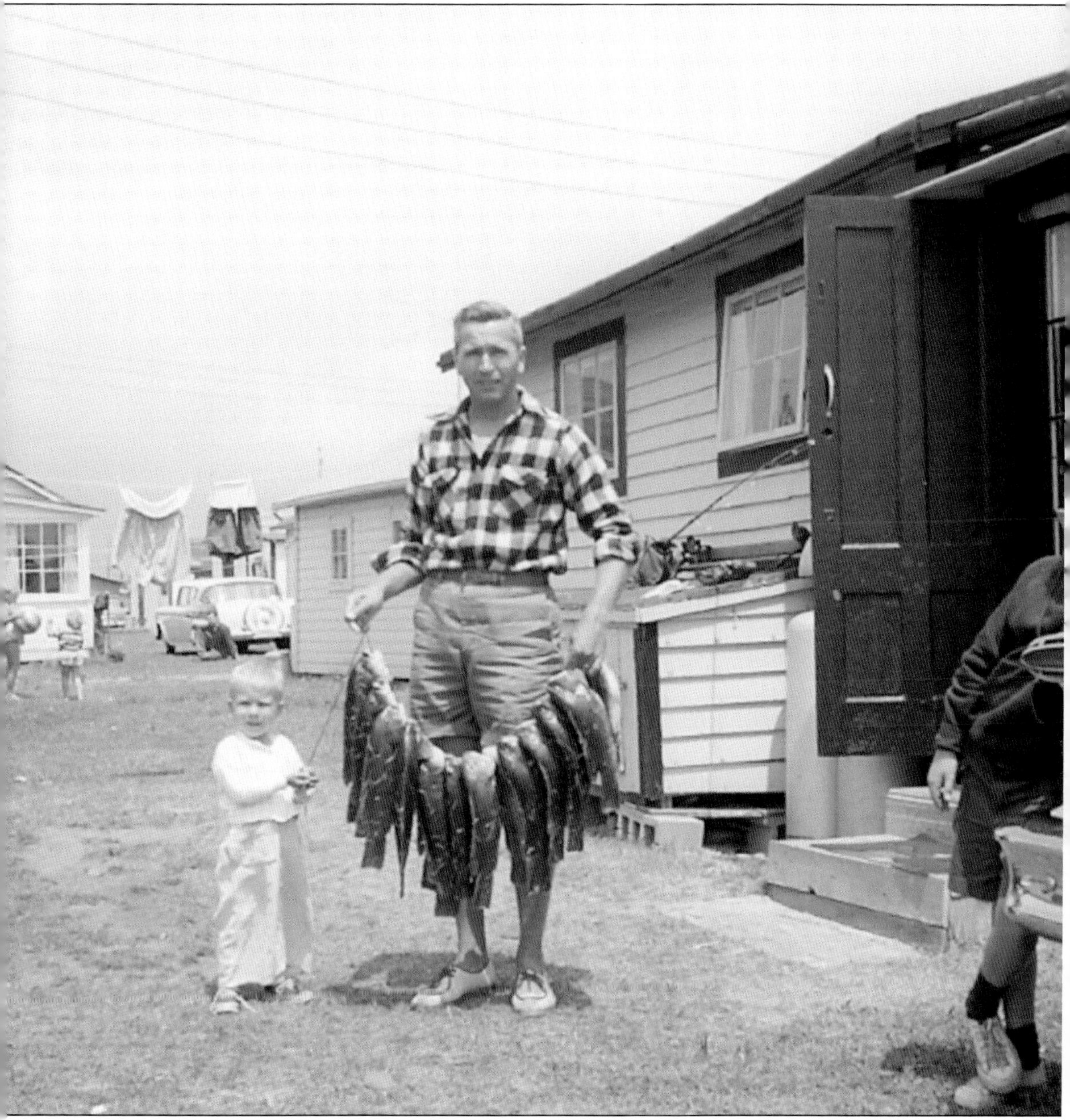

John Szymanski is with his father, Frank Szymanski, at their cottage at Roy Carpenter's Beach in the summer of 1962. Frank and his wife, Frances, bought the cottage in July 1961. John is still a resident of Roy's and owns a different cottage. (Courtesy of John Szymanski.)

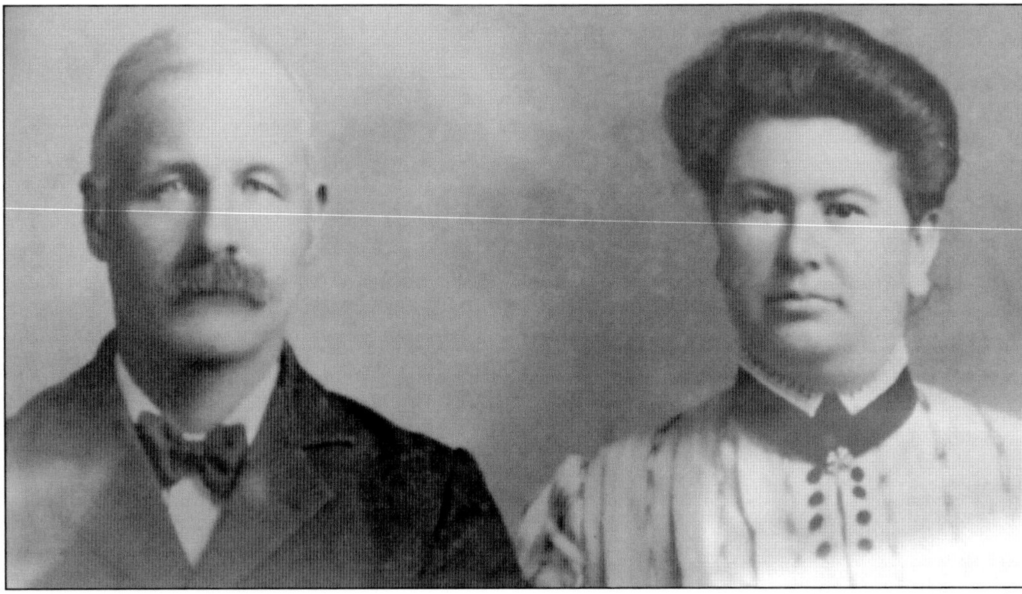

In 1898, Etta and George I. Champlin built the Dewey Cottage at Matunuck Beach Road, a 15-bedroom family-style boardinghouse. The Champlins named the cottage after Adm. George Dewey (1837–1917), who was an instructor at Newport's Naval Academy and the victor of the 1898 Battle of Manila Bay. (Courtesy of Levon Kasparian.)

The Dewey Cottage, now known as the Admiral Dewey Inn, was operated by the Champlins until the late 1930s. By the early 1970s, the cottage had become vacant and would remain so until Joan LeBel rescued it in 1986. LeBel had the cottage fully restored, including the installation of plumbing and heating and ensuring the building met all fire codes. This guest register is from opening day, June 23, 1898. (Courtesy of Levon Kasparian.)

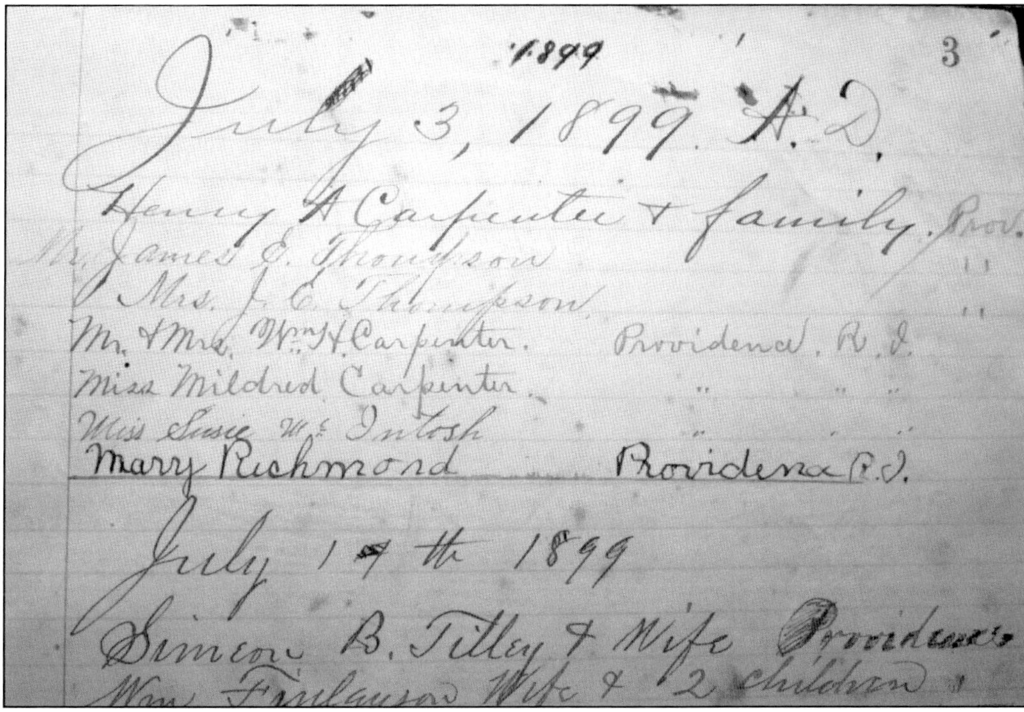

1899 3

July 3, 1899. A.D.

Henry A Carpenter & family. Prov.

Mr. James E. Thompson "

Mrs. J. E. Thompson "

Mr. & Mrs. Wm. H. Carpenter. Providence. R. I.

Miss Mildred Carpenter. " "

Miss Susie McIntosh " "

Mary Richmond Providence R.I.

July 14th 1899

Simeon B. Tilley & Wife Providence

Wm Finlayson Wife & 2 children "

In 2012, Levon Kasparian purchased the Admiral Dewey Inn from Joan LeBel. These guest register book pages are from July 3, 1899, and July 2, 1900. (Both, courtesy of Levon Kasparian.)

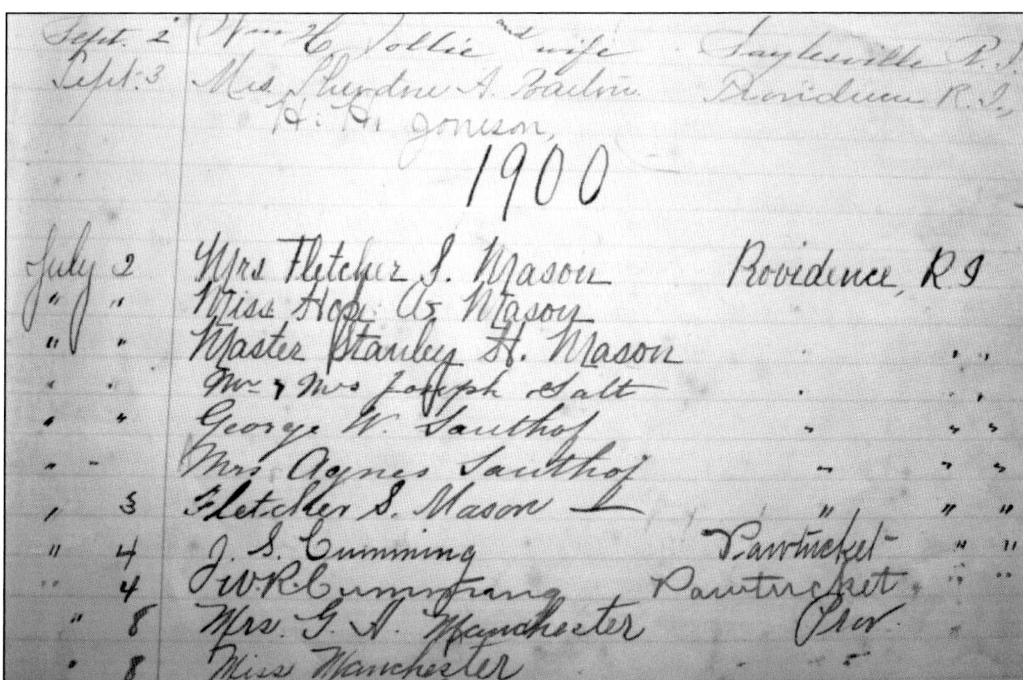

1900

July 2 Mrs Fletcher S. Mason Providence, R I

" " Miss Hope A. Mason

" " Master Stanley H. Mason " "

" " Mr & Mrs Joseph Salt " "

" " George W. Sauthof " "

" " Mrs Agnes Sauthof " "

" 3 Fletcher S. Mason " "

" 4 J. S. Cumming Pawtucket " "

" 4 J. W. R. Cumming Pawtucket " "

" 8 Mrs. G. A. Manchester Prov

" 8 Miss Manchester "

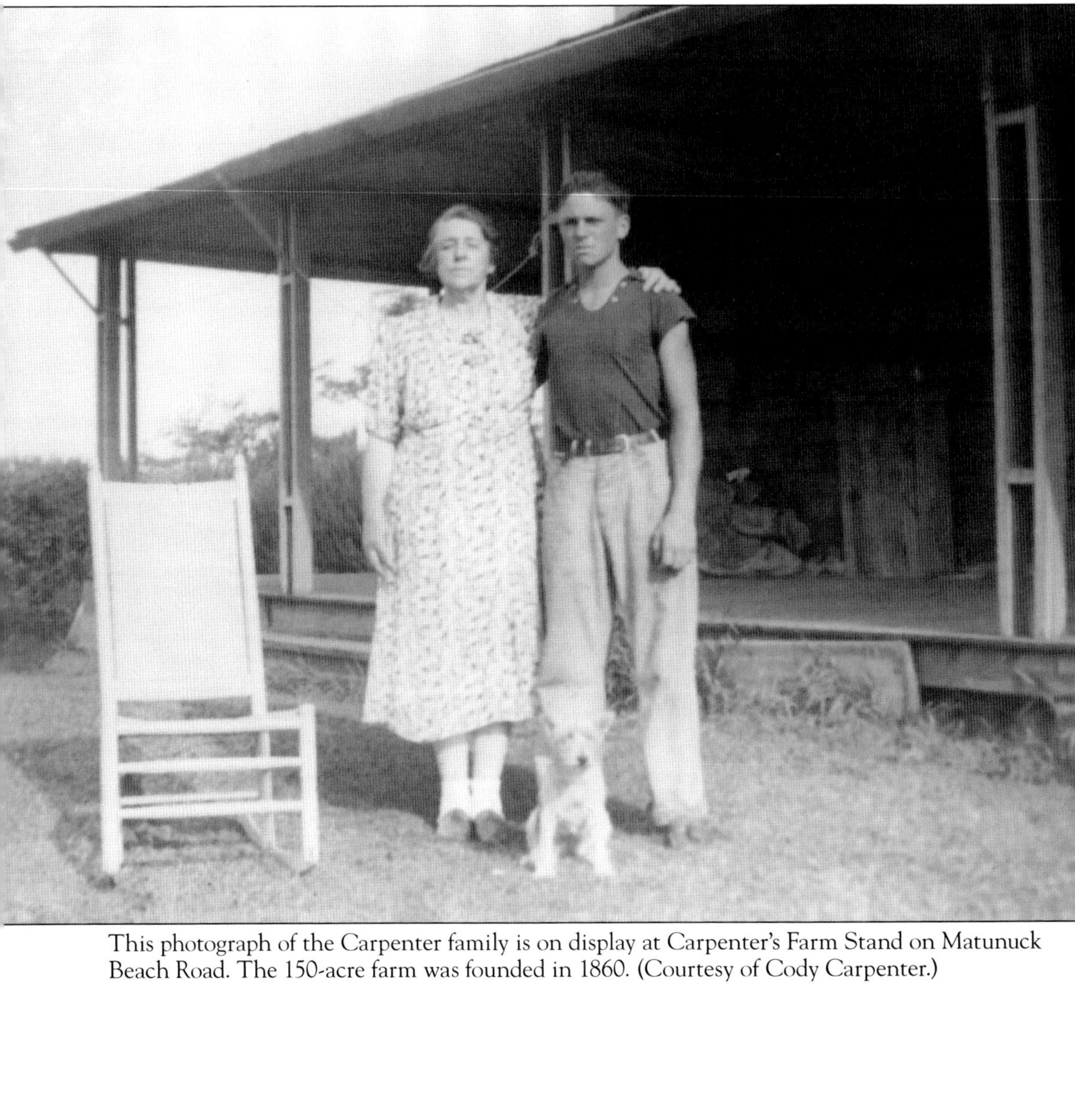

This photograph of the Carpenter family is on display at Carpenter's Farm Stand on Matunuck Beach Road. The 150-acre farm was founded in 1860. (Courtesy of Cody Carpenter.)

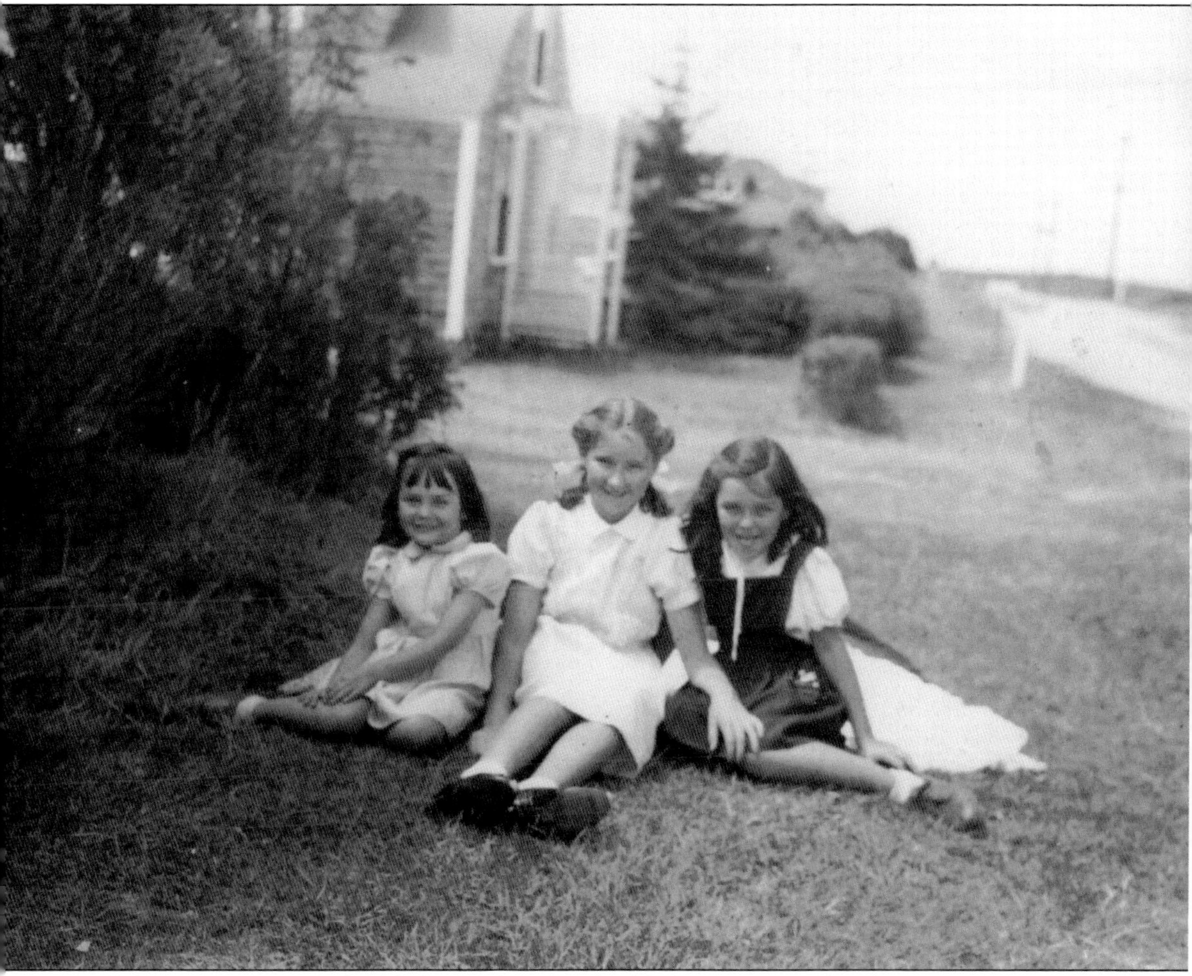

From left to right, Nancy Shields (age six), Joan Shields (age nine), and Helen Russell Henley (age 11), are pictured in Helen's yard on Atlantic Avenue in August 1945. (Courtesy of Regina Russell Goodwin.)

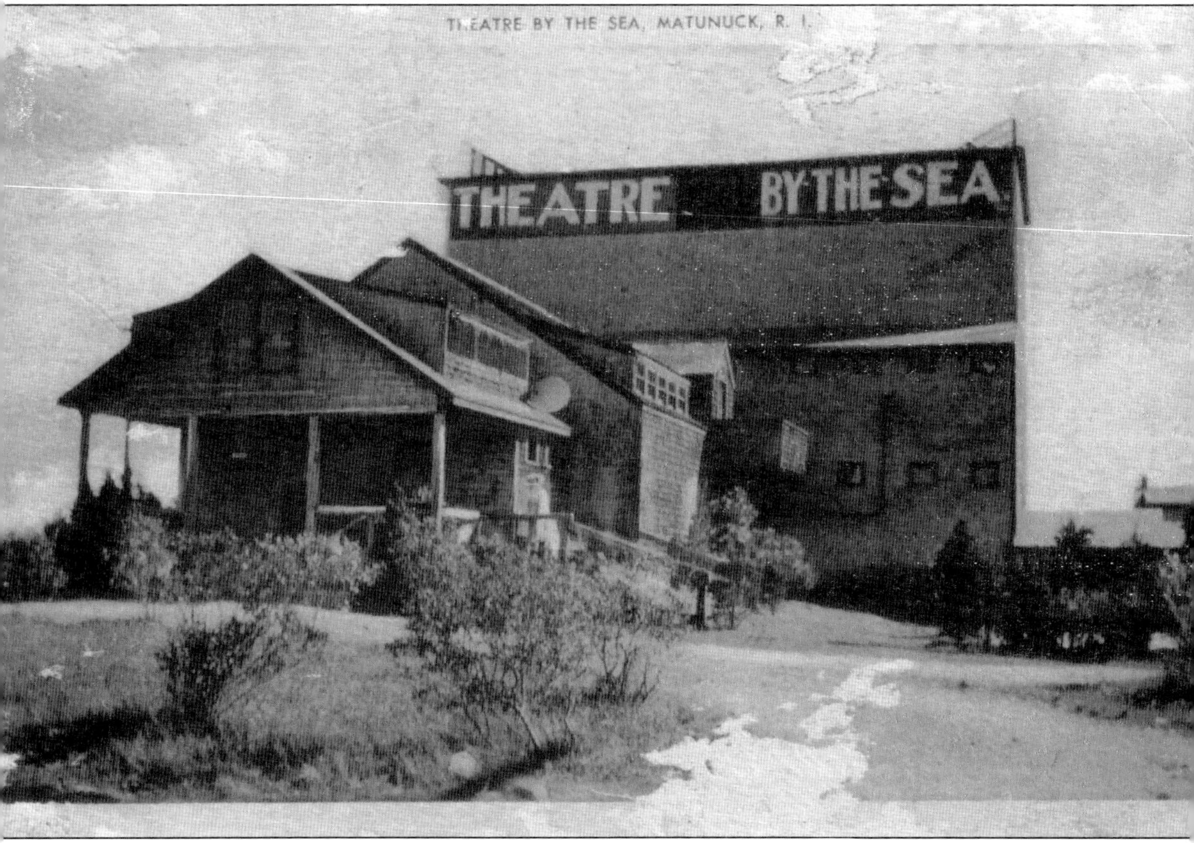

From 1928 to 1933, Alice Jaynes Tyler ran a summer camp for girls on the property of her summer home on Cards Pond Road. On August 7, 1933, her barn was transformed into a 300-seat theater called Theatre by the Sea. The property was originally owned by George N. Browning. He died in 1914, and his widow continued to run the Ocean Star Cottage inn there until 1919. (Courtesy of David Yale.)

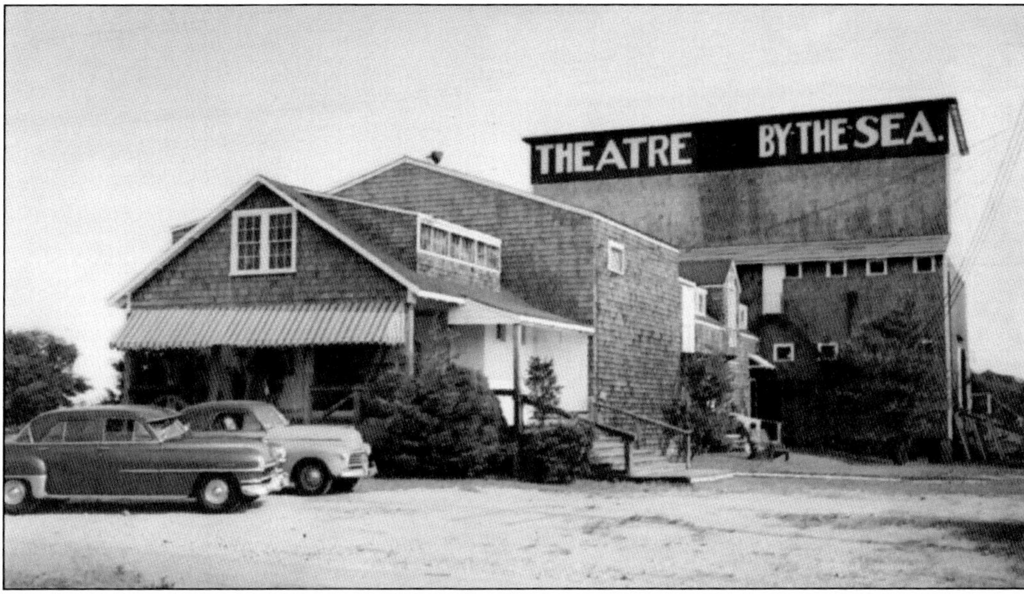

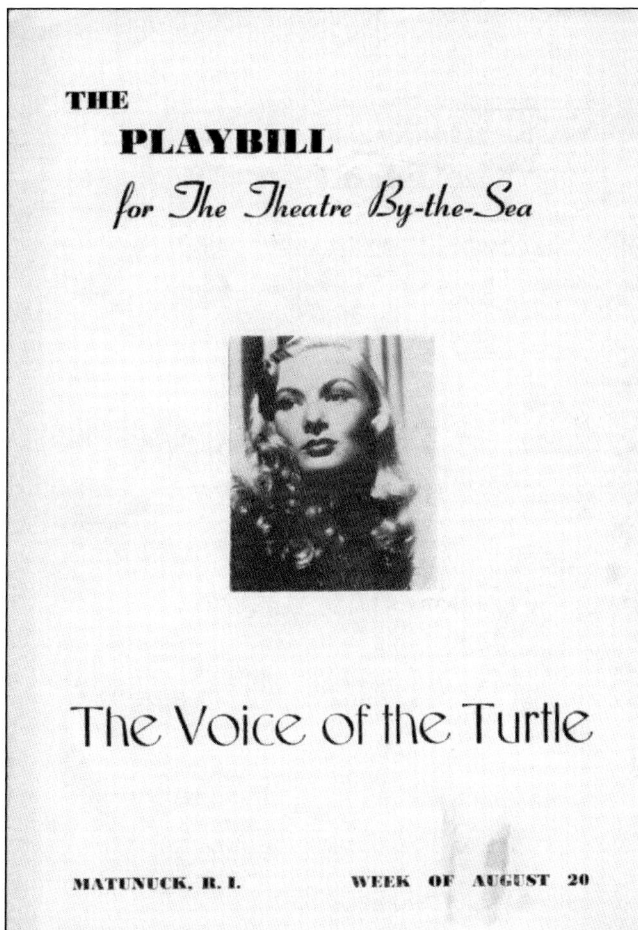

During the golden era of summer stock, Theatre by the Sea hosted world-renowned talent. The playbill at right advertises Veronica Lake in *The Voice of the Turtle*. (Both, courtesy of the University of Rhode Island Special Collections.)

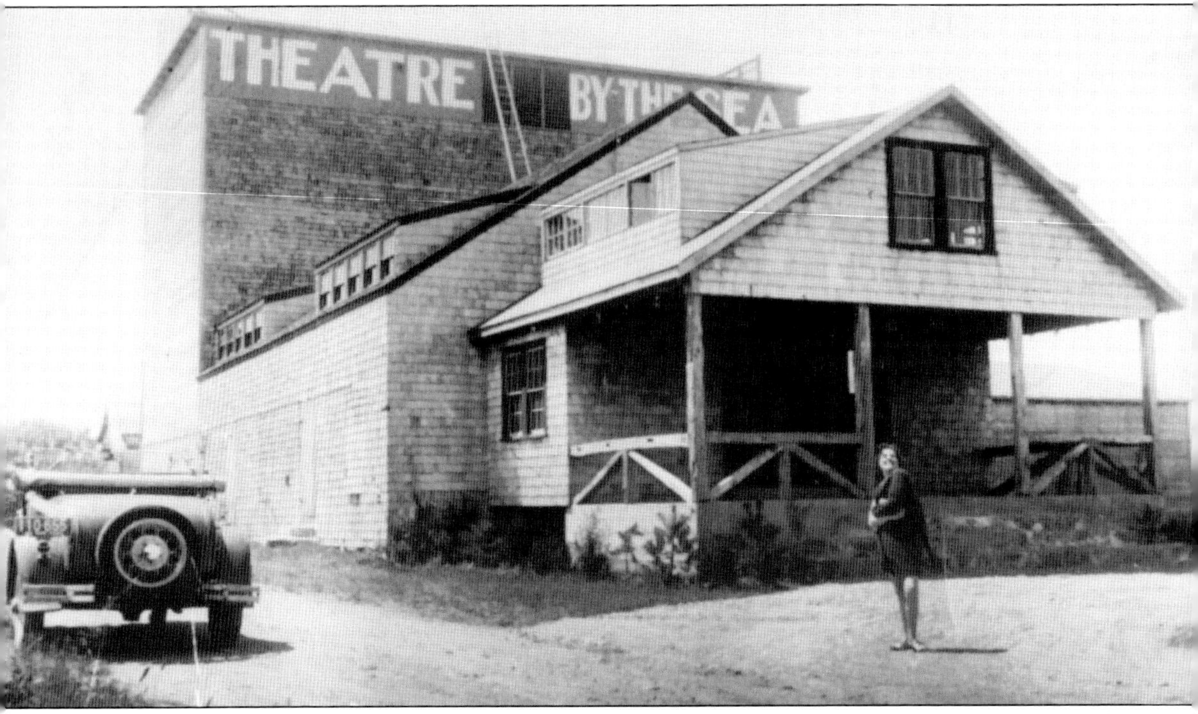

The hurricane of 1938 caused extensive damage to Theatre by the Sea. It is said the building was cut in half with a hand saw, and the box office was pulled forward by a dump truck. Then, a new section of balcony and theater were added. (Courtesy of the University of Rhode Island Special Collections.)

In the 1940s, Theatre by the Sea went dark, and was a target spot for military planes to practice diving maneuvers during World War II. It operated as a movie house in 1944 and 1945. By 1947, and for nearly the entirety of the following decade, the theater was up and running with some of the most popular actors of the time. Mae West (right) and Marlon Brandon (below) are shown on playbills. The theatre closed after the 1962 season. Tommy Brent came to the theater in 1967, when it was in great disrepair, and put it back into proper working order. It reopened on June 18 that year. (Both, courtesy of the University of Rhode Island Special Collections.)

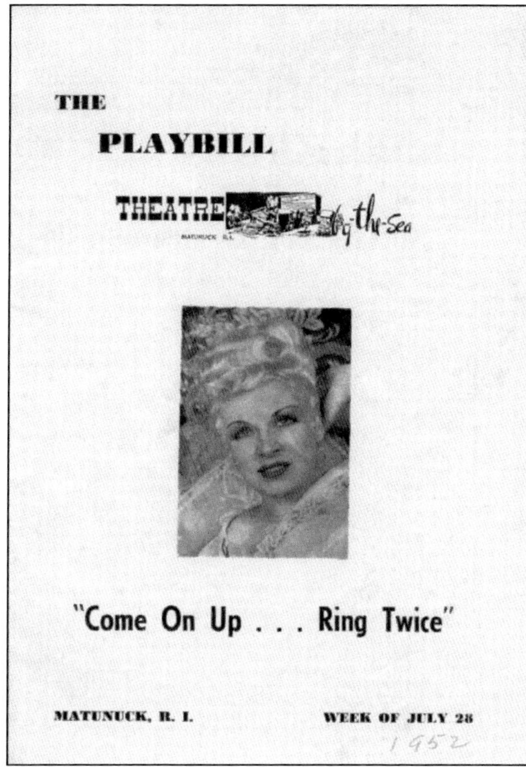

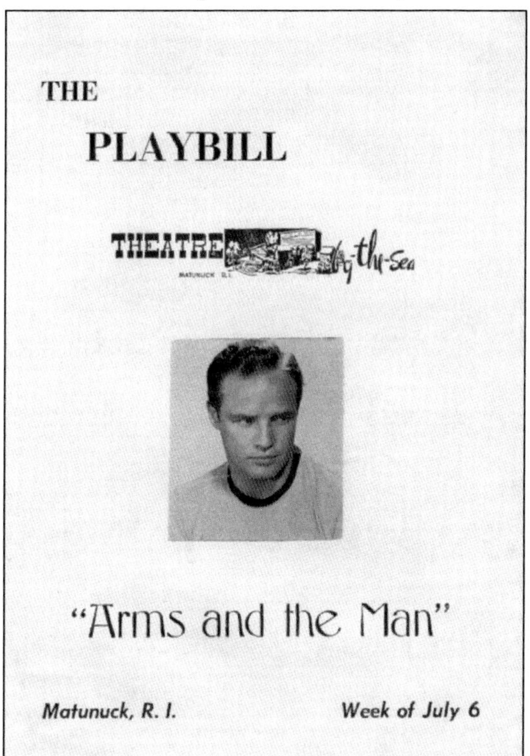

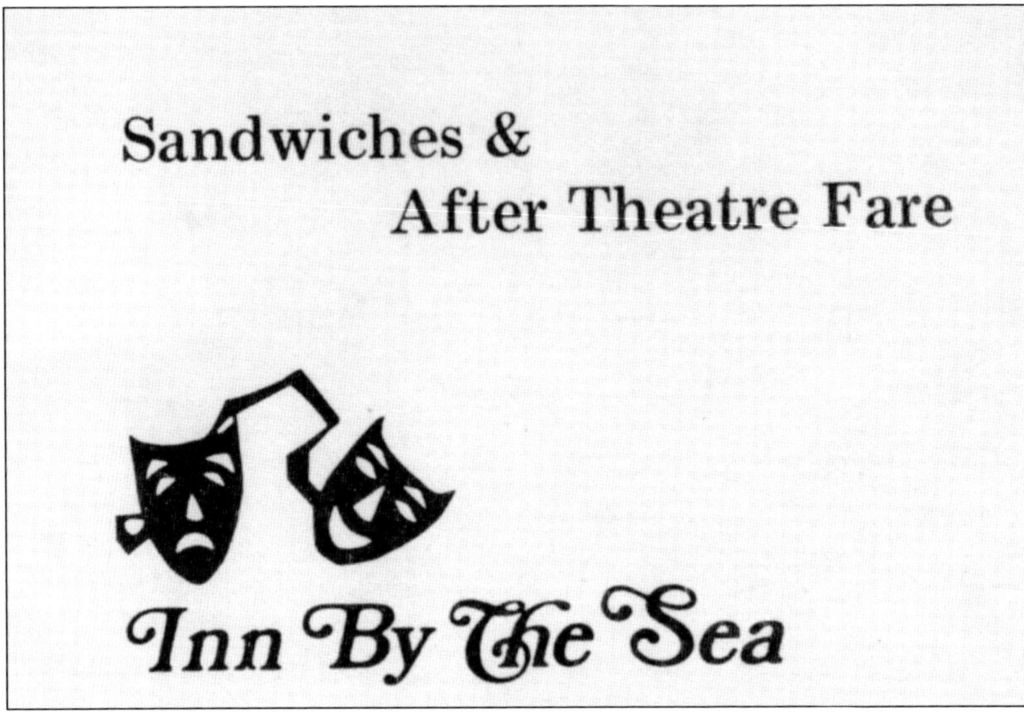

Bistro by the Sea is the current restaurant at Theatre by the Sea. Throughout the years, there have been cafés and tearooms on the property. This old menu lists a selection of sandwiches and specialties. (Both, courtesy of the University of Rhode Island Special Collections.)

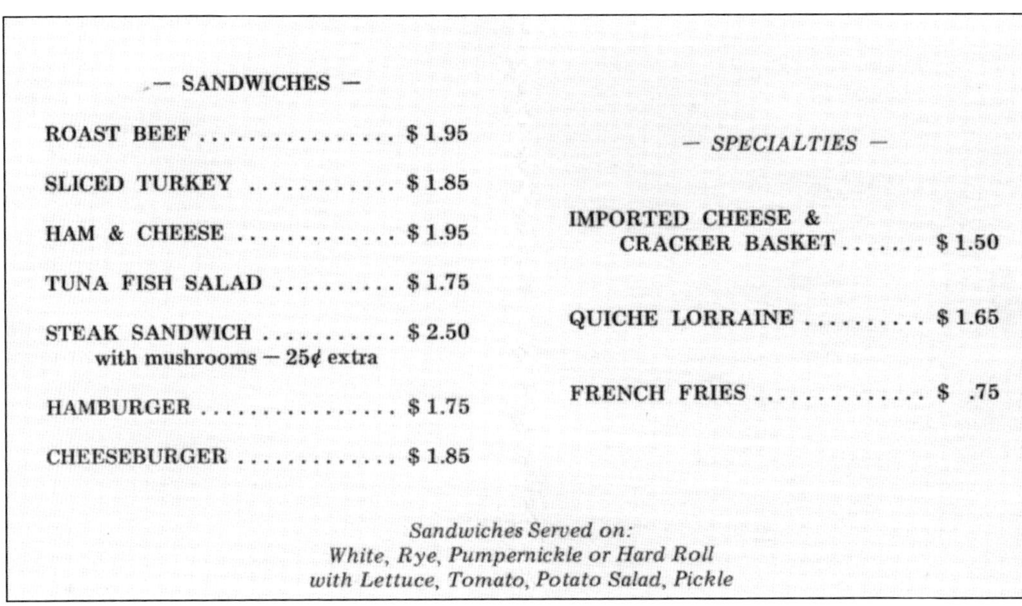

— SANDWICHES —

ROAST BEEF	$ 1.95
SLICED TURKEY	$ 1.85
HAM & CHEESE	$ 1.95
TUNA FISH SALAD	$ 1.75
STEAK SANDWICH with mushrooms — 25¢ extra	$ 2.50
HAMBURGER	$ 1.75
CHEESEBURGER	$ 1.85

— SPECIALTIES —

IMPORTED CHEESE & CRACKER BASKET	$ 1.50
QUICHE LORRAINE	$ 1.65
FRENCH FRIES	$ .75

Sandwiches Served on:
White, Rye, Pumpernickle or Hard Roll
with Lettuce, Tomato, Potato Salad, Pickle

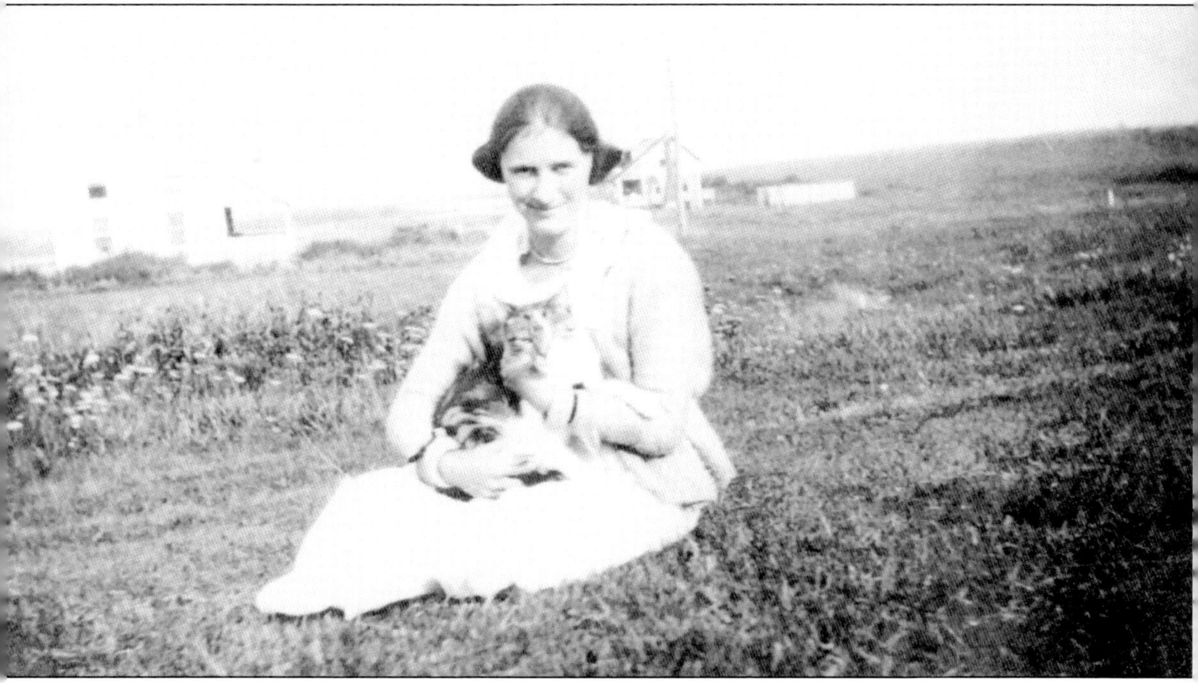

In 1919, Margaret Cummings McHenry and her cat are pictured at the summer home on Atlantic Avenue where she grew up. In 1927, she married John L. McHenry Sr., and they purchased a house next door on Park Avenue. (Courtesy of Jeanne McHenry Helma.)

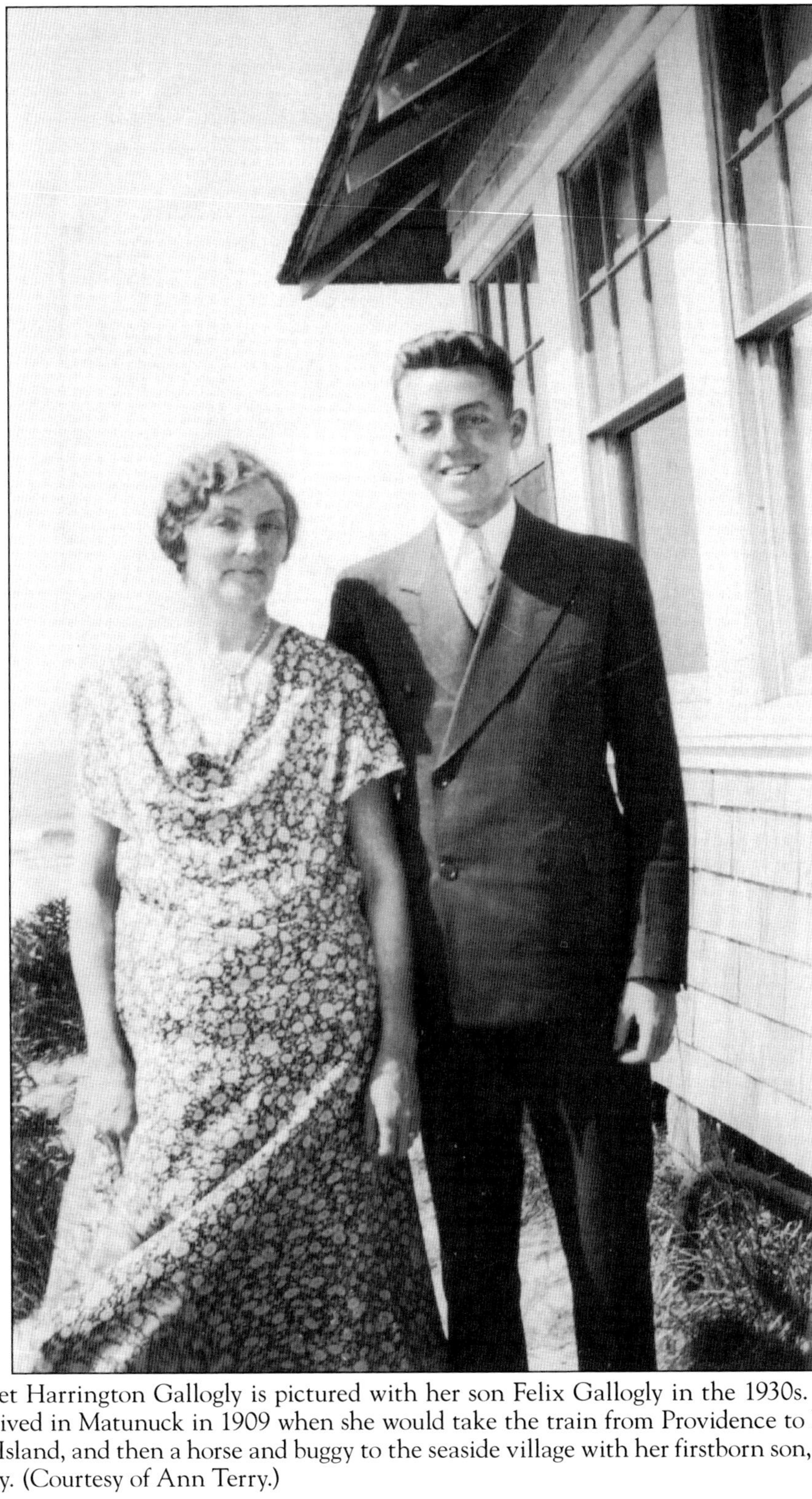

Margaret Harrington Gallogly is pictured with her son Felix Gallogly in the 1930s. Margaret first arrived in Matunuck in 1909 when she would take the train from Providence to Kingston, Rhode Island, and then a horse and buggy to the seaside village with her firstborn son, J. Francis Gallogly. (Courtesy of Ann Terry.)

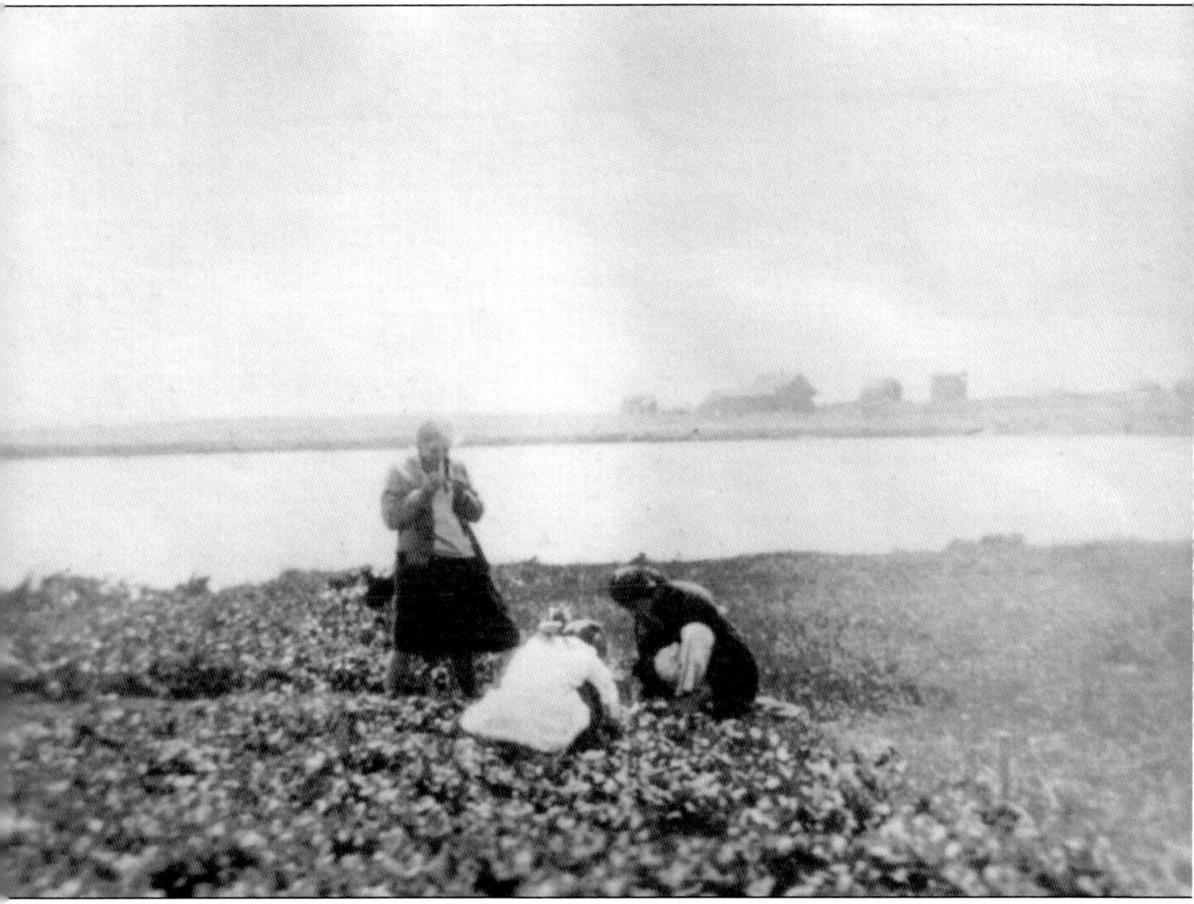

Women garden in a backyard on Prospect Road. One of them is Esther Rebecca Weeden Broome, maternal grandmother of David Yale, who lives on the same road today. Potter's Pond can be seen in the background. (Courtesy of David Yale.)

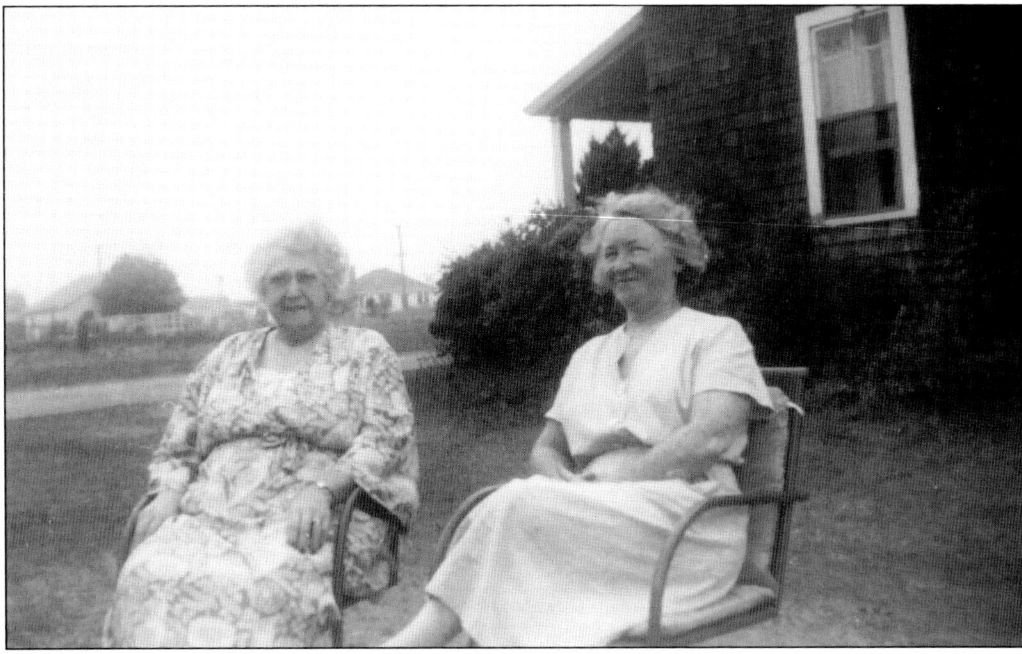

Esther McGuiggan and Helen Grady Russell relax on a summer's day in August 1949 at Helen's home on Atlantic Avenue. (Courtesy of Regina Russell Goodwin.)

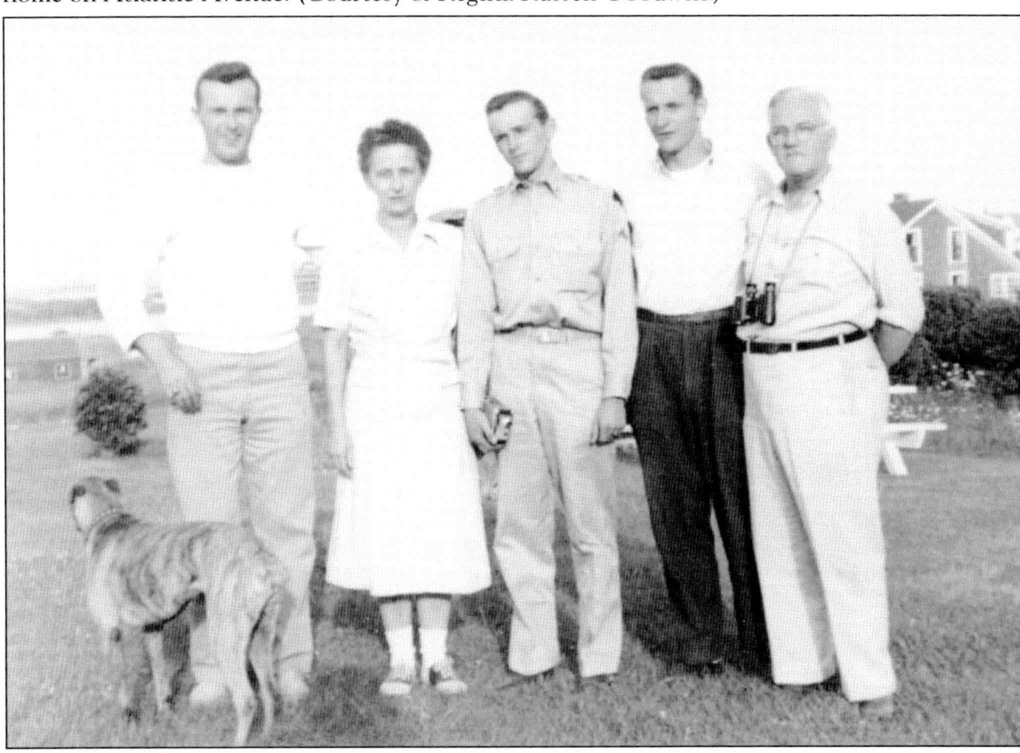

The McHenry family are at their beach homes at Park and Atlantic Avenues in 1950. From left to right are John L. Jr., Margaret, Robert, Matthew, and John L. McHenry Sr. (Courtesy of Jeanne McHenry Helma.)

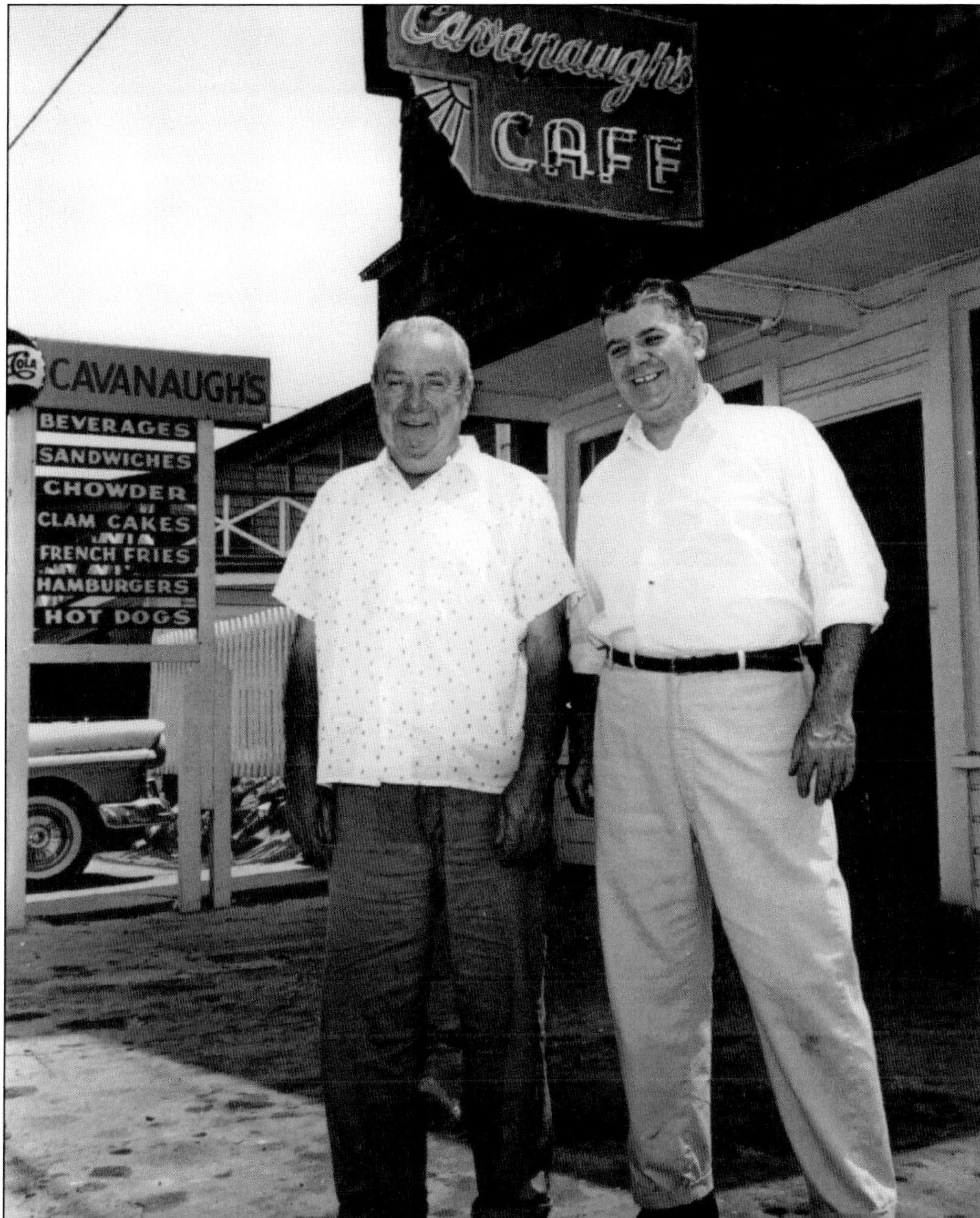

John Cavanaugh, owner of Cavanaugh's Café, stands in front of the building with his son-in-law John McAllister in the late 1950s. According to Cavanaugh's grandson Dennis McAllister, John Cavanaugh and his wife, Bridget, bought the café around 1933 and ran it until John's death in 1961. John McAllister then took over the business until he sold it to Vinnie Joyce in 1976. It became the Joyce Family Pub. Today, it is owned by Tara Mulroy and is called Tara's Tipperary Tavern. (Courtesy of Dennis McAllister.)

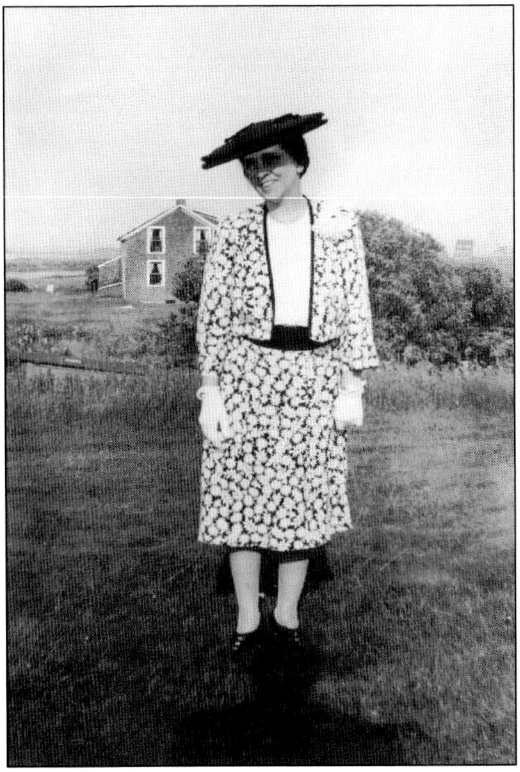

Grace King poses in a fancy hat near Hogg's House in the early 1930s. (Courtesy of Mary Ann Gallogly Scott.)

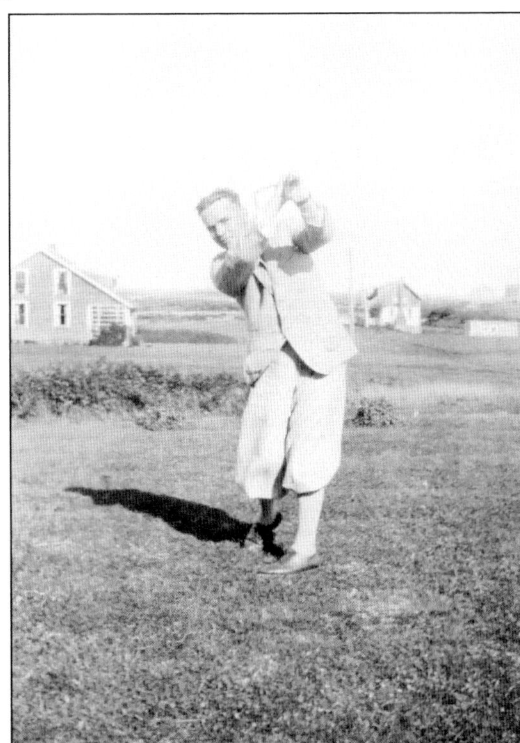

In 1929, John L. McHenry Sr. swings a golf club at the home of his in-laws, Mary and Matthew Joseph Cummings Sr., on Atlantic Avenue. (Courtesy of Jeanne McHenry Helma.)

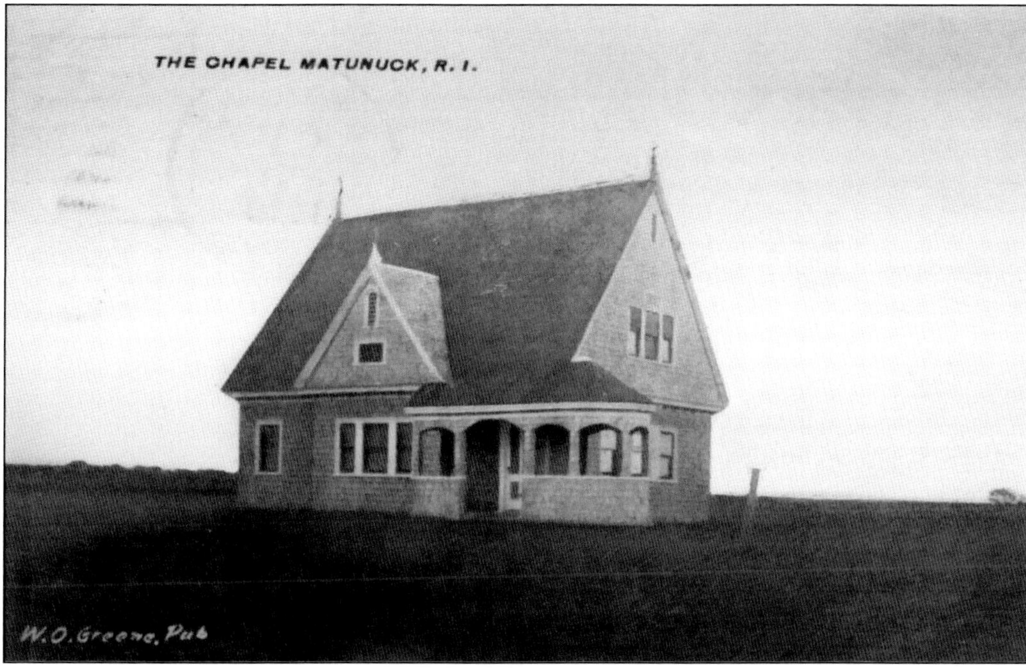

Pictured here is the Matunuck Park Chapel, which was located on Lake Avenue. The building no longer stands. (Courtesy of the Robert Beverly Hale Library.)

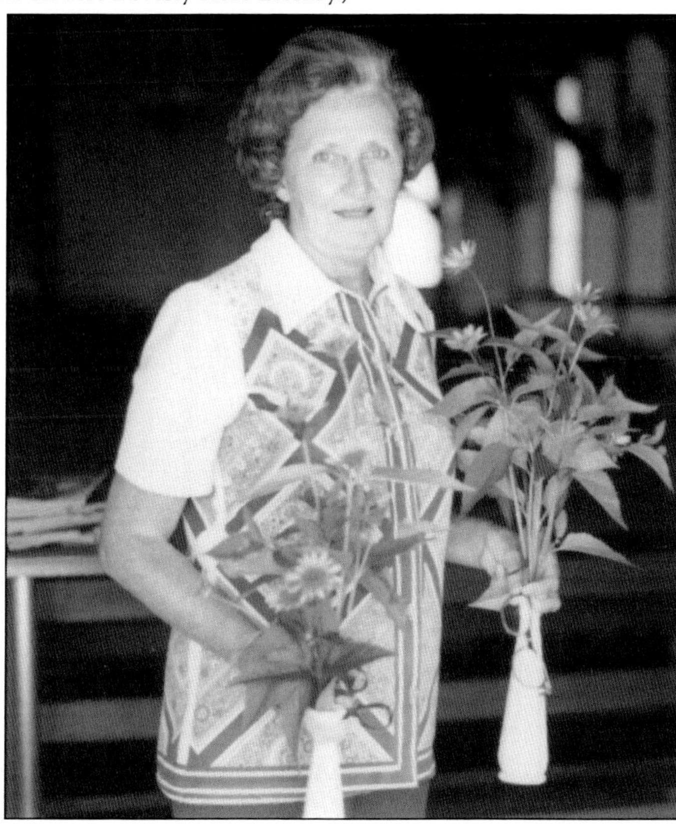

Margaret Gallogly Terry is rearranging floral decorations inside St. Romuald's Chapel in the late 1960s. It is said birds fly in the open windows, and an occasional cat or dog wanders in. Terry described the beauty of Matunuck in the many articles she wrote for the *South County Independent*, where she was the village columnist. (Courtesy of Ann Terry.)

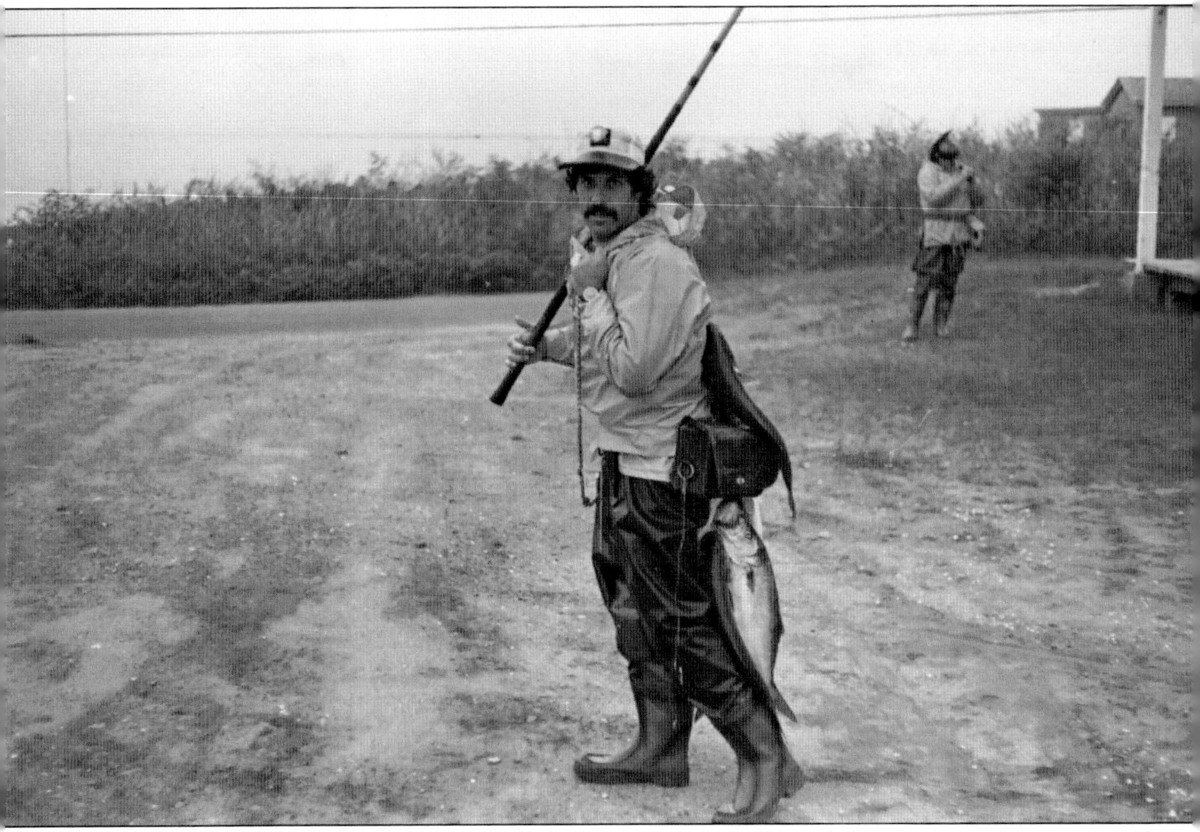

A member of the Narragansett Salt Water Fishing Club walks with his catch on the grounds of the club property on Matunuck Beach Road. Originally the site of the Atlantic Hotel, the club moved to the location in 1954. (Courtesy of the Narragansett Salt Water Fishing Club.)

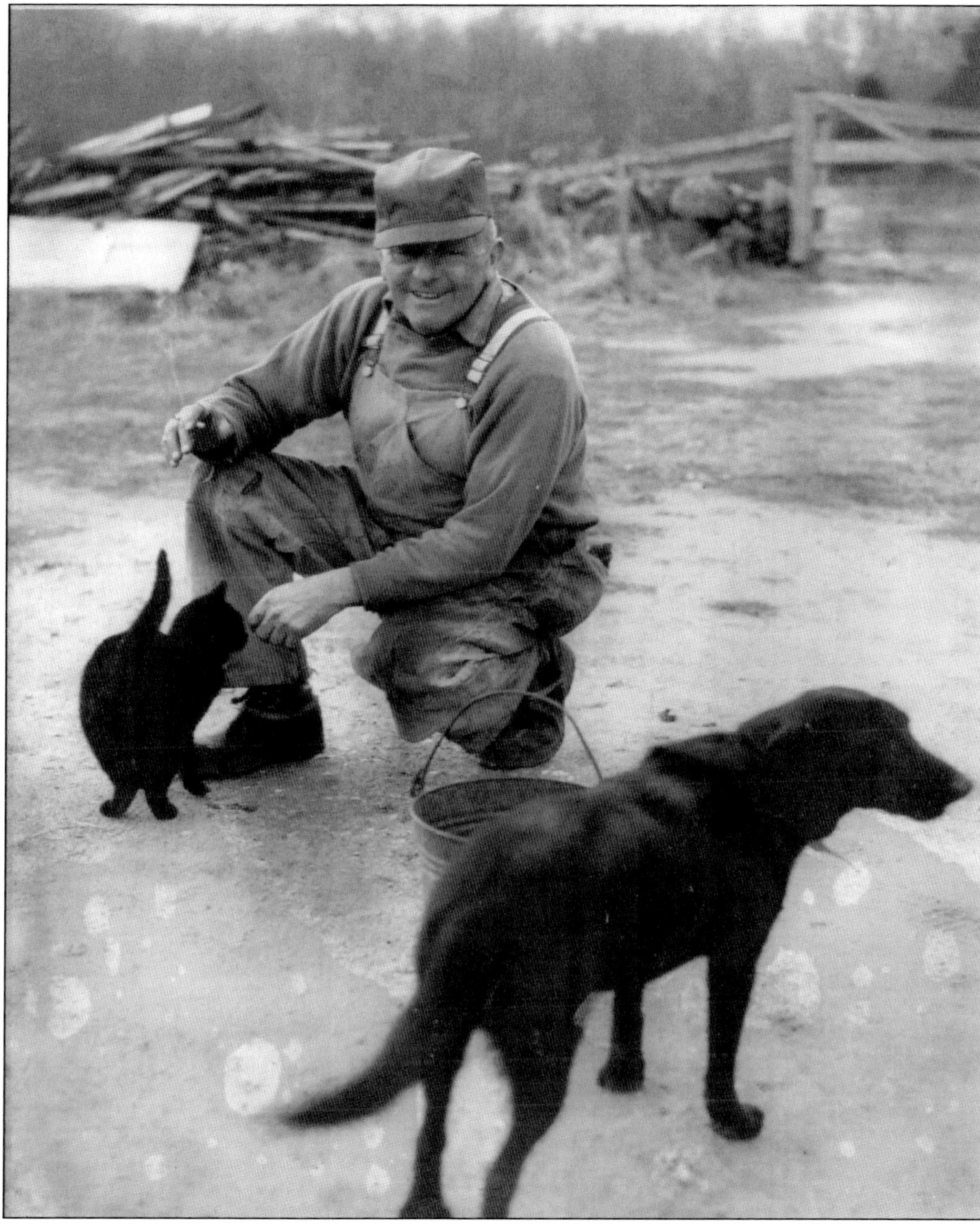

Benjamin S. Carpenter Jr. owned Carpenter's Farm on Matunuck Beach Road for many years. The Carpenters are well known as one of the early farming families in the community. (Courtesy of Cody Carpenter.)

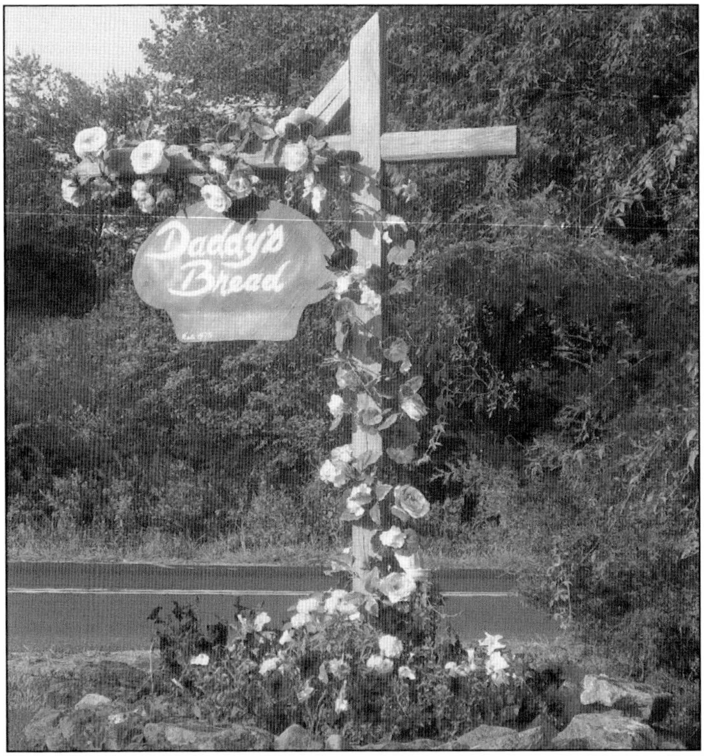

Everett J. Hopkins opened Daddy's Bread on Moonstone Beach Road in 1975. Customers use the honor system to pay for artisan breads. There are as many as 19 varieties at a time to choose from, including parmesan, dill and garlic, rosemary spice, and blueberry apple cinnamon. Daddy's daughter, Jennifer Hopkins Manzo, has run the business for more than 14 years. Everett J. Hopkins passed away in 2012. (Both, courtesy of Jennifer Hopkins Manzo.)

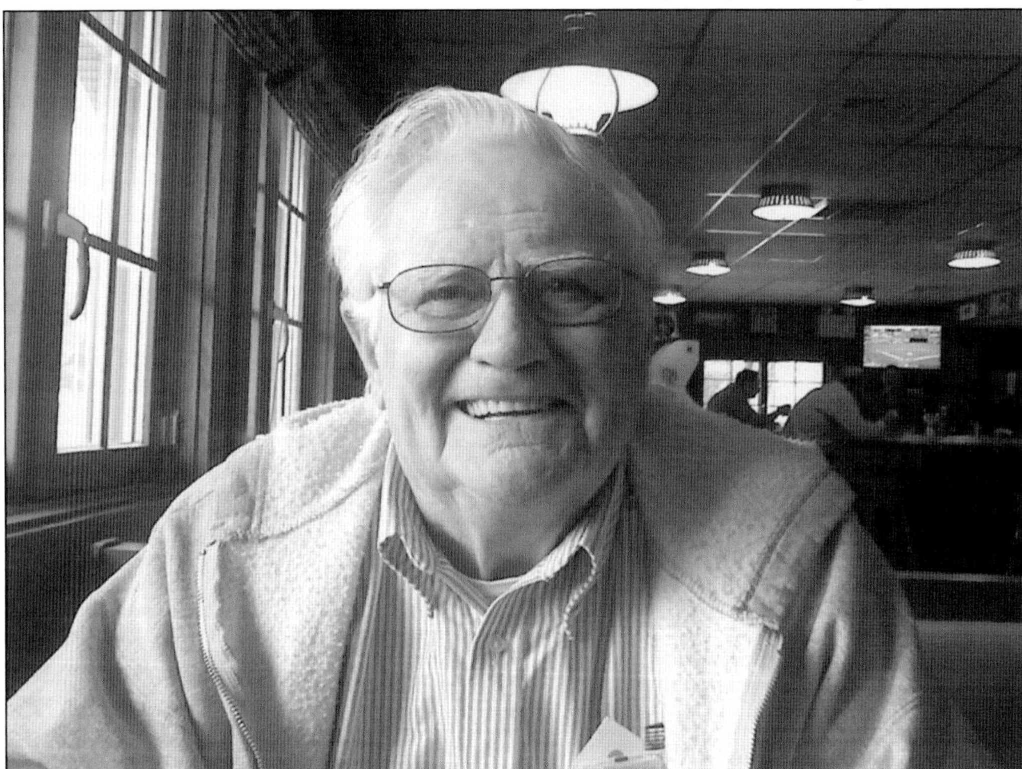

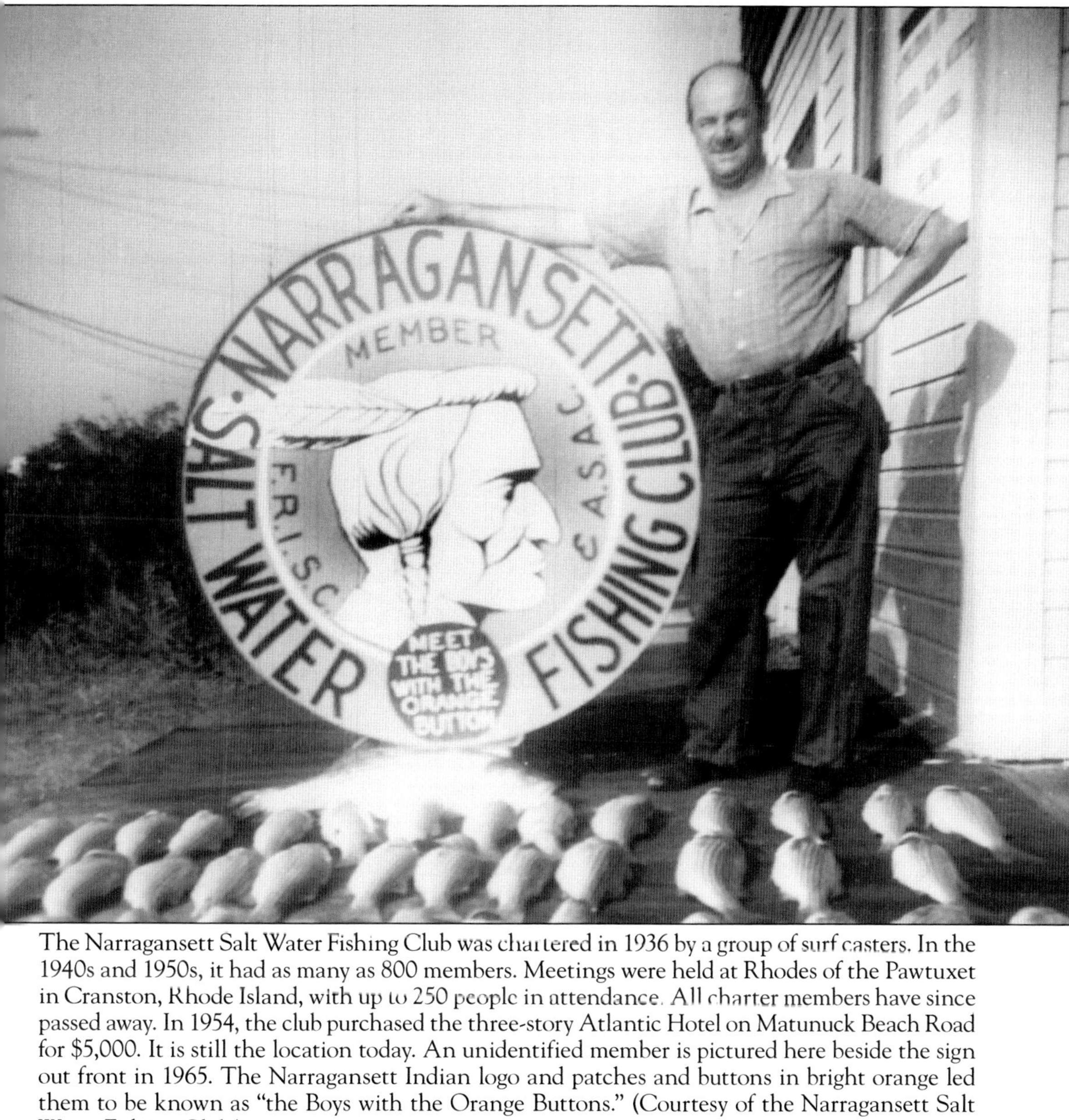

The Narragansett Salt Water Fishing Club was chartered in 1936 by a group of surf casters. In the 1940s and 1950s, it had as many as 800 members. Meetings were held at Rhodes of the Pawtuxet in Cranston, Rhode Island, with up to 250 people in attendance. All charter members have since passed away. In 1954, the club purchased the three-story Atlantic Hotel on Matunuck Beach Road for $5,000. It is still the location today. An unidentified member is pictured here beside the sign out front in 1965. The Narragansett Indian logo and patches and buttons in bright orange led them to be known as "the Boys with the Orange Buttons." (Courtesy of the Narragansett Salt Water Fishing Club.)

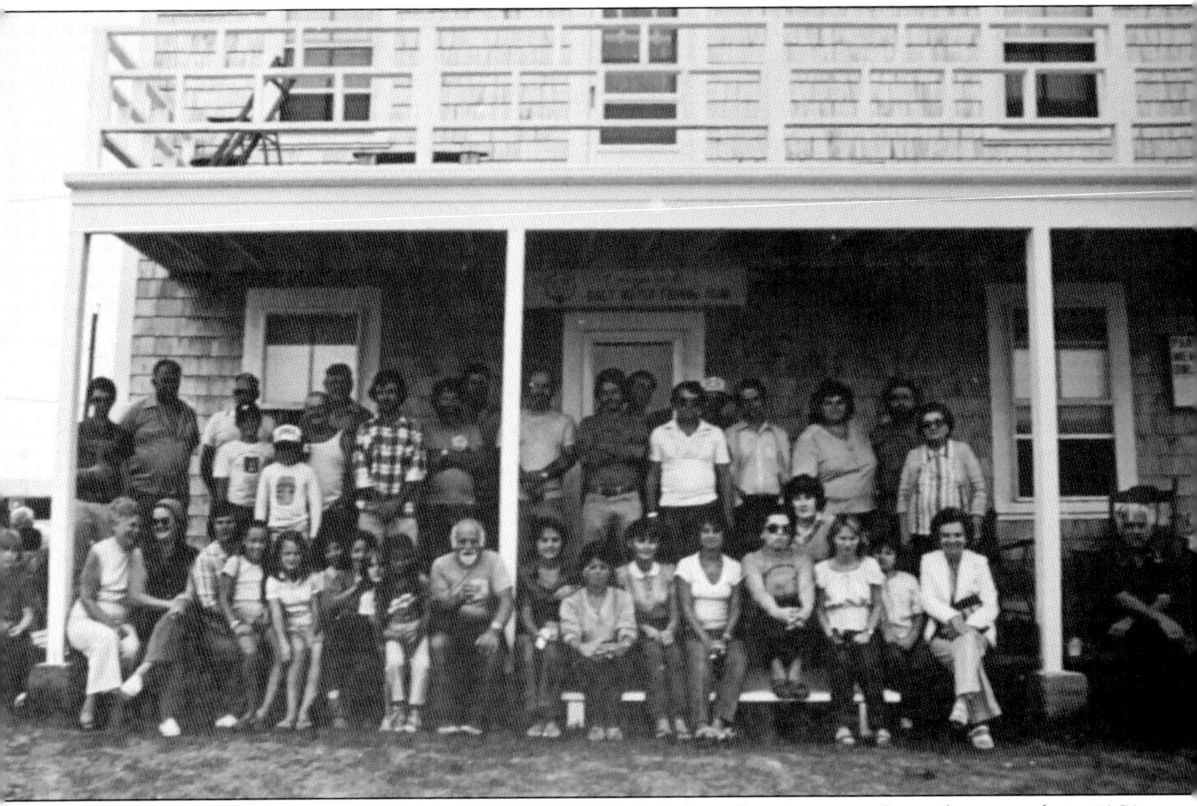

Narragansett Salt Water Fishing Club members and their families pose for a photograph in 1981. (Courtesy of the Narragansett Salt Water Fishing Club.)

Mr. and Mrs. Stusick clean fish at the Narragansett Salt Water Fishing Club. (Courtesy of the Narragansett Salt Water Fishing Club.)

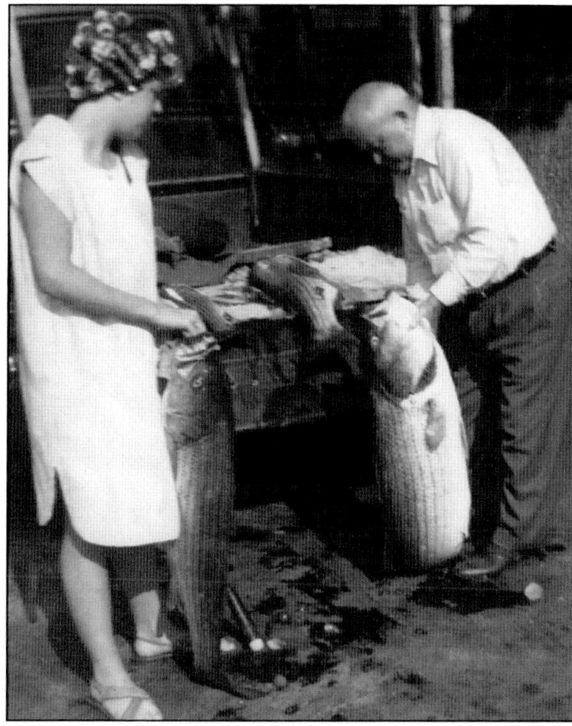

William Kramer goofs around with a table of fish. In 2005, Kramer, a life member, made a generous donation that allowed the club to remove the building's deteriorated siding and replace it with maintenance-free vinyl shingling. (Courtesy of the Narragansett Salt Water Fishing Club.)

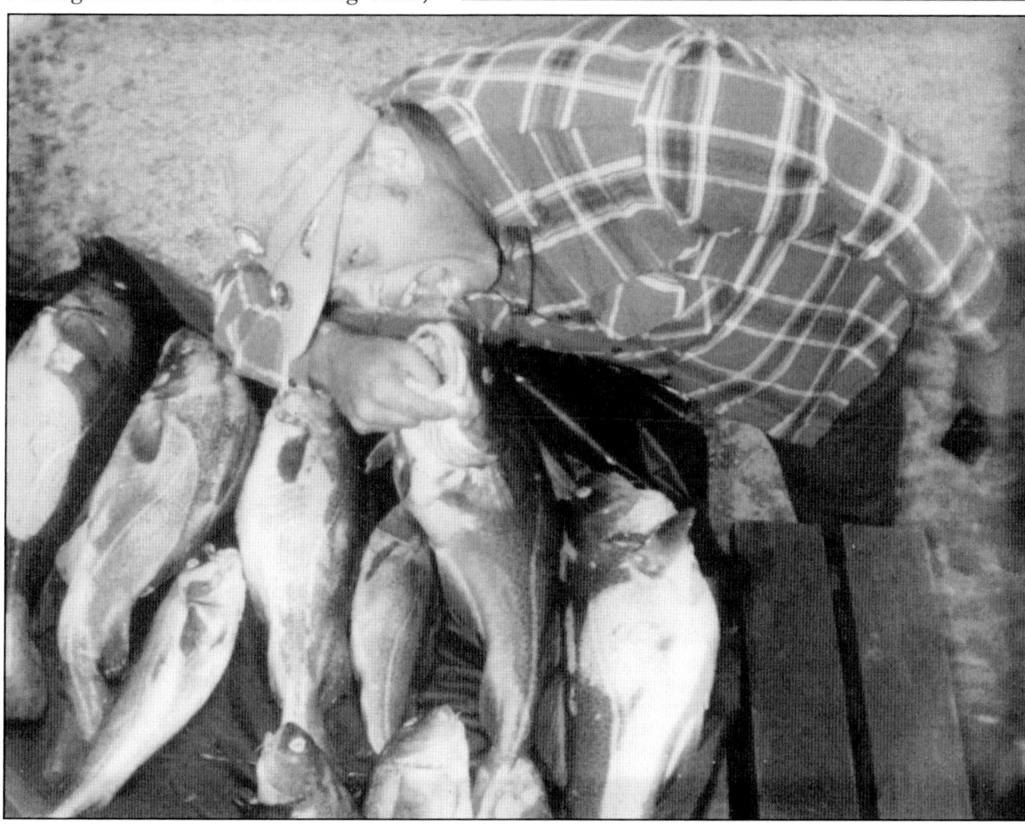

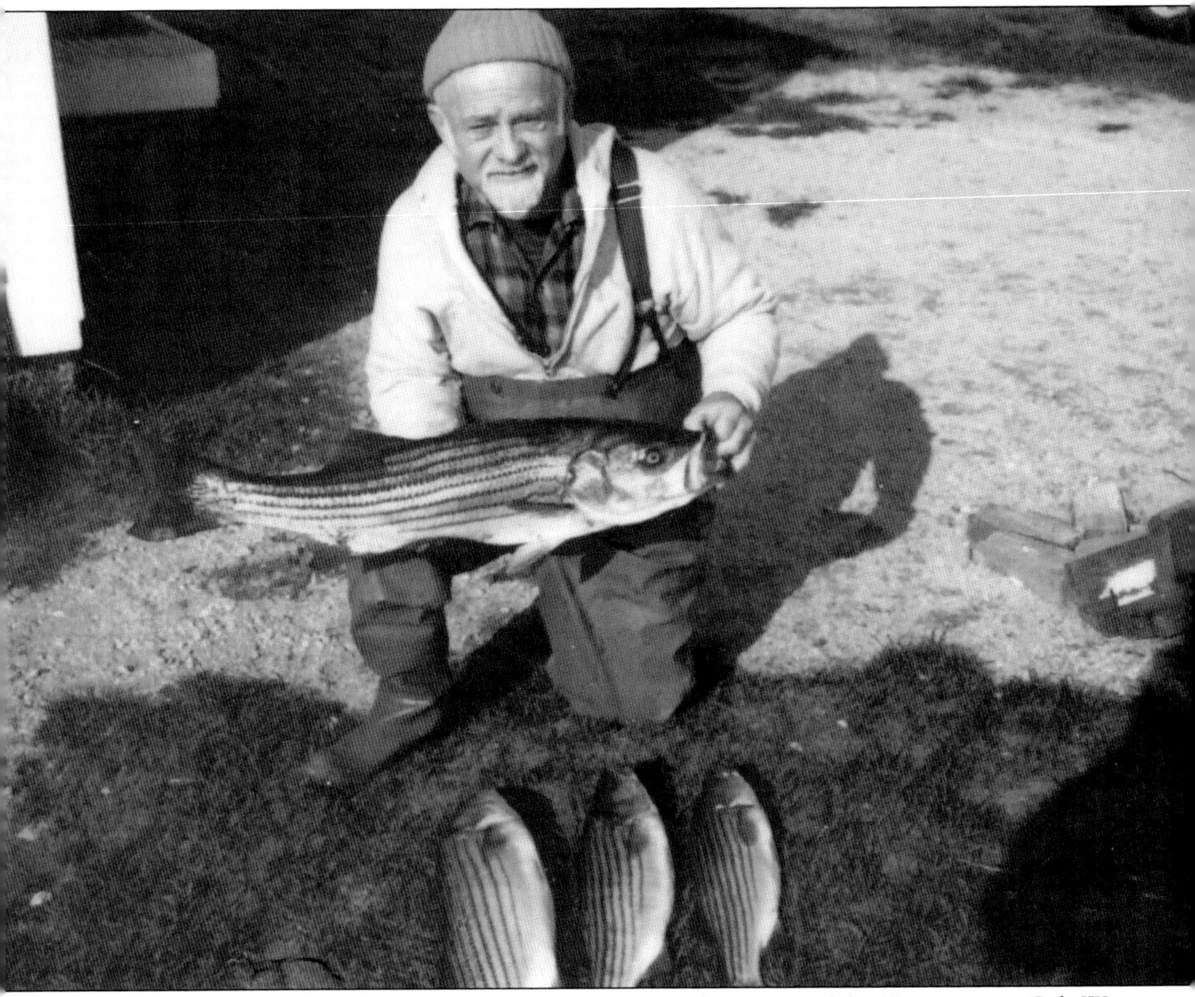

Nick Manzo displays his catch on November 2, 1975. (Courtesy of the Narragansett Salt Water Fishing Club.)

John LaCroix and his father, Horace LaCroix, hang out on the porch of their house on Matunuck Beach Road in 1953. (Courtesy of John LaCroix.)

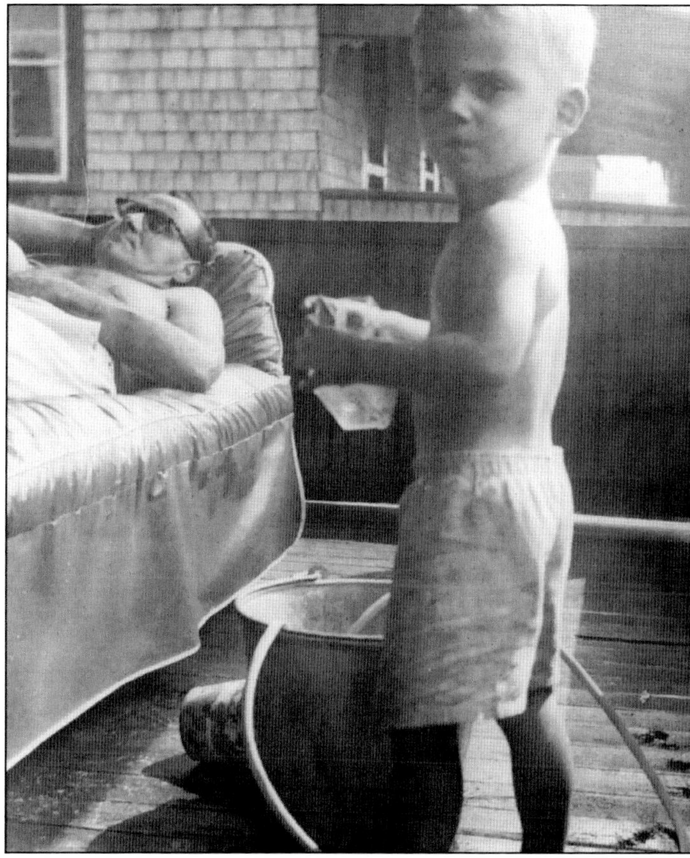

John LaCroix stands in the middle of Matunuck Beach Road in August 1960. The Breakers can be seen on the right. LaCroix is still a summer resident of Matunuck. (Courtesy of John LaCroix.)

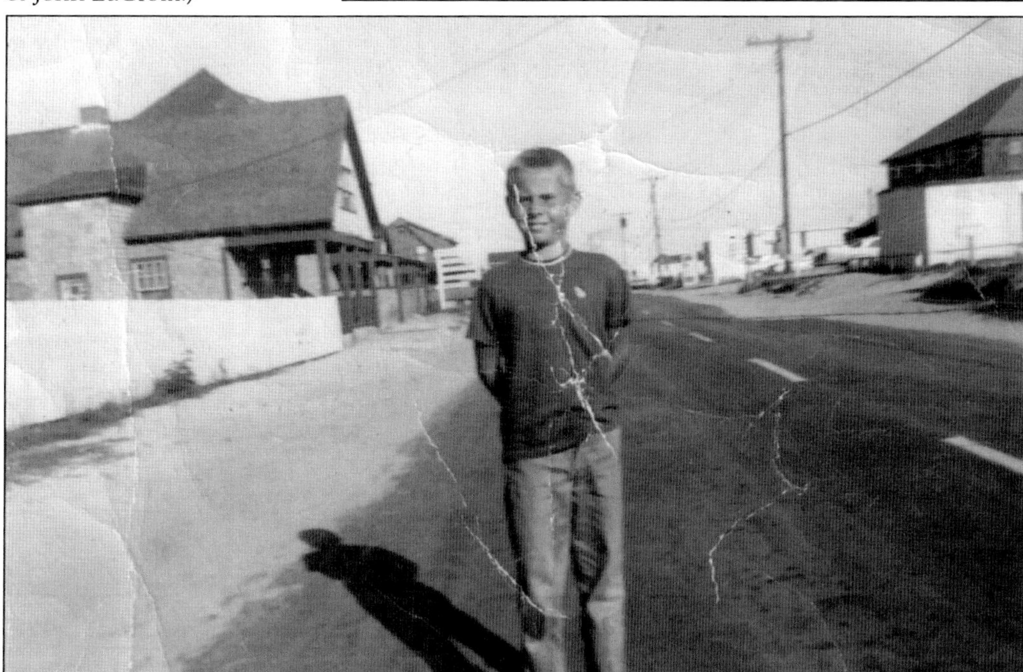

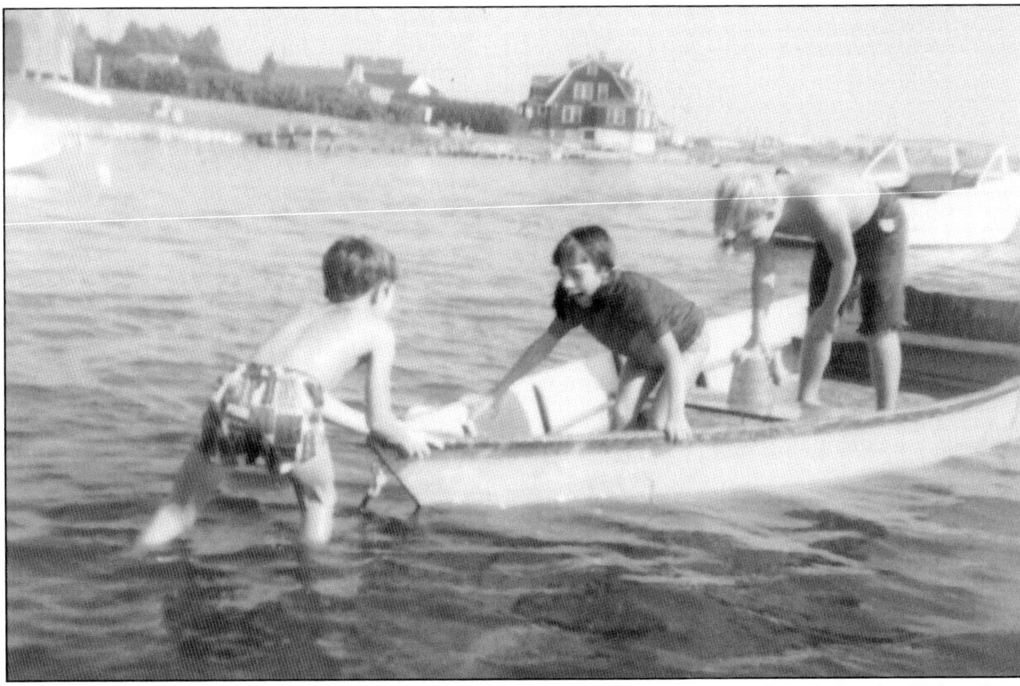

Siblings Buster Rivera (left) and Robyn Rivera (center) are pictured with Ricky Whitehead on Potter's Pond in 1966. From the time Robyn and Buster were born in the early 1960s, they spent their summers in Matunuck. The family would arrive after school let out in June and stay through Labor Day, explained their sister Susan Rivera Russo. They would stay in Matunuck the first three days of the school year, commuting from Cranston, Rhode Island. Once heat was put in the family home on Prospect Road, Robyn and Buster spent most weekends there year-round except at the holidays. (Courtesy of Susan Rivera Russo.)

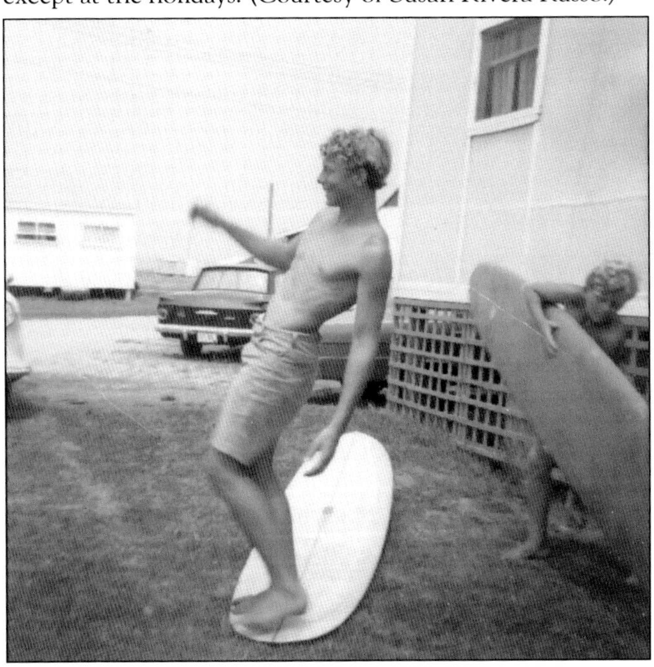

Bill Arcand (left) and his younger brother, Brian Arcand, play on their surfboards at Roy Carpenter's Beach in August 1966. Missing from the photograph is their brother Kevin Arcand. Their parents, Walter and Mary Jiles Arcand, bought the family cottage in 1965. Today, the brothers are all residents of Roy's. (Courtesy of Bill Arcand.)

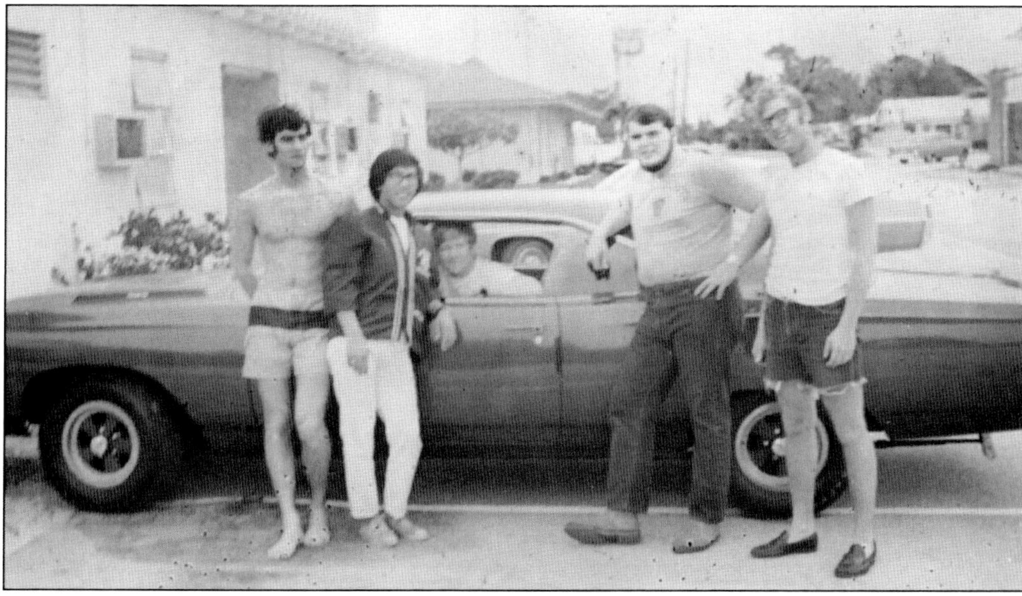

Members of Matunuck Surfing Association (MSA) take a vacation to Fort Lauderdale, Florida, in April 1969. Bob Stockley, now a resident of Carpenter's Beach Meadow, is in the car. MSA is still an active group with a mission to continue the long-standing tradition of wave riding activities in the Matunuck area while supporting the local community through an organization based on sport, camaraderie, and charity. (Courtesy of Bob Stockley.)

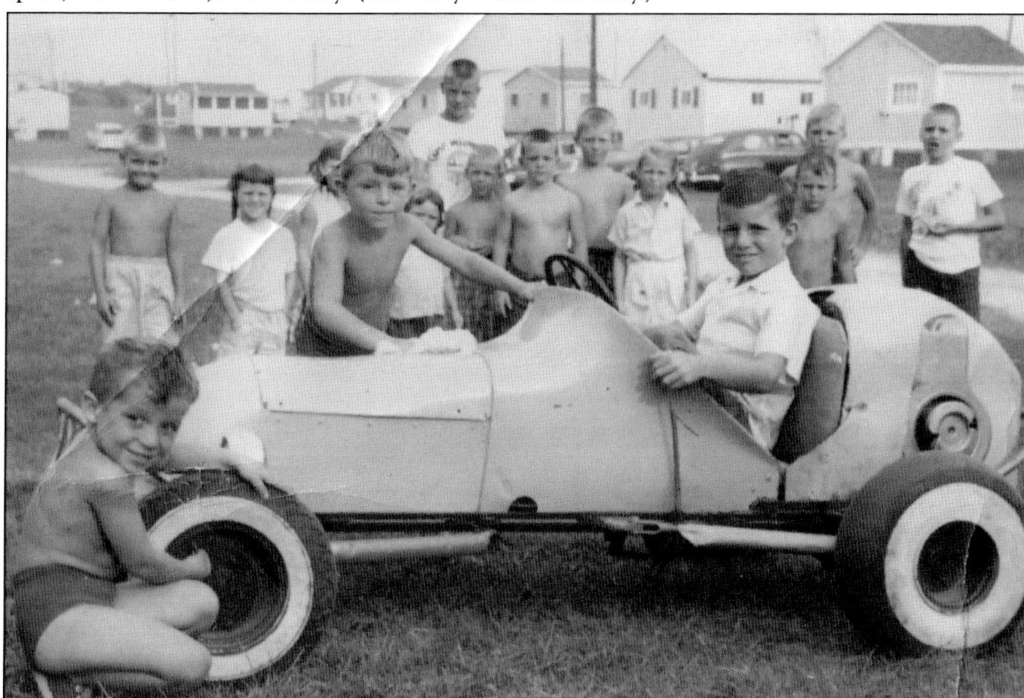

Neighborhood children have fun with a toy car at Roy Carpenter's Beach in the early 1960s. Alan Enos is sitting in the car, Paul Enos is fixing the wheel, and Gary Enos is wiping the hood. Many of these children are still Matunuck residents. (Courtesy of Bob McKenna.)

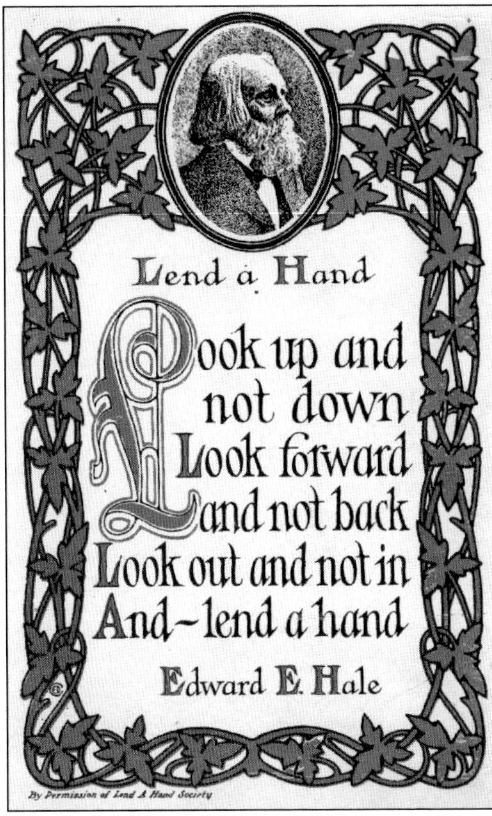

Pictured here is a postcard featuring a quote by Edward Everett Hale (1822–1909). Hale, an author, historian, and Unitarian minister, had a summer home in Matunuck. His house was listed in the National Register of Historic Places in 2007. (Courtesy of the Robert Beverly Hale Library.)

The Meadows clan is enjoying the outdoors at a summer home on Park Avenue in 1960. From left to right are (first row) John McHenry and Karen McHenry; (second row) Marcia Easterling, Jeanne McHenry Helma, and Mary Madelyn Meadows; (third row) Madelyn Anderson, Cookie Easterling, Catheryn Easterling, Anne McHenry, and Stephen McHenry. (Courtesy of Jeanne McHenry Helma.)

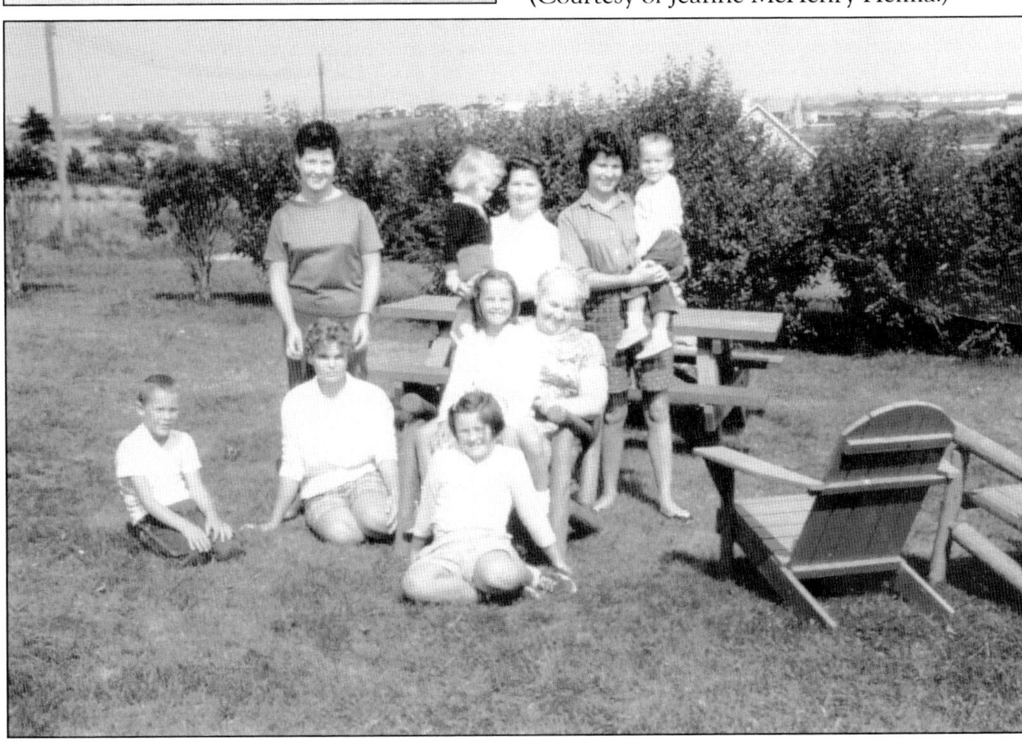

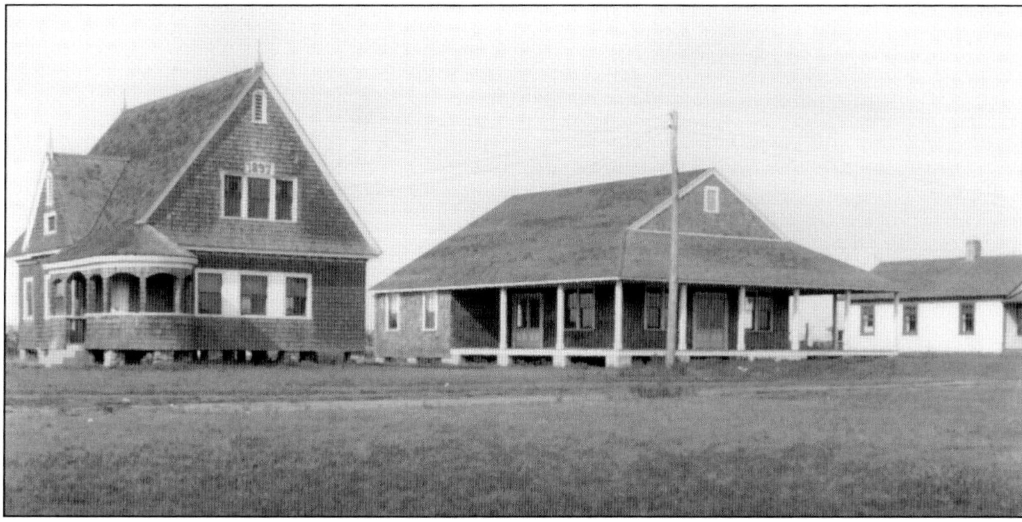

The Matunuck Community House was built on Lake Avenue in 1897, near the Matunuck Park Chapel. This photograph was taken sometime between 1897 and 1935. In 1935, the building was moved to 42 Community Drive, after the Ladies' Auxiliary of the chapel sold the land. It was moved again in May 1964 to its present location at 619 Matunuck Beach Road. An expansion took place in 1997 when the porch and deck were enlarged. The new deck was dedicated in memory of Bill Ellsbree in 1998 with a plaque in his honor. In 2010, a butterfly garden was dedicated to Dorothy Sarni, a longtime friend and benefactor of Matunuck Community Association. In 2012, the flag memorial circle was dedicated to Dennis DeGrass, a board member for many years and ongoing benefactor of the club. The organization will celebrate its 100th anniversary in 2015. (Courtesy of David Gallogly.)

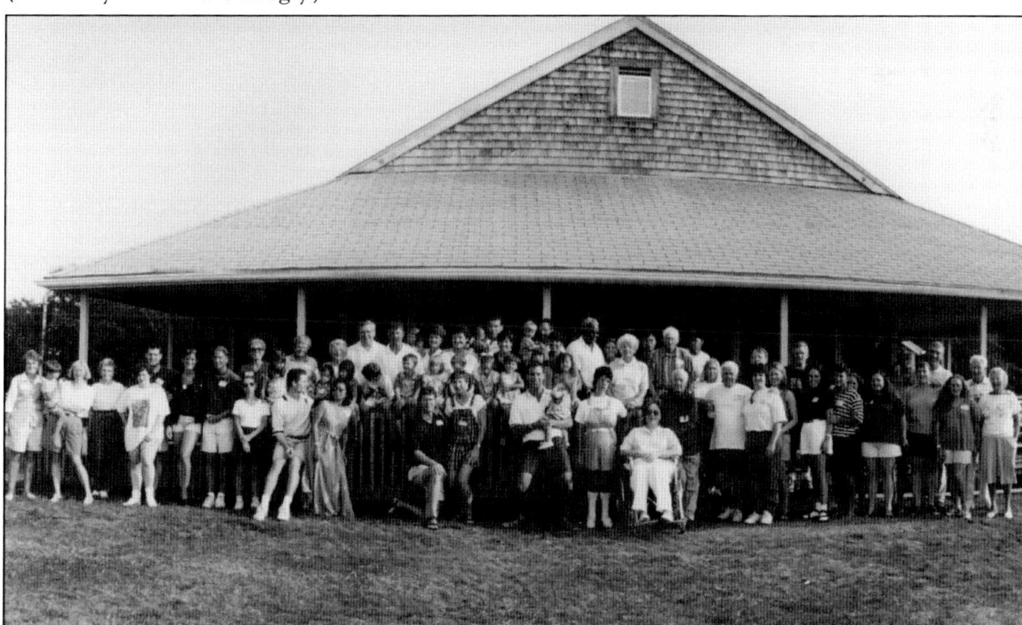

A Gallogly family reunion took place at the Matunuck Community House on August 2, 1997. Members of the Gallogly family have lived in Matunuck for more than a century. (Courtesy of David Gallogly.)

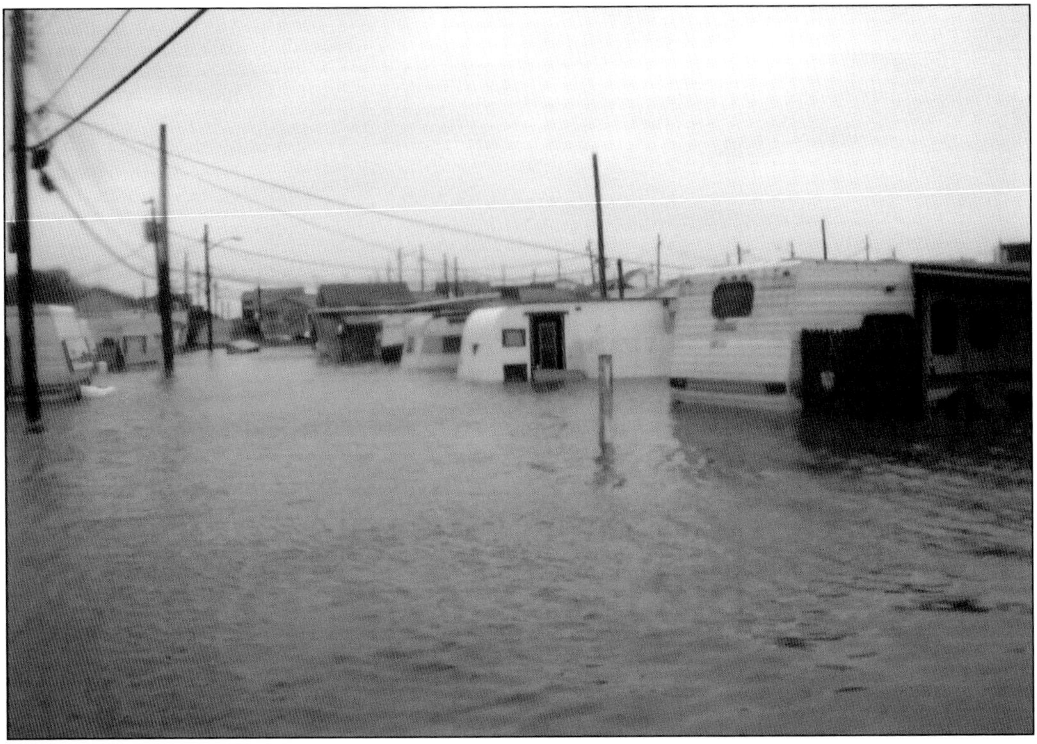

After a storm in October 2006, severe flooding hit Carpenter's Beach Meadow. (Both, courtesy of Mike McKenna.)

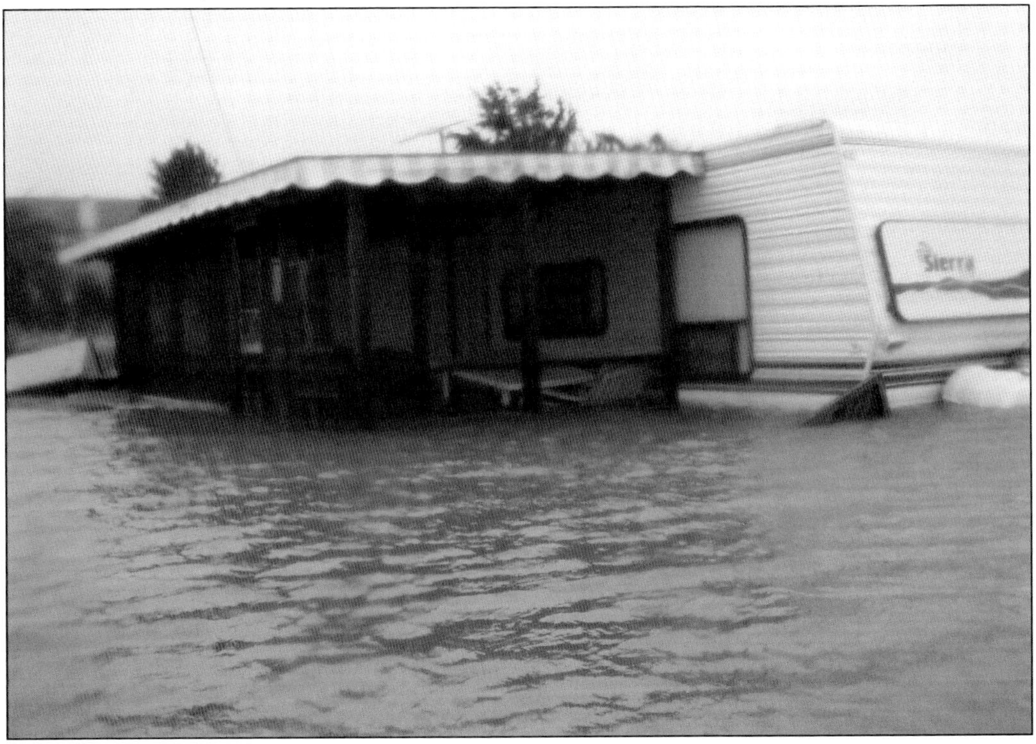

Two

The Beach

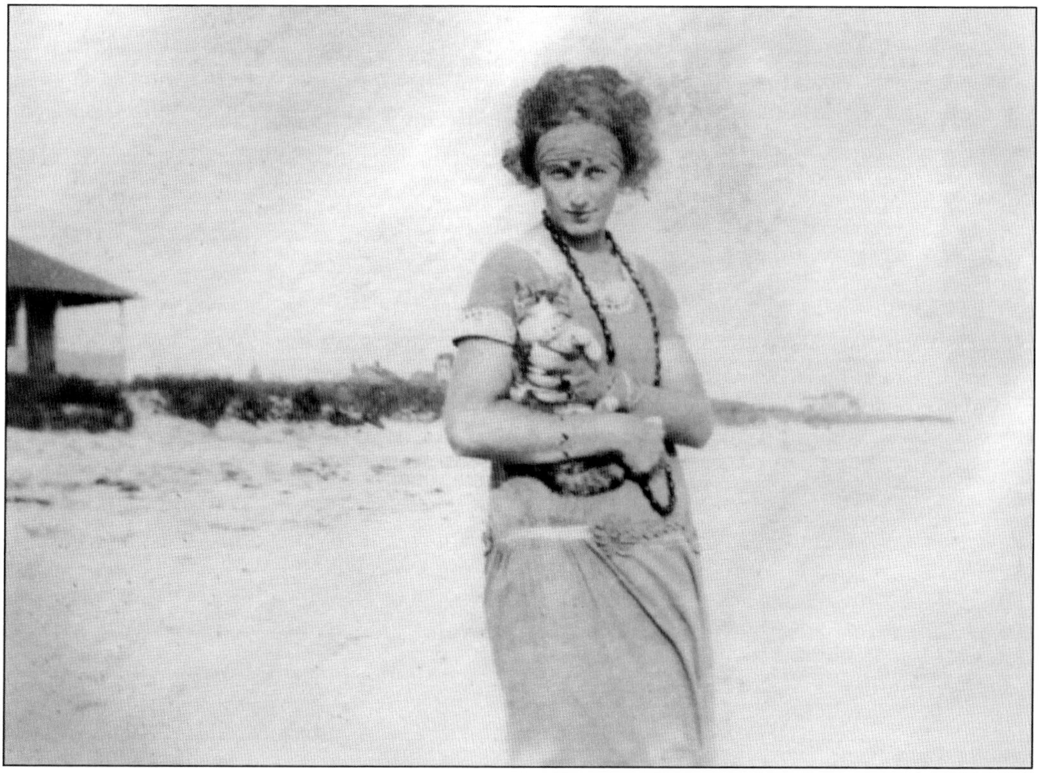

Fashionably dressed Virginia Broome Yale and her cat pose on Matunuck Beach in the 1920s. Virginia became a permanent summer resident at age eight when her parents, Charles and Esther Rebecca Weeden Broome, built a home there. (Courtesy of David Yale.)

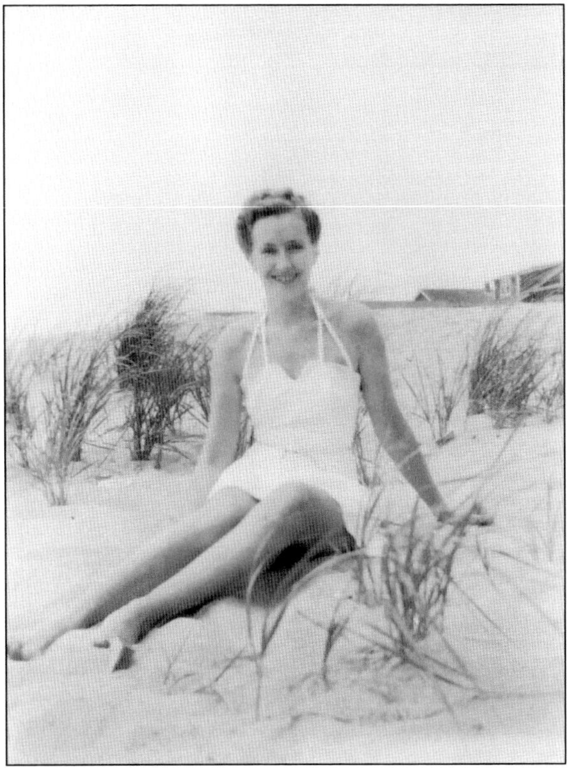

Margaret Gallogly Terry looks lovely in the dunes of Matunuck Beach in the late 1930s. (Both, courtesy of Ann Terry.)

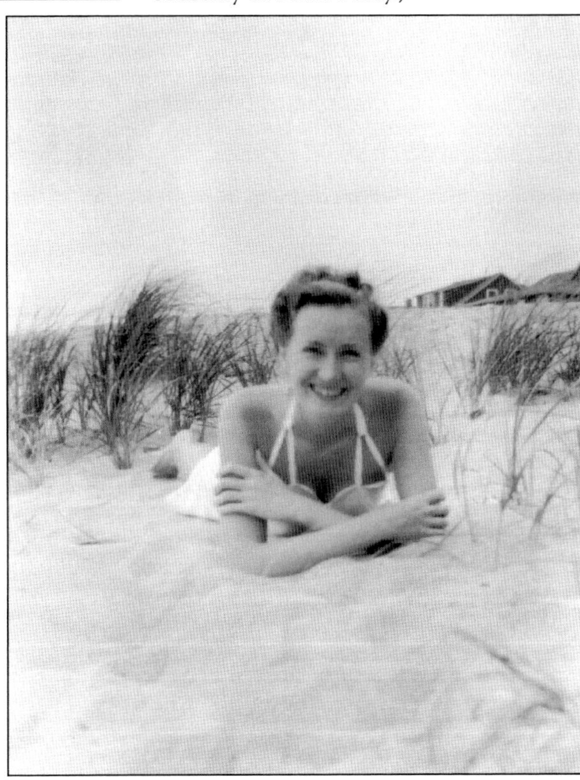

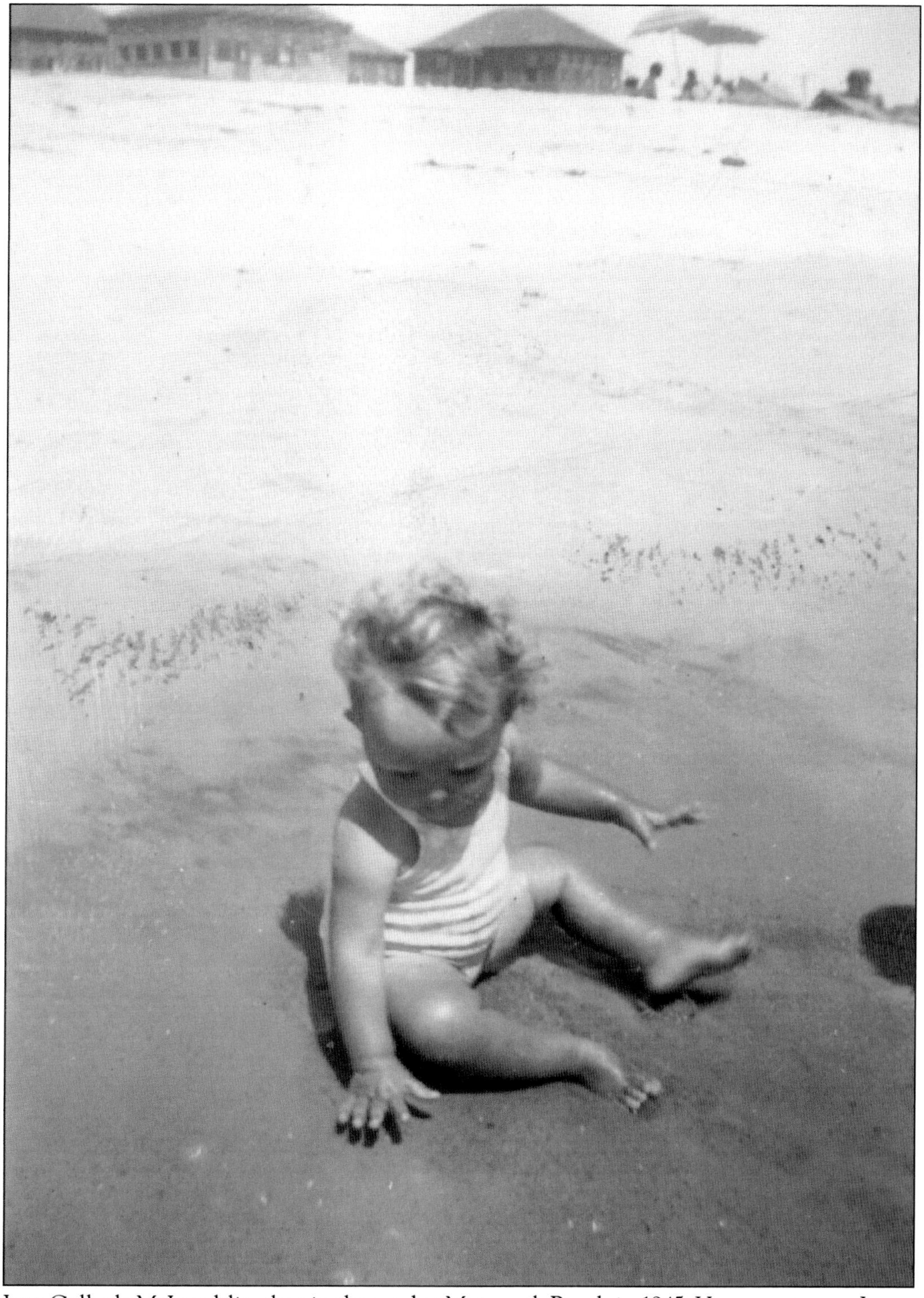

Jane Gallogly McLaughlin plays in the sand at Matunuck Beach in 1945. Her parents were James and Cecile Clarkin Gallogly. Her brother David Gallogly stills resides in Matunuck. (Courtesy of David Gallogly.)

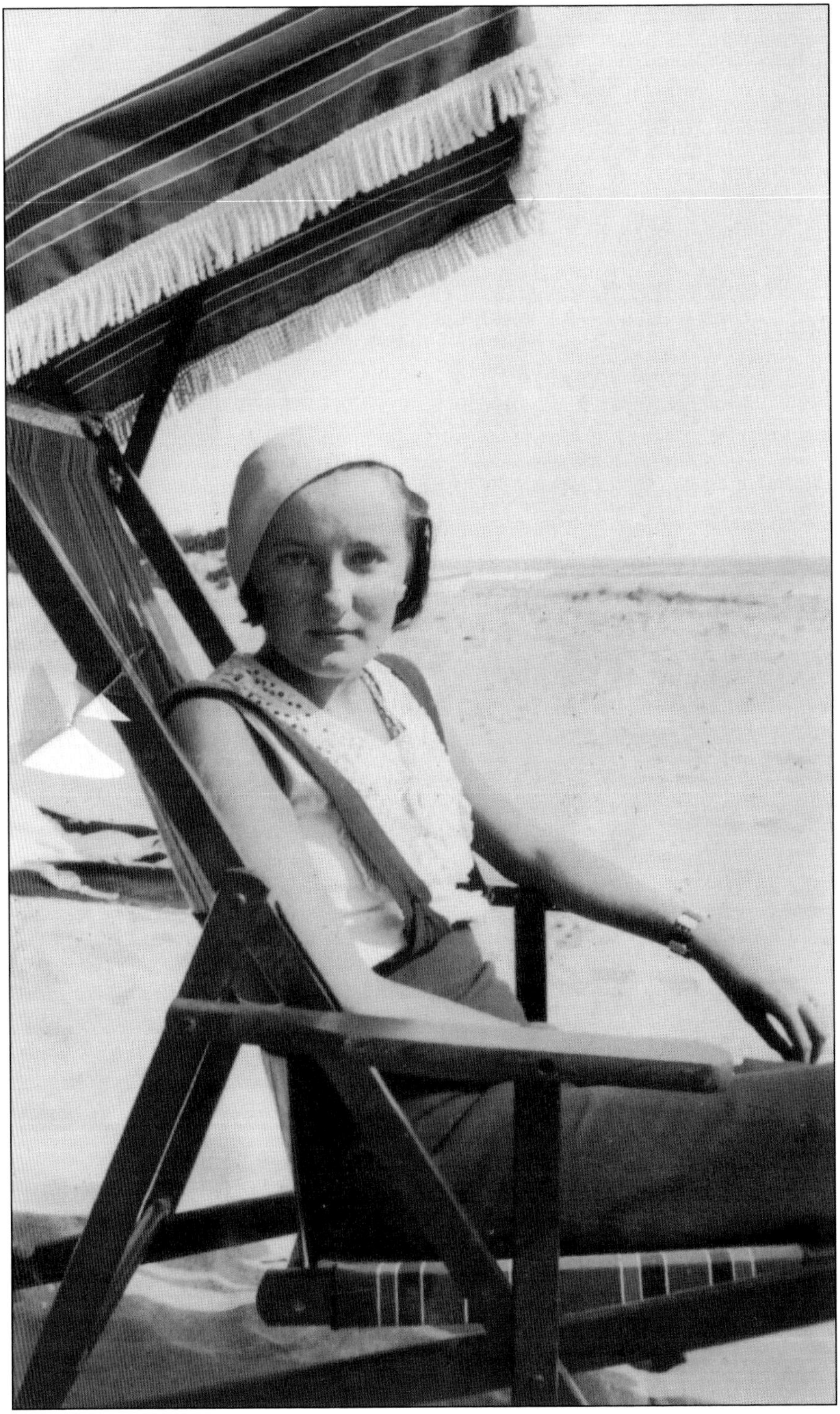

Margaret Gallogly Terry lounges in her beach chair around 1936. (Courtesy of Eleanor Gallogly Mullaney and Margaret Gallogly Navin.)

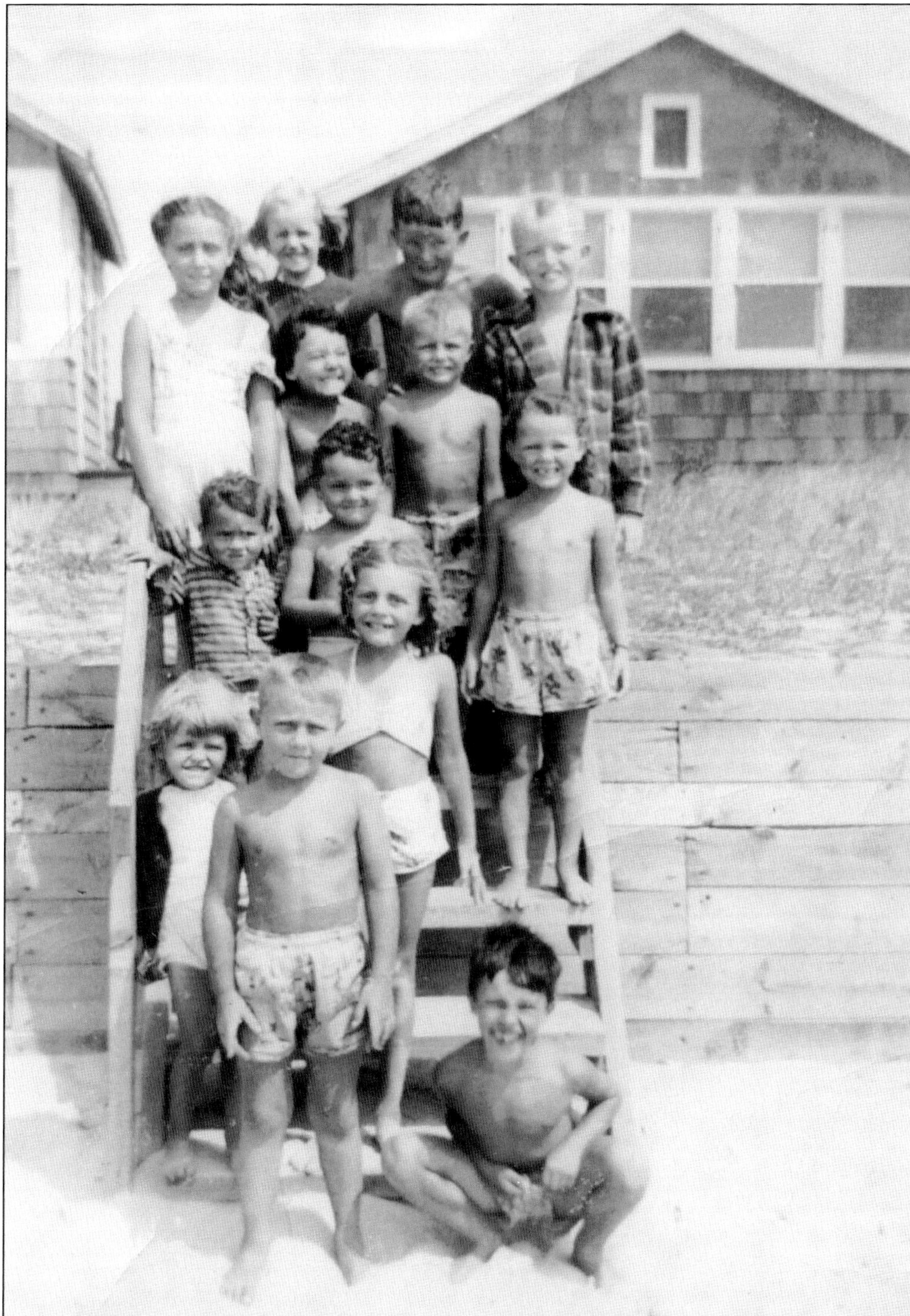

Children stand on the steps at the Ahearn Cottages on Matunuck Beach Road in 1949. Owned by James and Mary Callahan Ahearn, two of the three cottages were available for rent. They are still in existence today. (Courtesy of Mary Ann Gallogly Scott.)

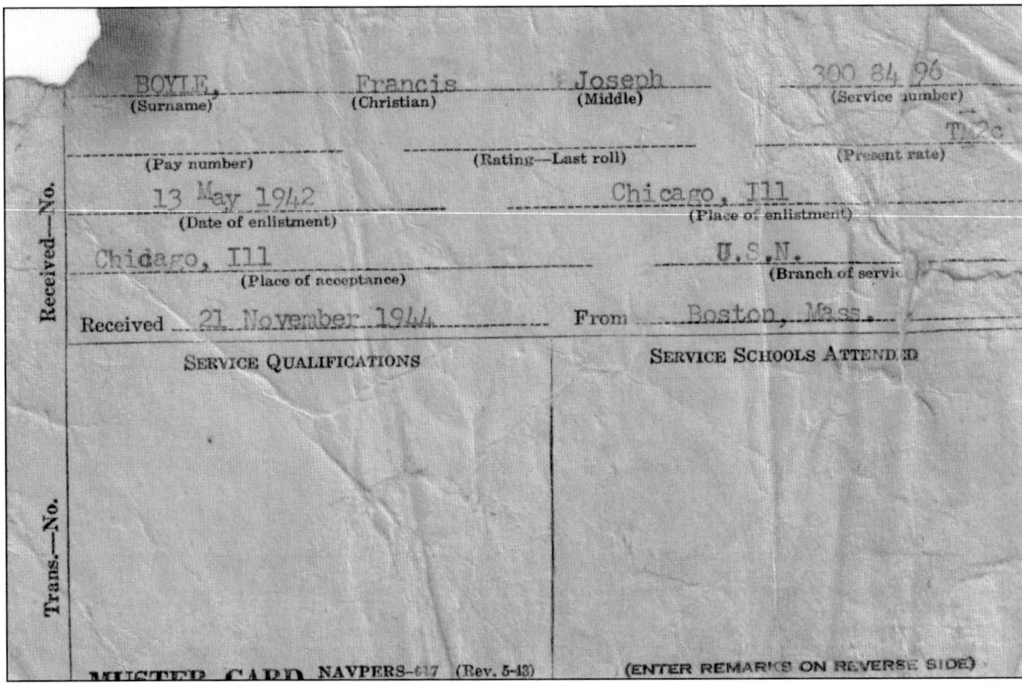
BOYLE, (Surname) Francis (Christian) Joseph (Middle) 300 84 96 (Service number)

(Pay number) (Rating—Last roll) TM2c (Present rate)

13 May 1942 (Date of enlistment) Chicago, Ill (Place of enlistment)

Chidago, Ill (Place of acceptance) U.S.N. (Branch of servic

Received 21 November 1944 From Boston, Mass.

Received—No.

Trans.—No.

SERVICE QUALIFICATIONS

SERVICE SCHOOLS ATTENDED

MUSTER CARD NAVPERS-617 (Rev. 5-43) (ENTER REMARKS ON REVERSE SIDE)

Like many young Matunuck children in the early 1940s, David Yale often went for a walk along the beach after dinner. Just around twilight one day, he came across these muster cards floating in an oil slick. (Both, courtesy of David Yale.)

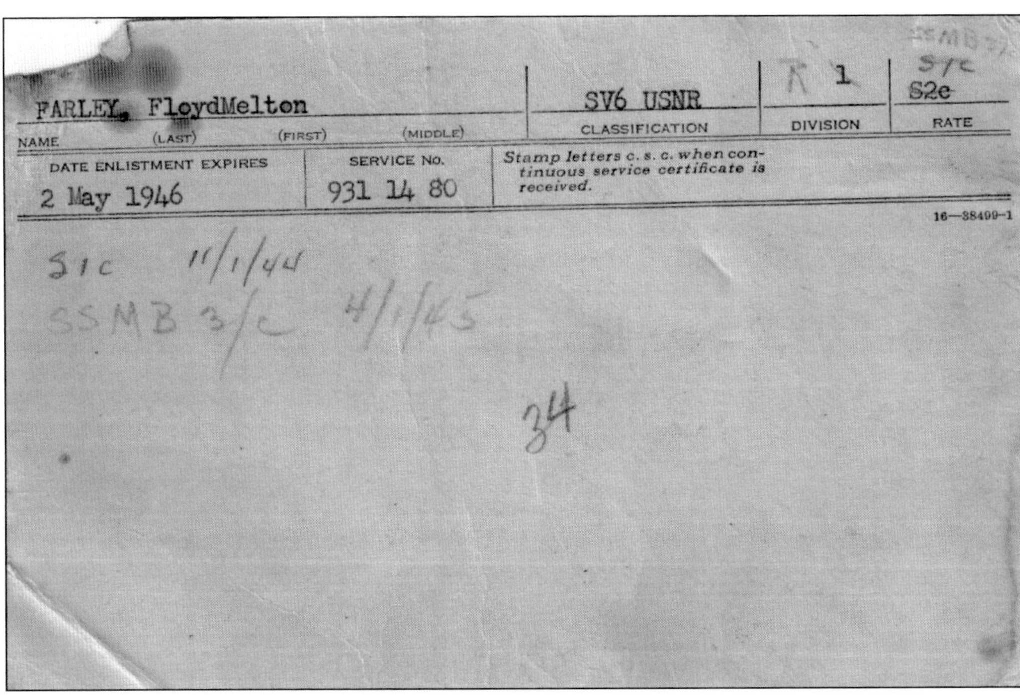
NAME FARLEY, FloydMelton (LAST) (FIRST) (MIDDLE)

CLASSIFICATION SV6 USNR

DIVISION R 1

RATE S2e S/c

DATE ENLISTMENT EXPIRES 2 May 1946

SERVICE No. 931 14 80

Stamp letters c. s. c. when continuous service certificate is received.

16—38499-1

S1c 11/1/44

SSMB 3/c 4/1/45

34

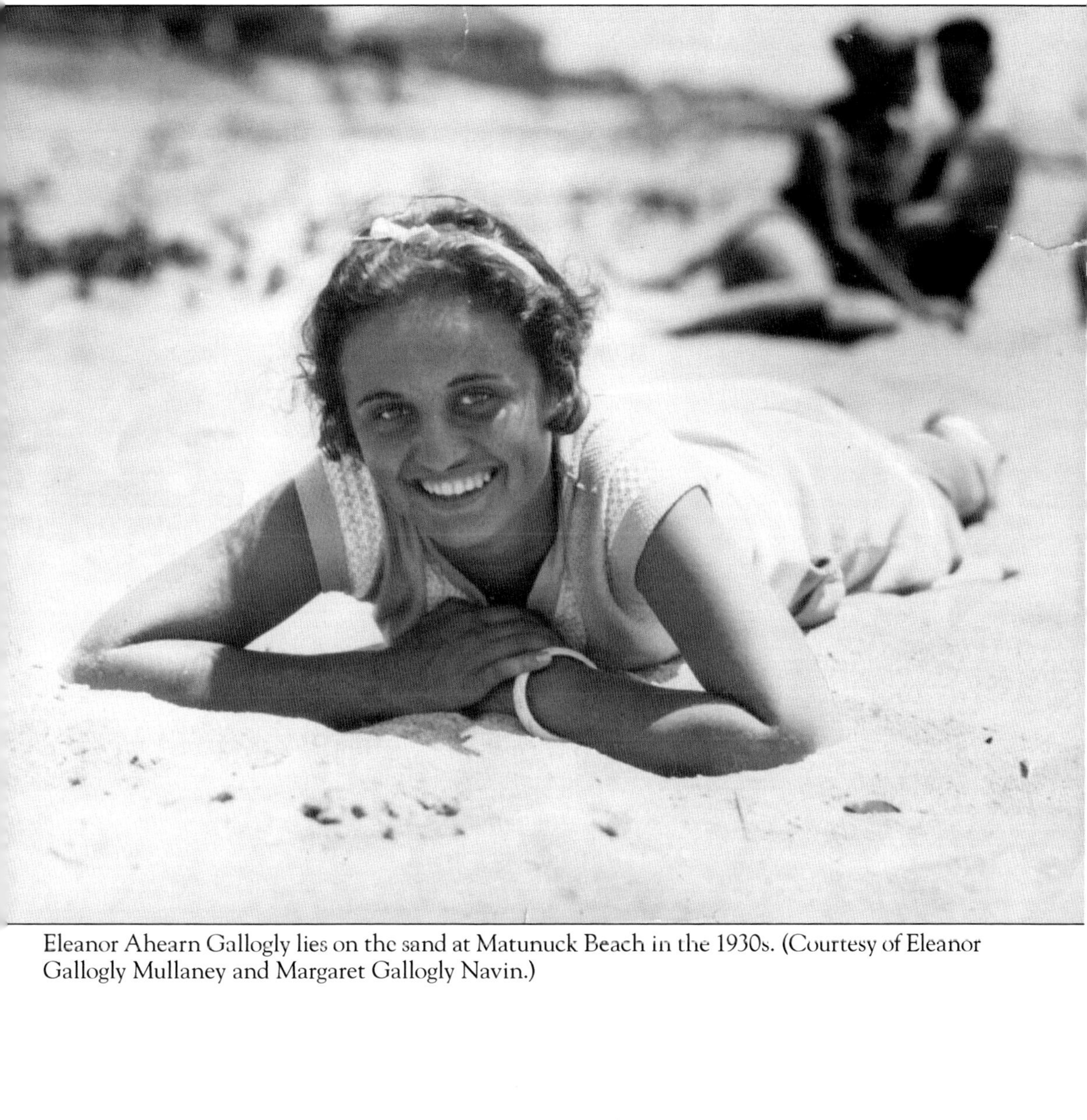

Eleanor Ahearn Gallogly lies on the sand at Matunuck Beach in the 1930s. (Courtesy of Eleanor Gallogly Mullaney and Margaret Gallogly Navin.)

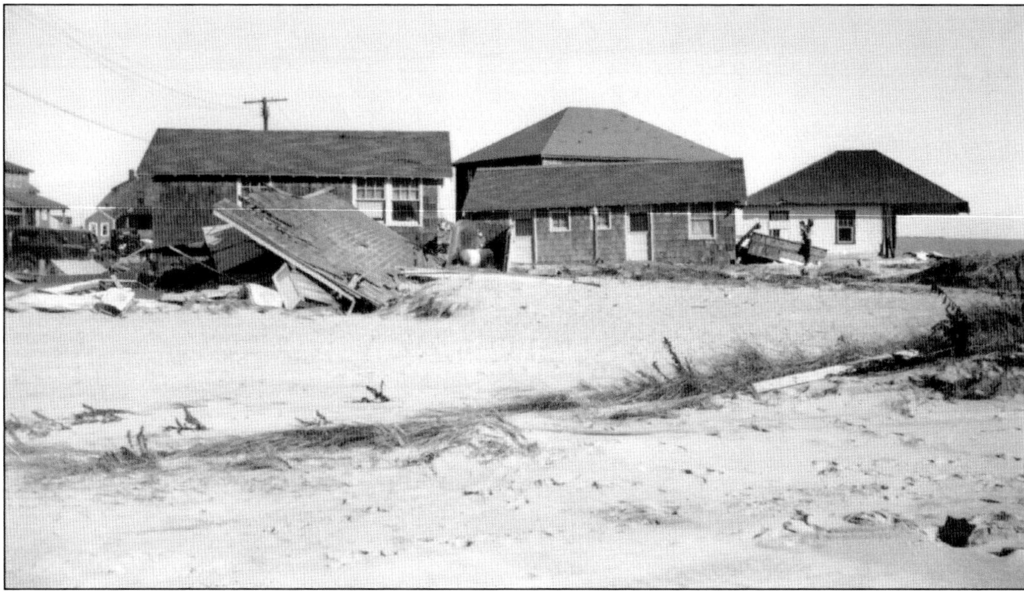

This is how the Ahearn Cottages on Matunuck Beach Road looked just after the hurricane of 1938. They were owned by James and Mary Callahan Ahearn, the maternal grandparents of Eleanor Gallogly Mullaney and Margarert Gallogly Navin. (Both, courtesy of Eleanor Gallogly Mullaney and Margaret Gallogly Navin.)

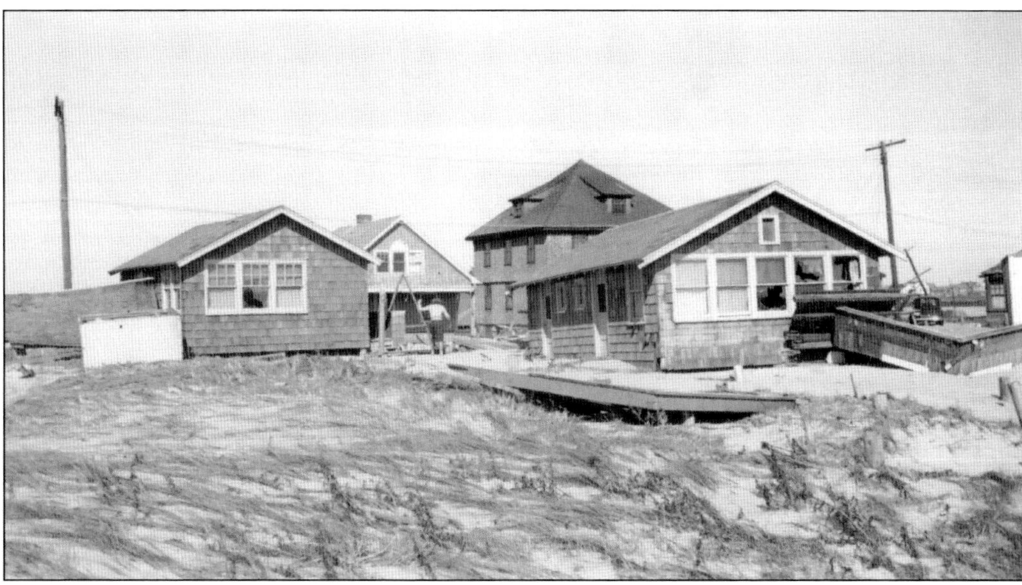

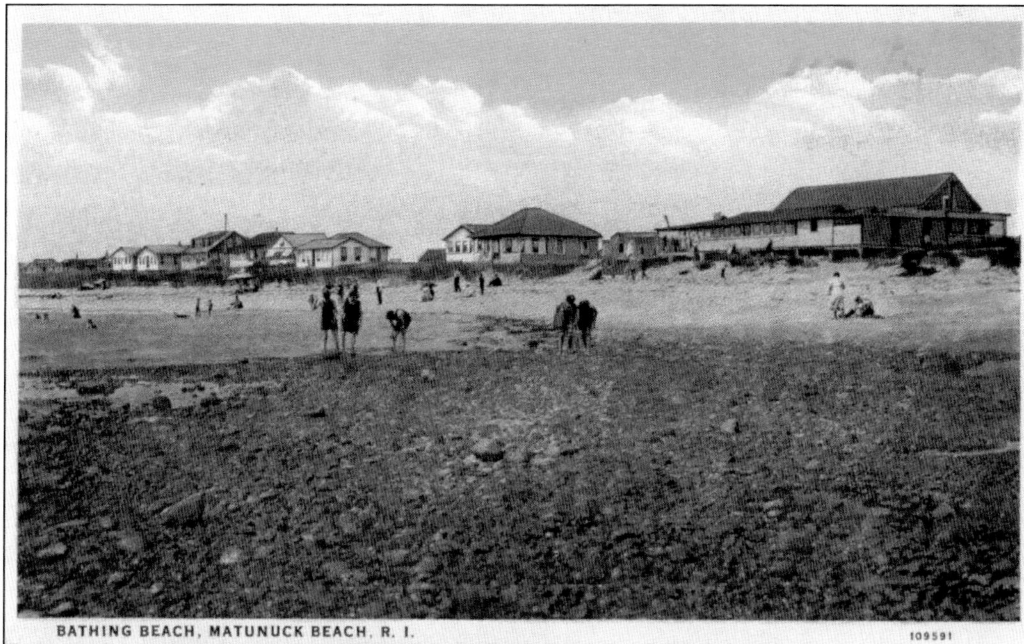

One of the buildings seen from Bathing Beach was La Bea's Restaurant, which later burned down. (Courtesy of the Robert Beverly Hale Library.)

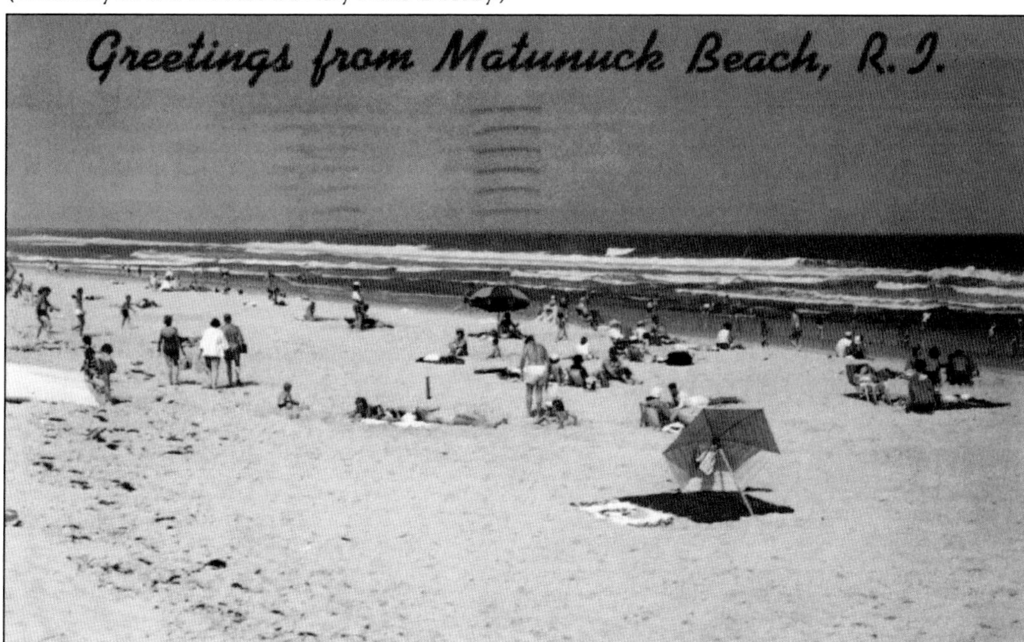

Matunuck Beach was the original name for the entire stretch of coast along the village. In the early 1900s, with the increased use of automobiles and improved highways, more visitors came to Matunuck Beach. They stayed at large boardinghouses or built summer cottages. More homes and cottages popped up after World War II. Today, summer residents make up the majority of the population; however, with great beaches, surfing, and fishing spots, Matunuck is popular with day trippers. (Courtesy of the Robert Beverly Hale Library.)

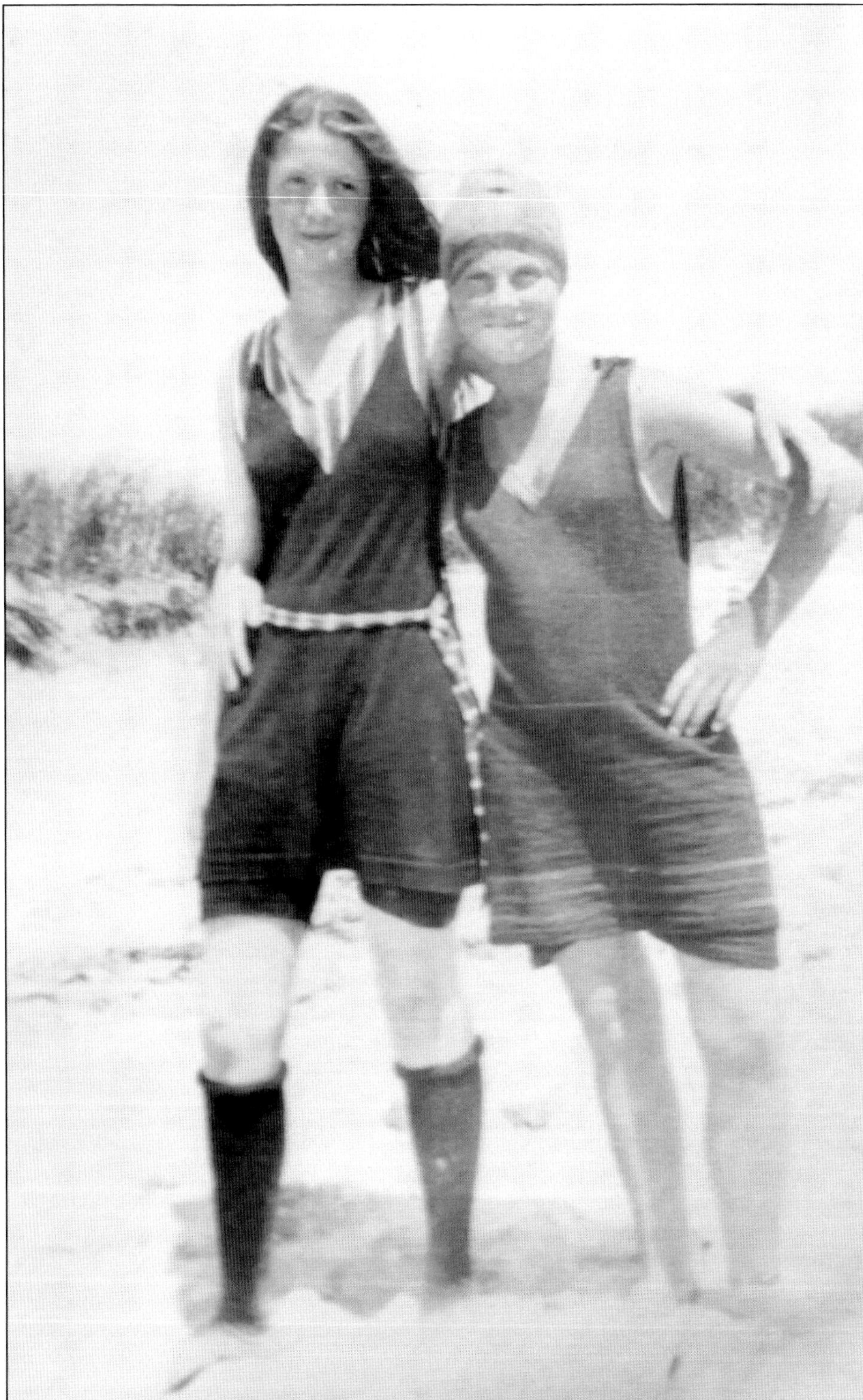

Two young women are pictured at Matunuck Beach in the 1920s. (Courtesy of David Yale.)

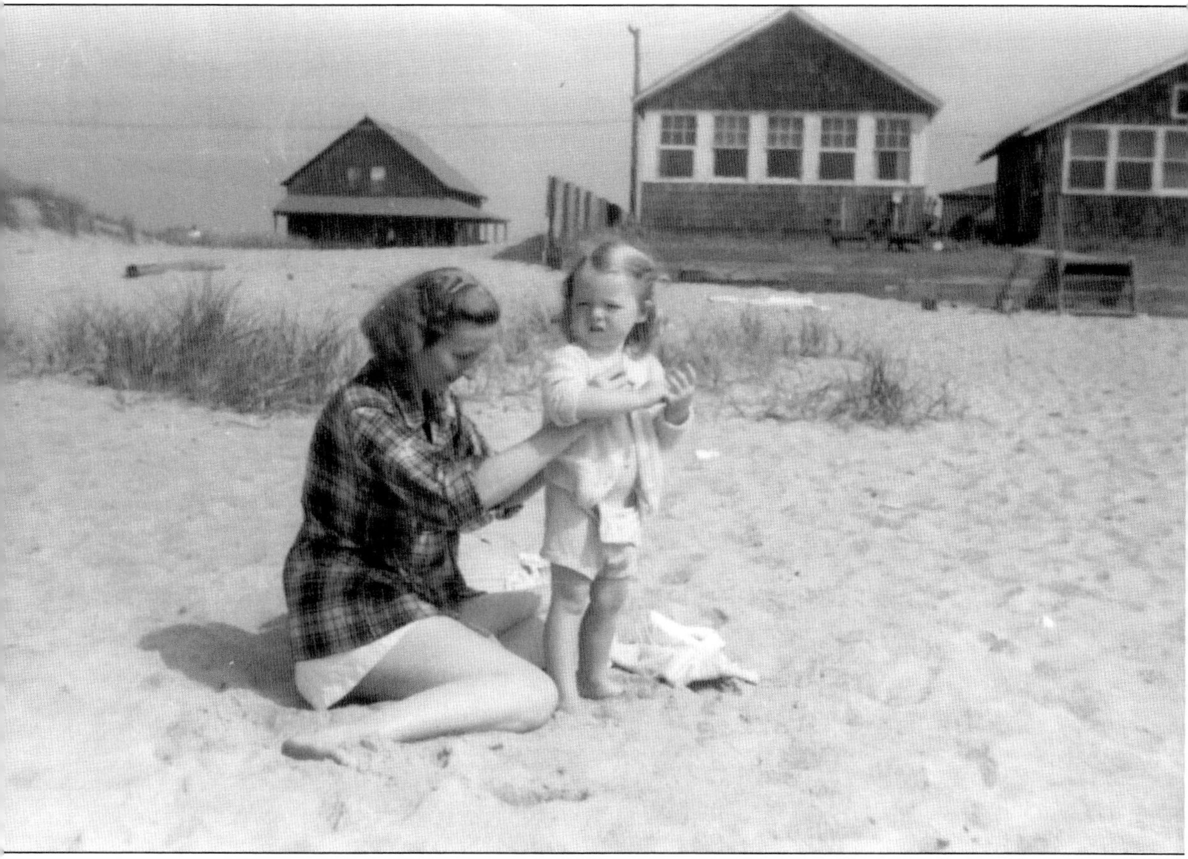

Margaret Gallogly Terry and her firstborn child, Marsha Terry Obusek, are at the Ahearn Cottages in the late 1940s. (Courtesy of Ann Terry.)

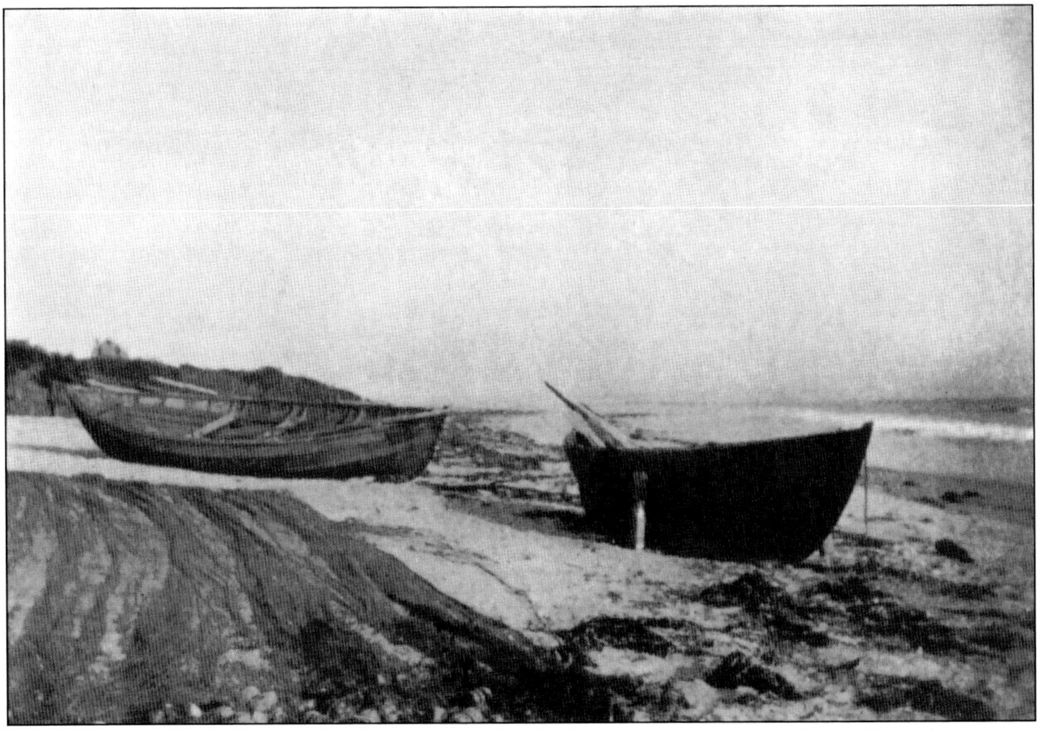

Fishermen's boats make the perfect scene for this letter card. (Courtesy of David Yale.)

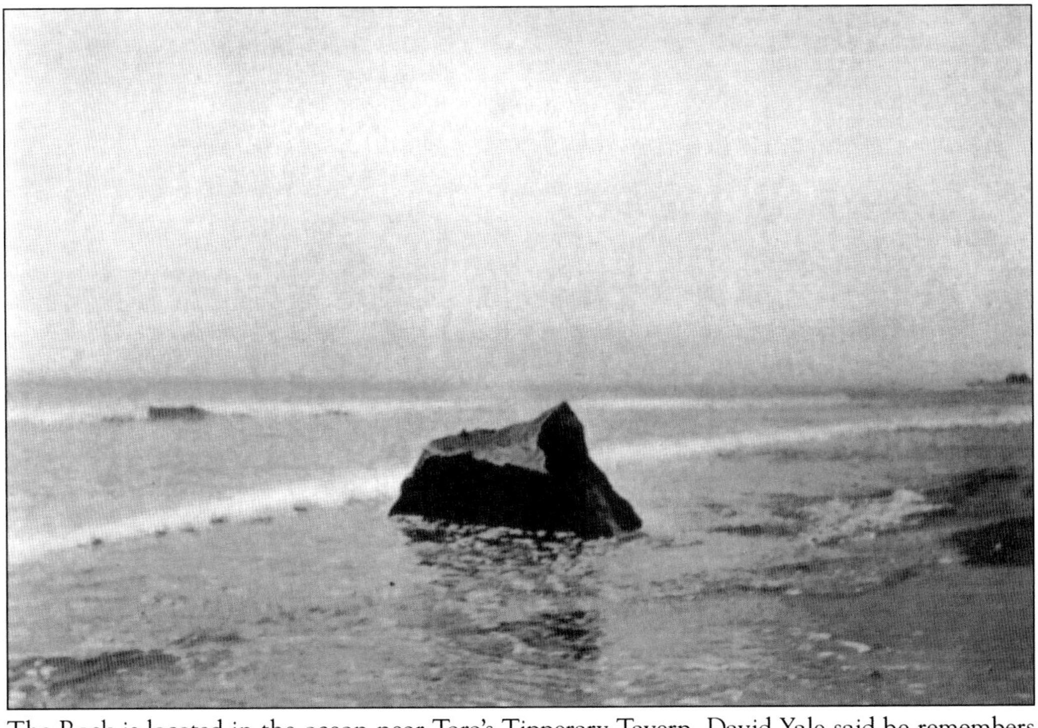

The Rock is located in the ocean near Tara's Tipperary Tavern. David Yale said he remembers first seeing it as a child in the late 1930s. (Courtesy of David Yale.)

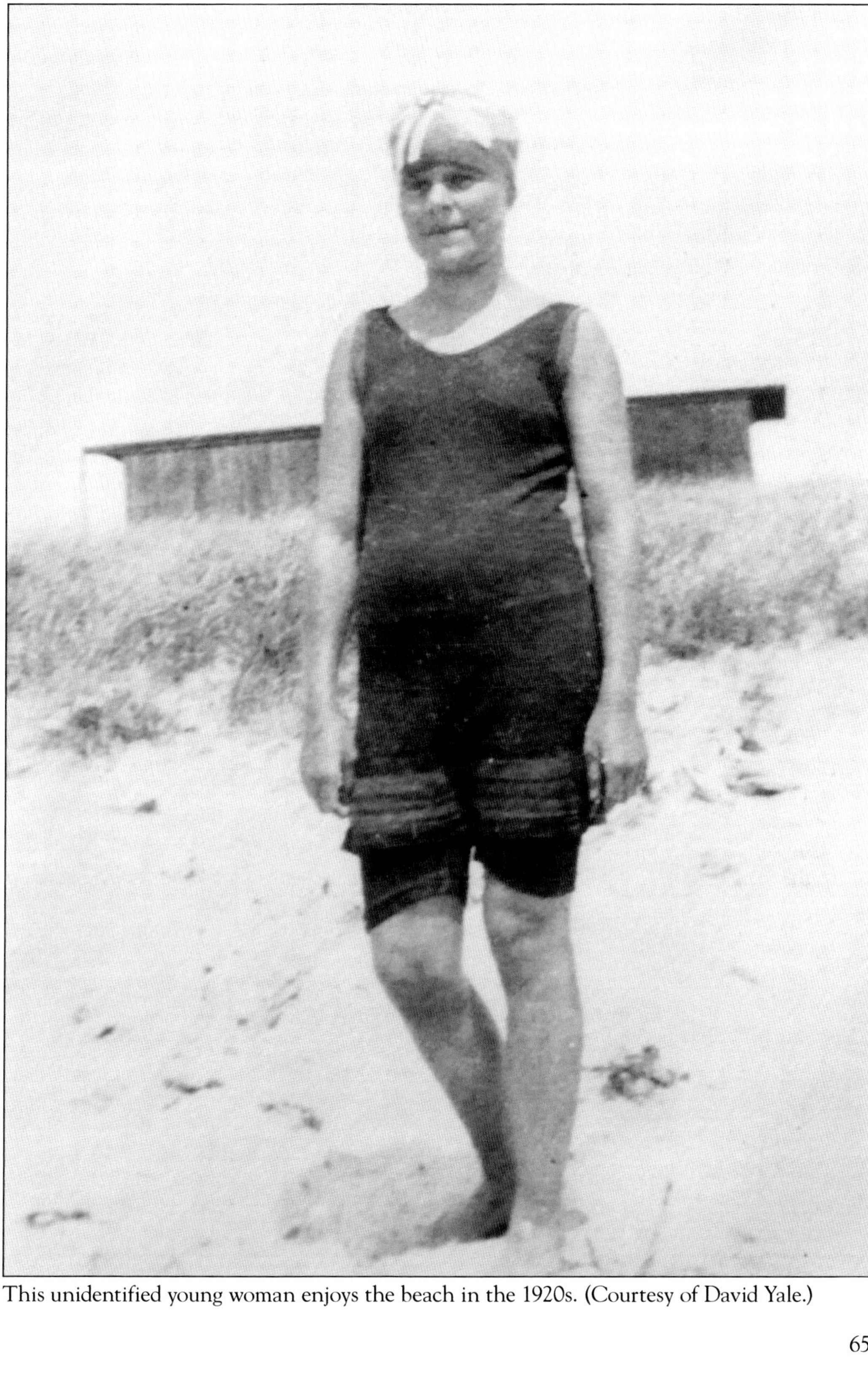

This unidentified young woman enjoys the beach in the 1920s. (Courtesy of David Yale.)

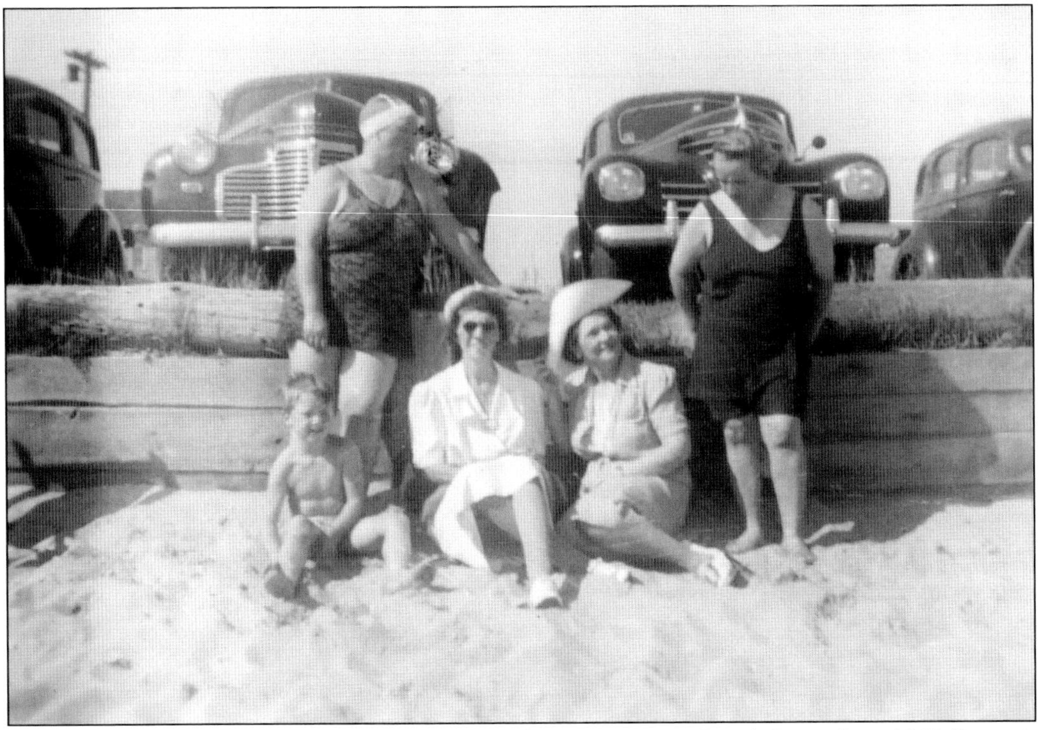

The family of Regina Russell Goodwin are near today's Ocean Mist Beach Bar in June 1943. Regina's parents moved to Matunuck in the early 1930s. (Courtesy of Regina Russell Goodwin.)

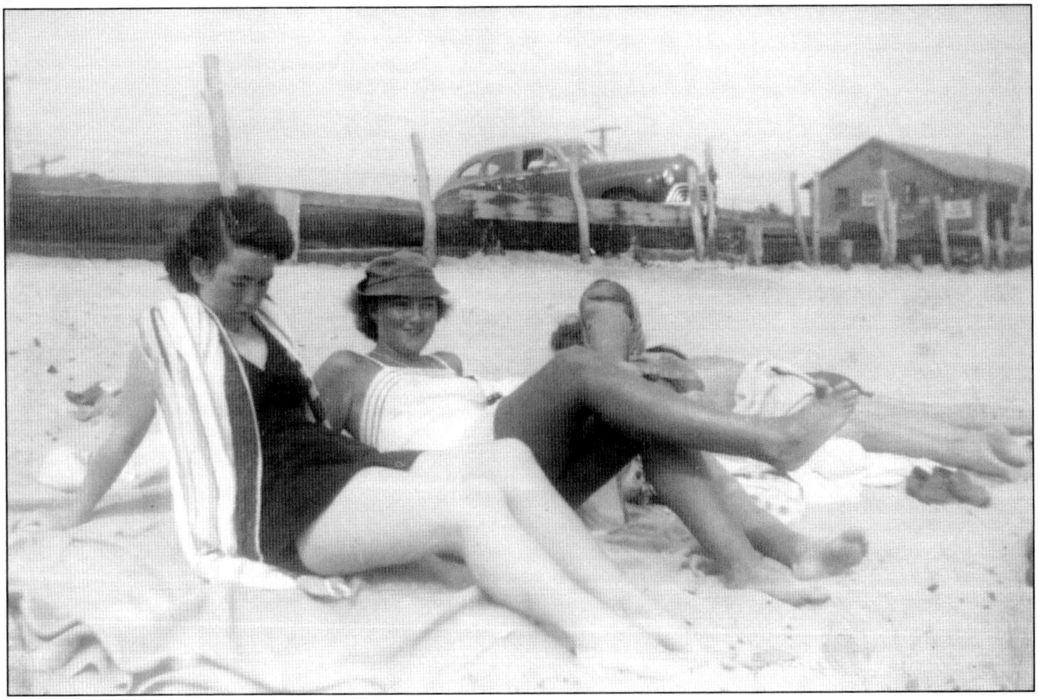

Mary McGuinness, Regina Russell Goodwin, and Marie Clark spread out on towels near today's Ocean Mist Beach Bar. (Courtesy of Regina Russell Goodwin.)

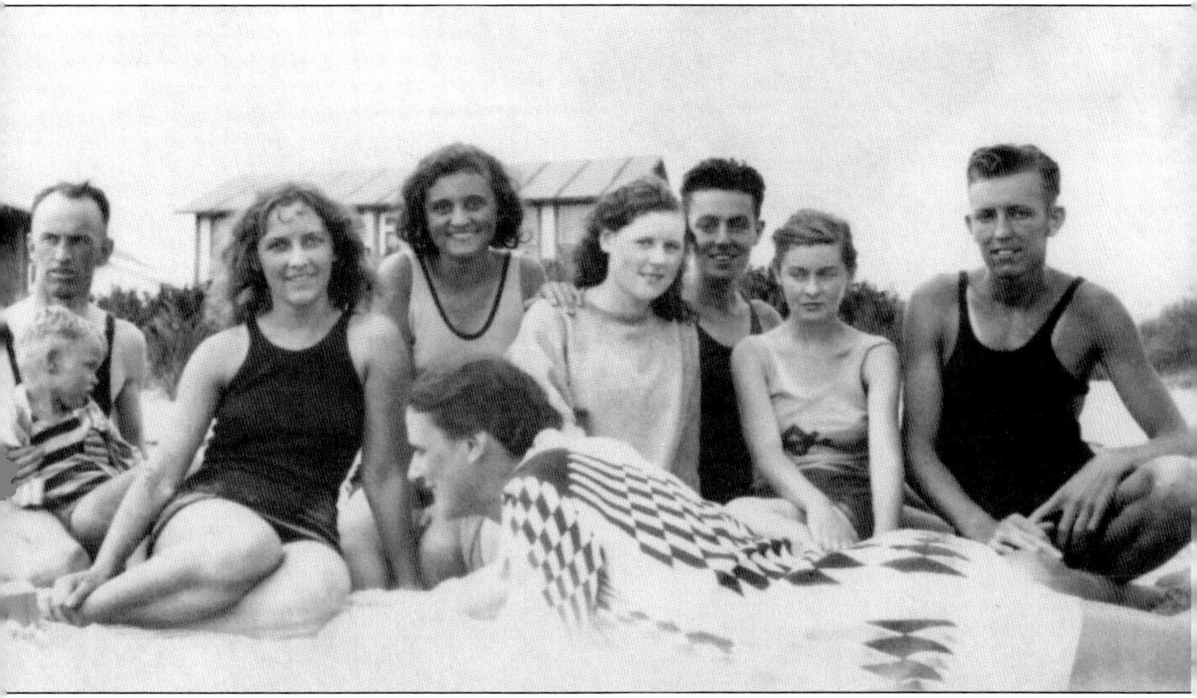

Friends and family hang out at Matunuck Beach in 1936. From left to right are an unidentified man and child, Claire McKenna McMillan, Eleanor Ahearn Gallogly, Rosalind Fleming Langlois, Felix F. Gallogly, unidentified, J. Francis Gallogly, and Mary Fleming, lying down. (Courtesy of Eleanor Gallogly Mullaney and Margaret Gallogly Navin.)

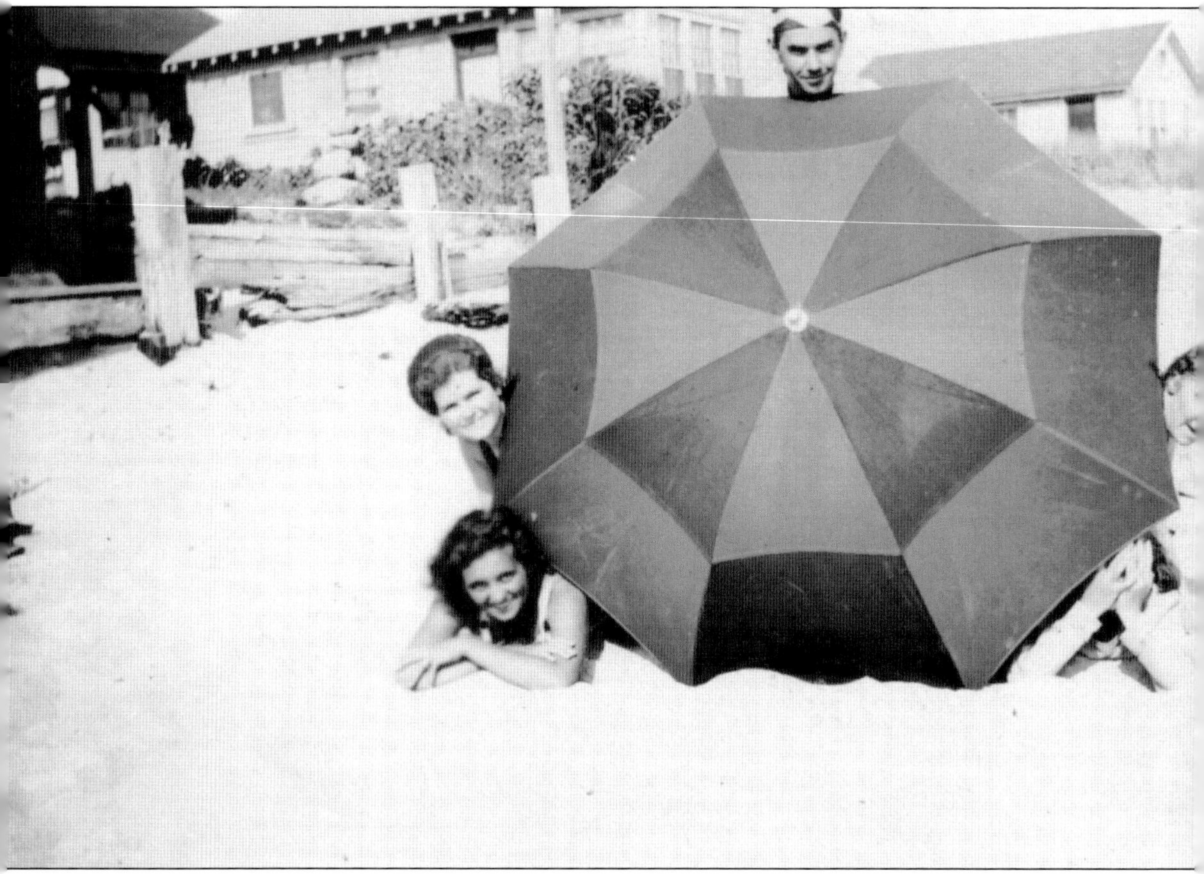

It was fun behind a beach umbrella in the 1930s. At bottom left is Eleanor Ahearn Gallogly, and just above her is Veronica Cavanaugh McAllister. (Courtesy of Eleanor Gallogly Mullaney and Margaret Gallogly Navin.)

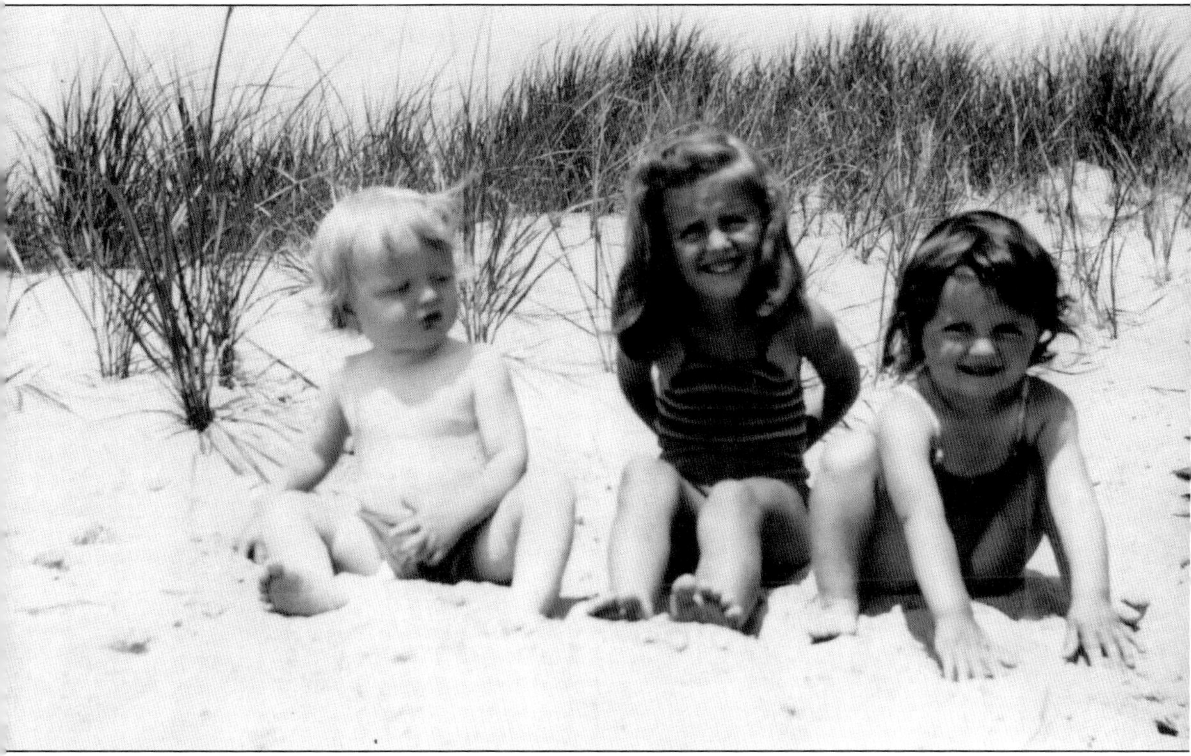

Donald Gallogly plays in the dunes with his cousins—sisters Eleanor Gallogly Mullaney and Margaret Gallogly Navin—in July 1942. (Courtesy of Mary Ann Gallogly Scott.)

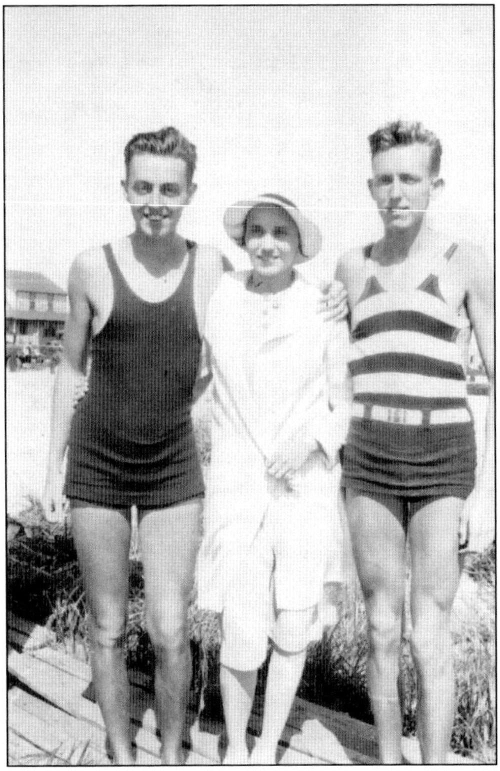

Felix F. Gallogly Jr. (left) is pictured at left with his future wife, Eleanor Ahearn Gallogly, and his brother J. Francis Gallogly, one of the first Matunuck lifeguards. J. Francis Gallogly is pictured below. (Both, courtesy of Eleanor Gallogly Mullaney and Margaret Gallogly Navin.)

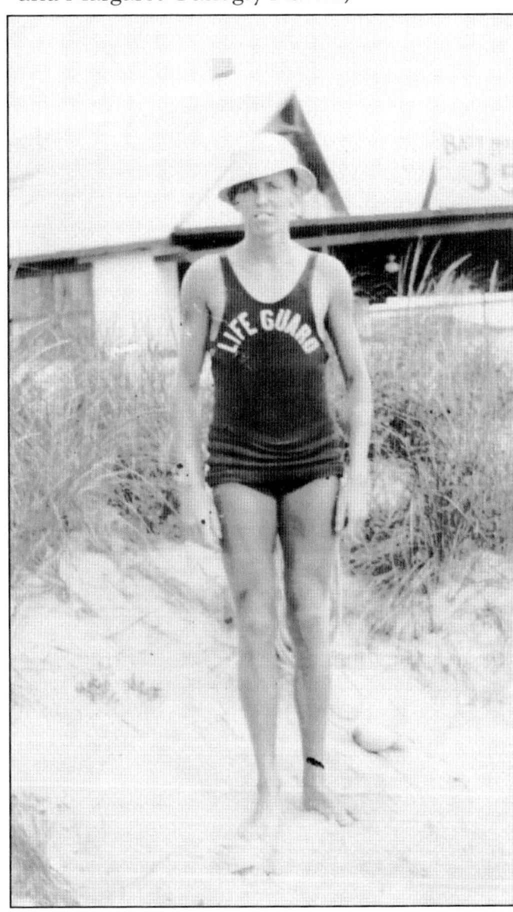

Seasonal storms have changed the face of Matunuck. Over the years, a series of beach clubs sprang up along the shore, and one of them, Blackberry Beach Club, was washed out to sea in a nor'easter in 1983. Jane Gallogly McLaughlin is pictured at right at the Blackberry Beach Club around 1961. Below, Ann Larkowich and Kathy McKinnon are there in the summer of 1960. (Both, courtesy of David Gallogly.)

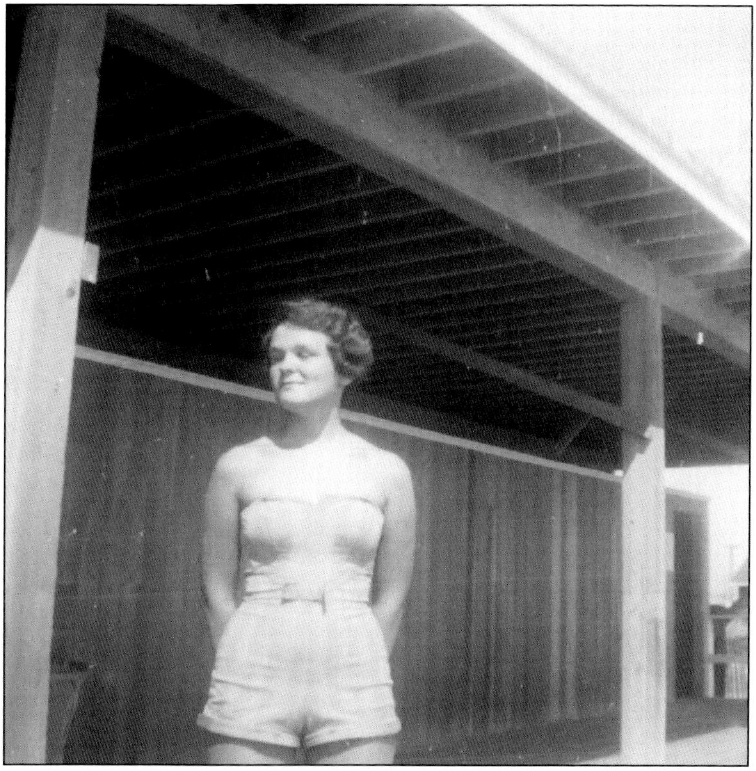

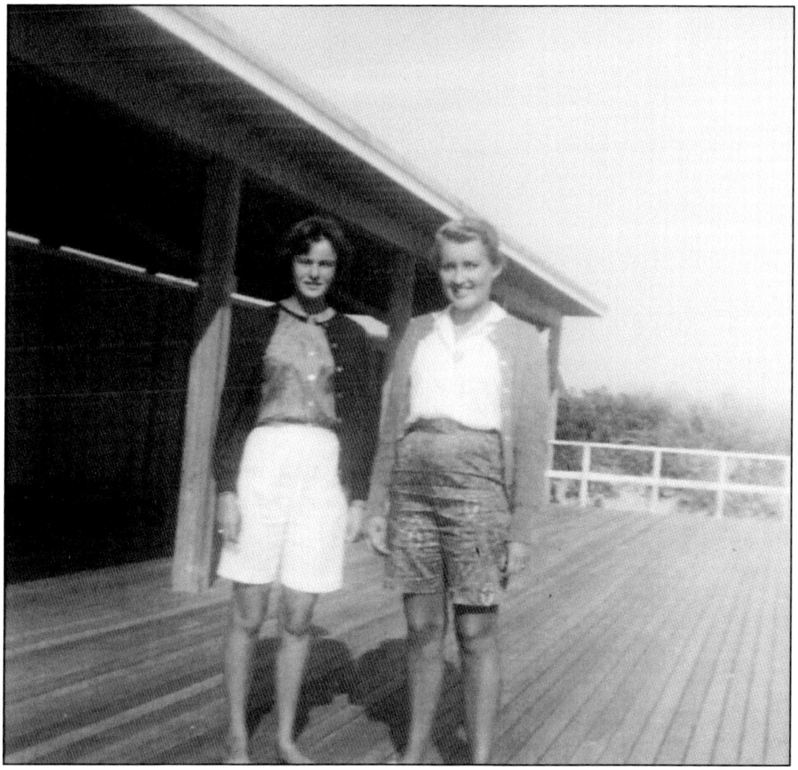

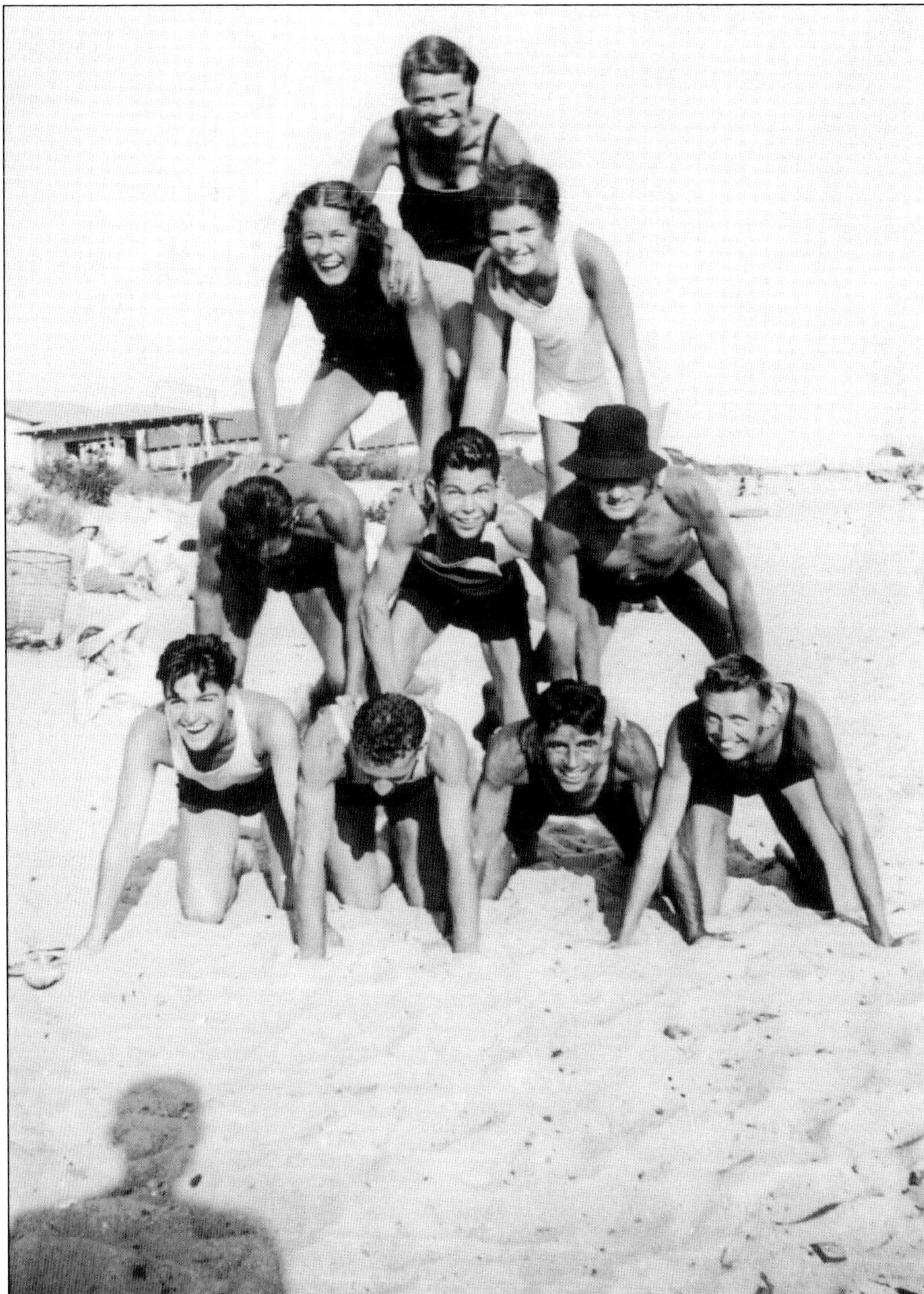

Friends have fun making a pyramid at Matunuck Beach. At top is Mary Gallogly O'Donnell, and Veronica Cavanaugh McAllister is just below her to the right. (Courtesy of Eleanor Gallogly Mullaney and Margaret Gallogly Navin.)

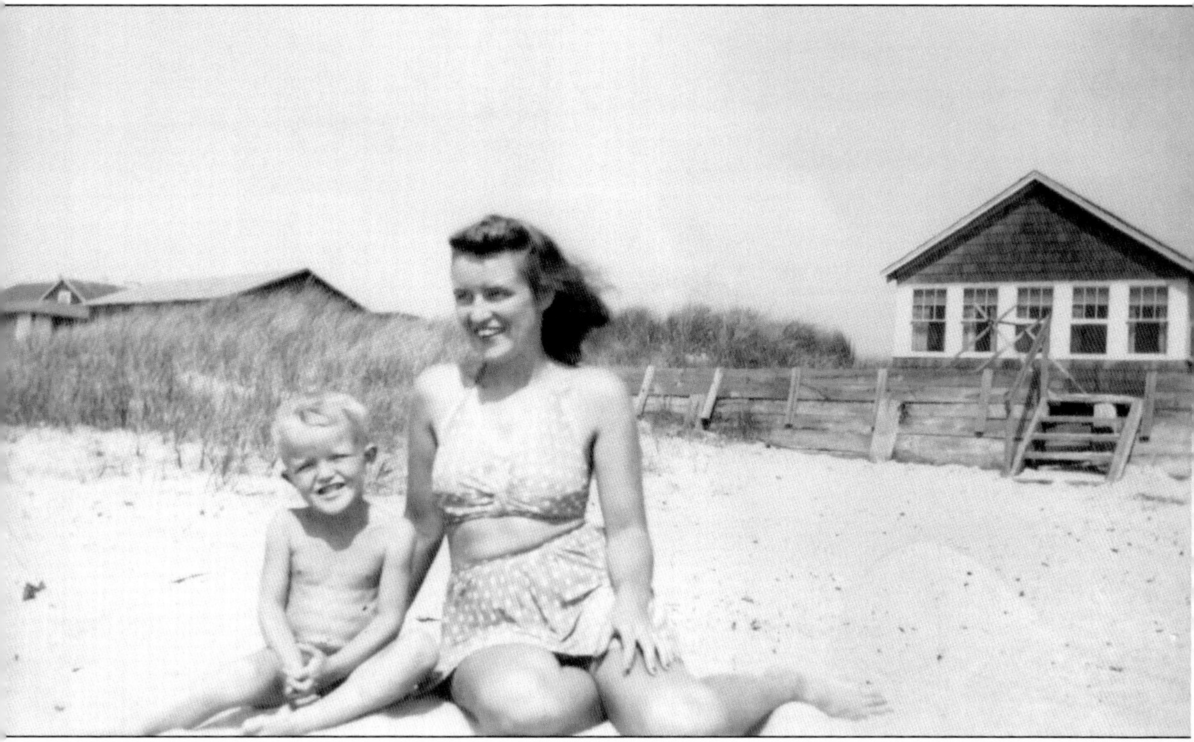
Helen King Gallogly and her son Donald are enjoying their day in September 1944. (Courtesy of Mary Ann Gallogly Scott.)

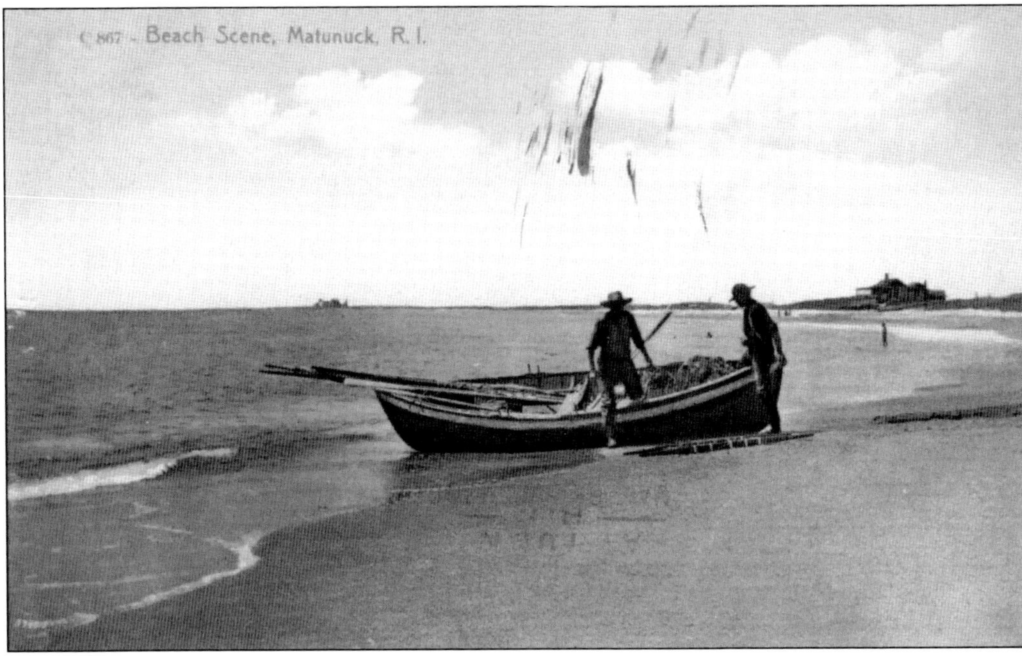

Matunuck's Robert Beverly Hale Library houses an extensive local postcard collection, which includes a fishing boat at the beach (above) and what is apparently the wreck of a barge on the shore (below). (Both, courtesy of the Robert Beverly Hale Library.)

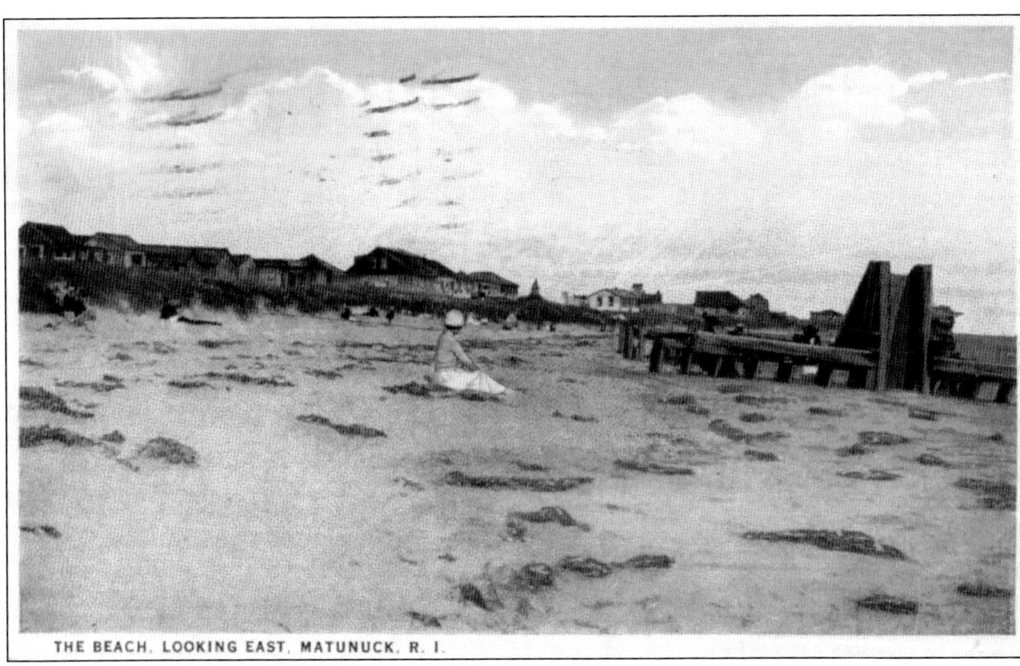

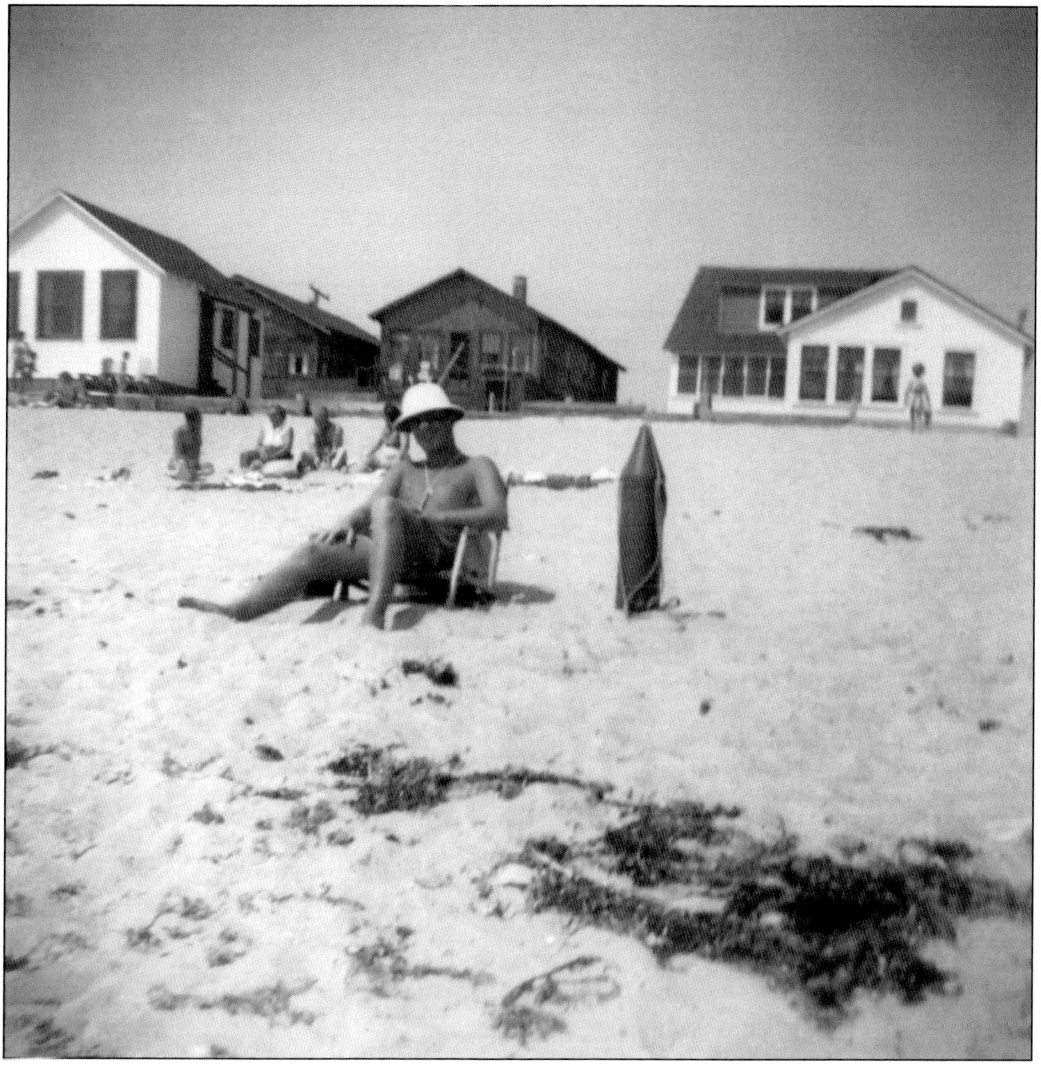

Clark Sammartino was one of the lifeguards at the Carpenter's (a restaurant and bar) and Cavanaugh's Café section of Matunuck Beach in 1958, according to Susan Rivera Russo. "He taught many of us how to swim and watched out for everyone," she said. (Courtesy of Susan Rivera Russo.)

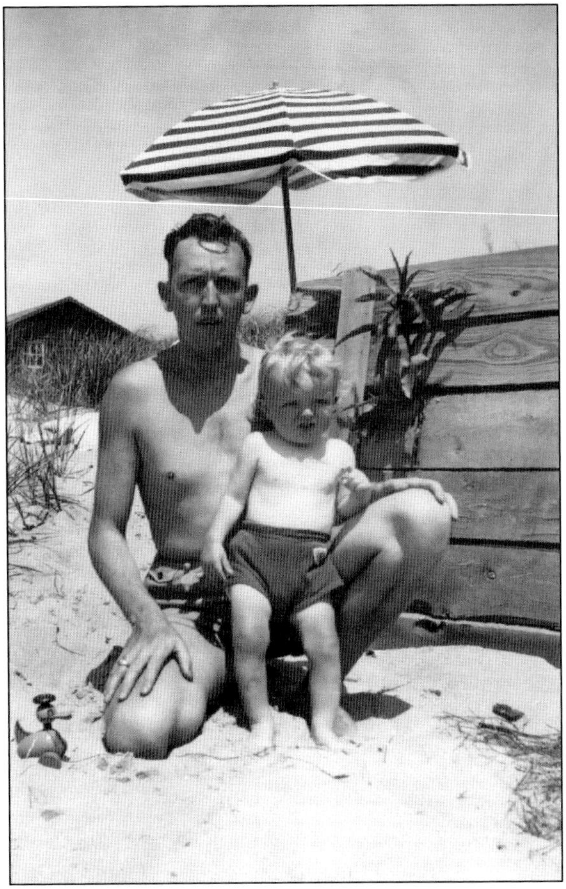

J. Francis Gallogly spends beach time with his son Donald in July 1942. (Courtesy of Mary Ann Gallogly Scott.)

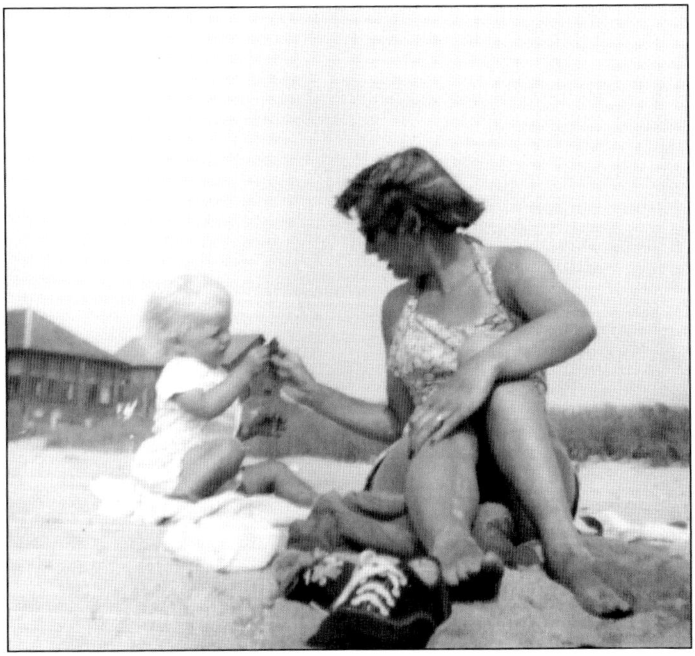

Mary Clarkin Murphy plays with her daughter Joan at Cardy Cottages on Matunuck Beach Road in September 1953. (Courtesy of David Gallogly.)

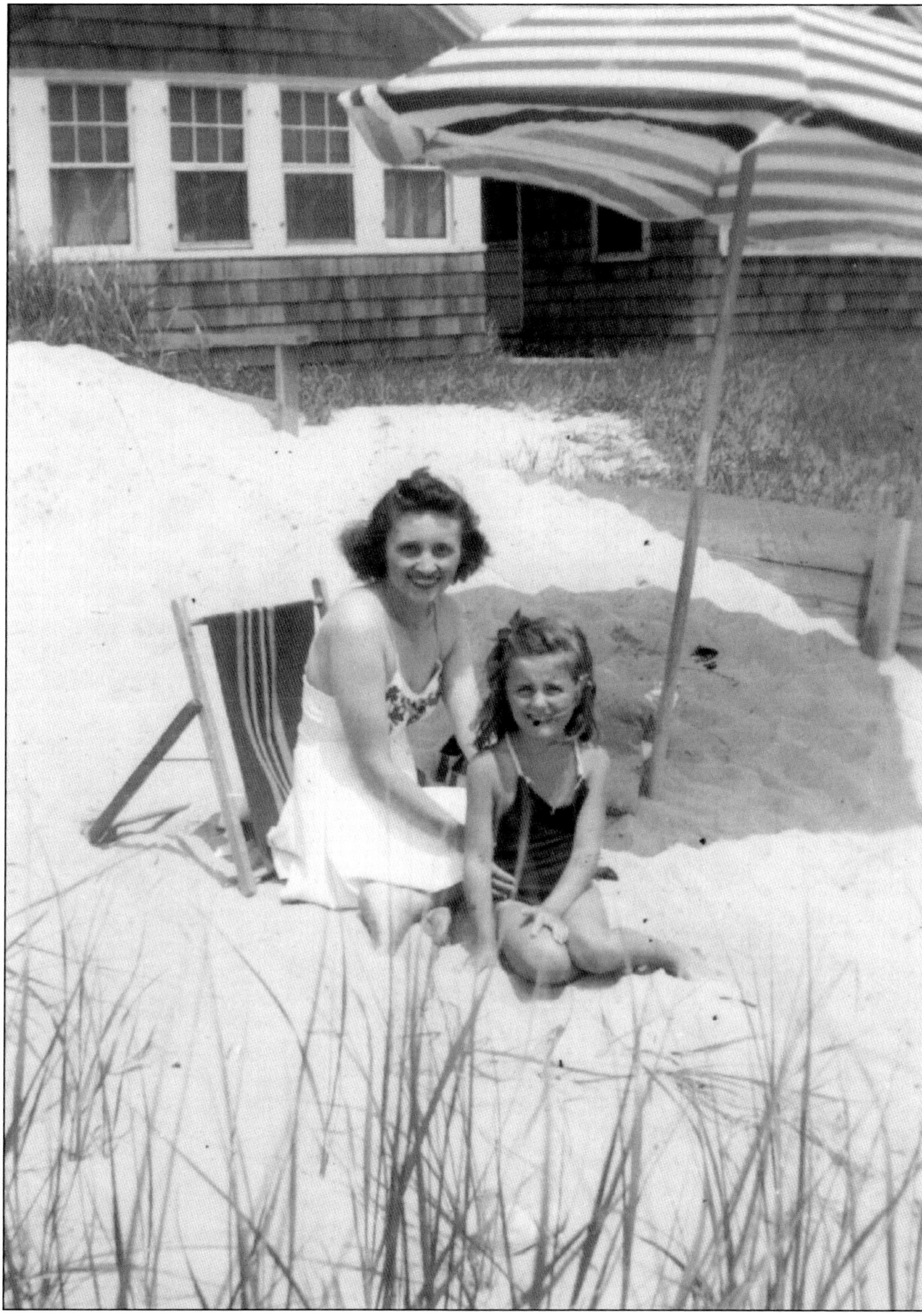

Eleanor Ahearn Gallogly's parents owned the Ahearn Cottages at the time this photograph was taken in 1942. She is enjoying the beach with her daughter Eleanor Gallogly Mullaney. (Courtesy of Eleanor Gallogly Mullaney and Margaret Gallogly Navin.)

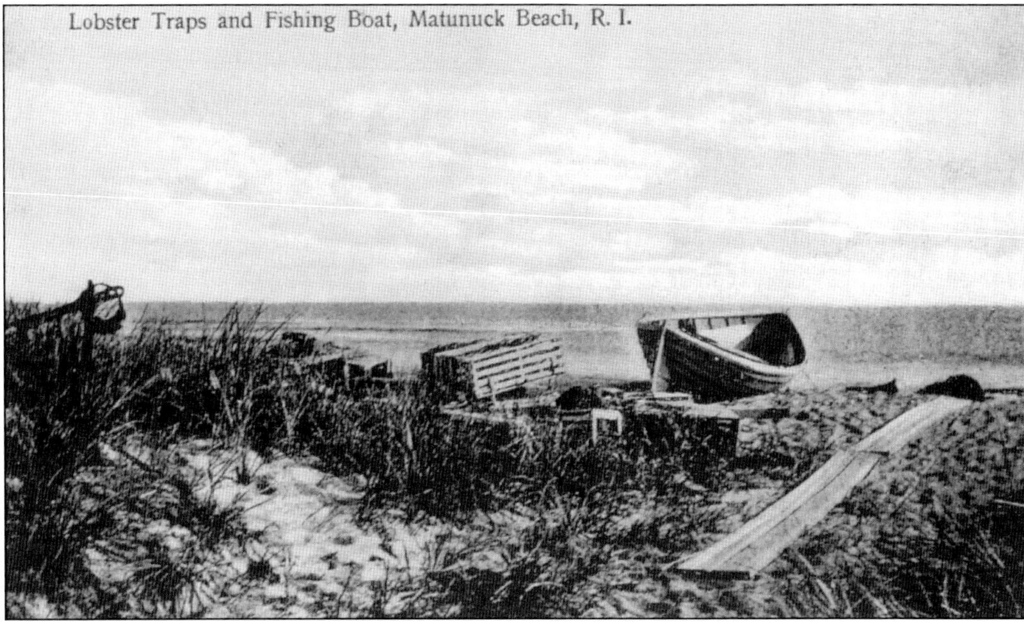

Some of the many postcard collections of Matunuck include these from local residents—lobster traps and fishing boat (above) and the beach (below). (Above, courtesy of Michael McKenna; below, courtesy of John LaCroix.)

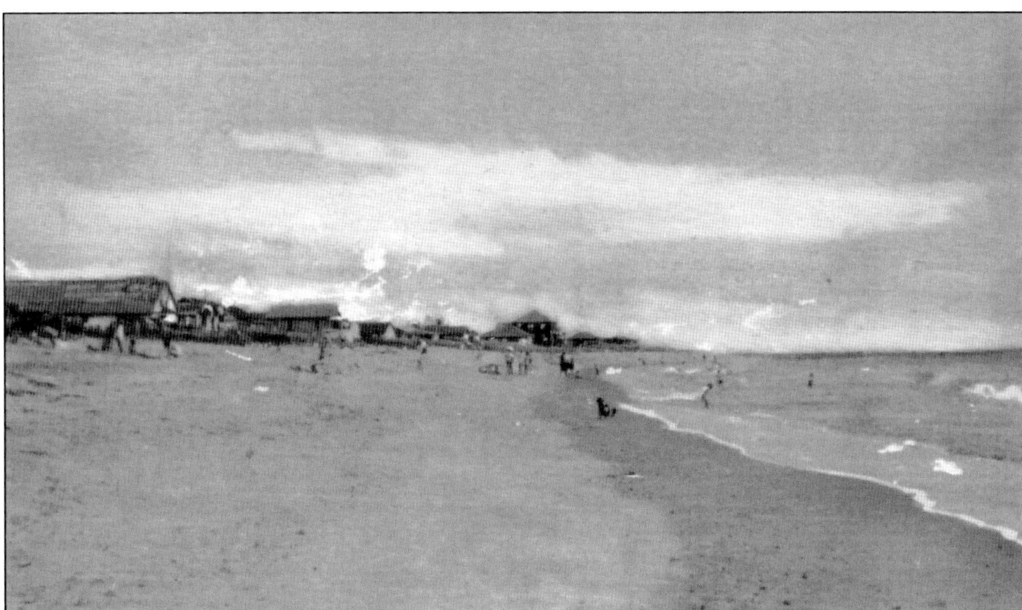

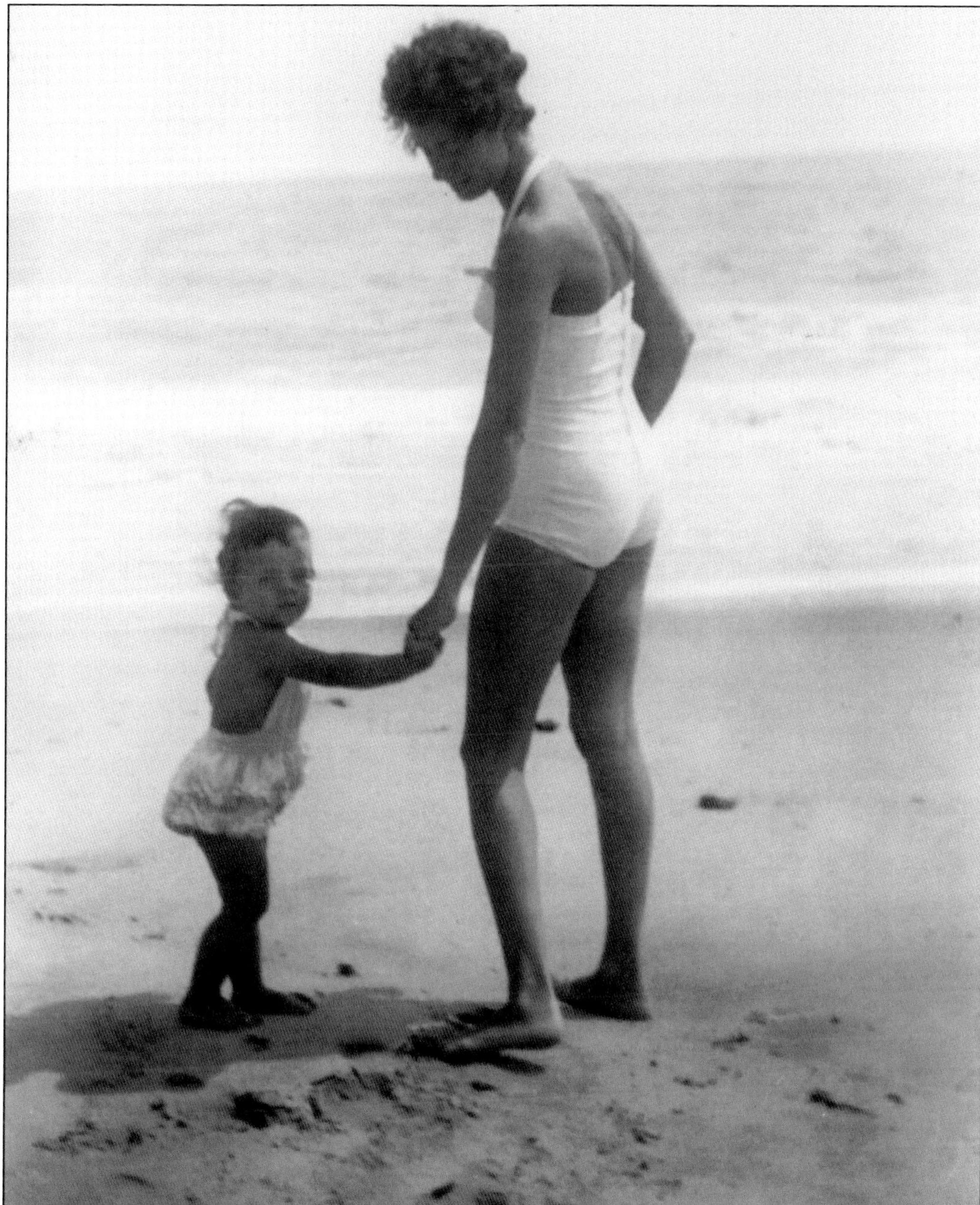

Grace Rivera and her daughter Susan Rivera Russo are at Roy Carpenter's Beach in 1953. Susan explained that they were day tripping at that time. A year or two later, her parents rented a green cottage next to Carpenter's Bar and Restaurant on Matunuck Beach Road. Around 1956–1957, the family rented a house on Prospect Road that they eventually purchased. (Courtesy of Susan Rivera Russo.)

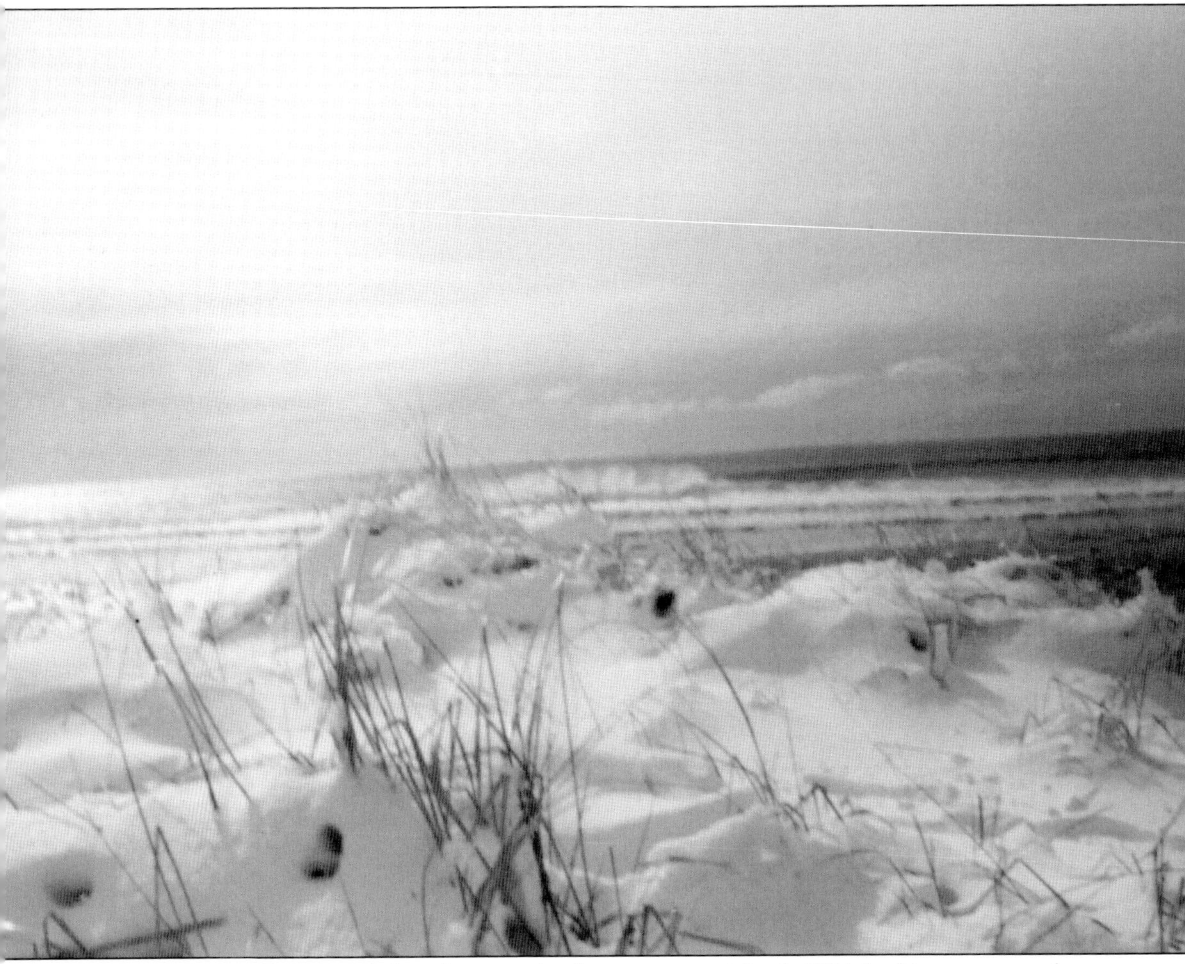

Susan Rivera Russo took this photograph after a storm in March 1974, looking out over the snow-covered dunes, glistening surf, and perfect waves. (Courtesy of Susan Rivera Russo.)

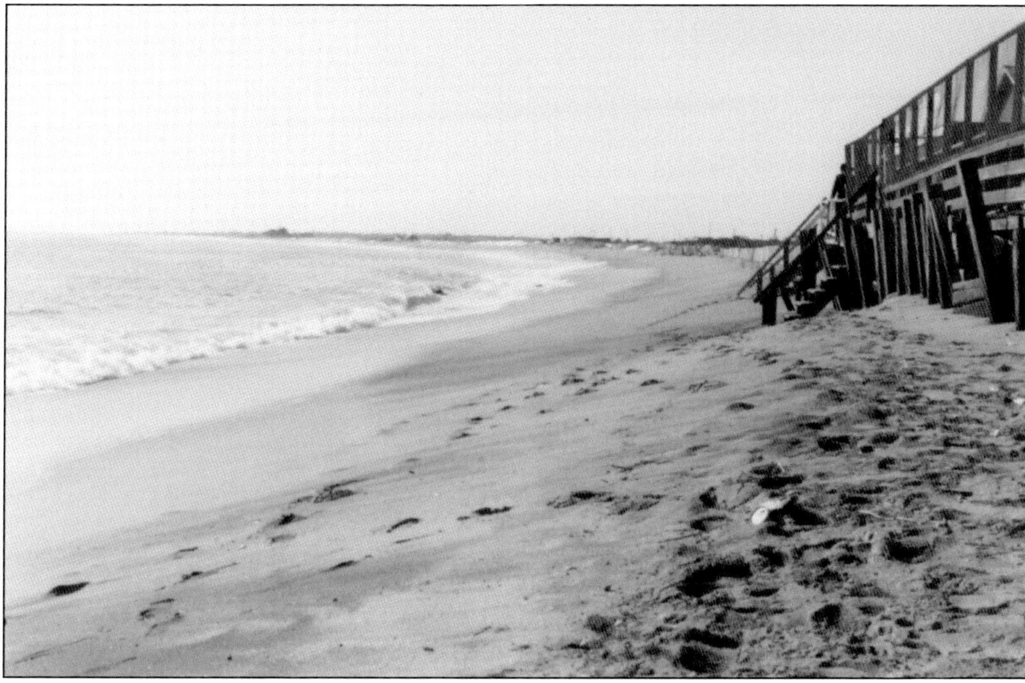

The photograph above was taken in front of Carpenter's Bar and Restaurant (today's Ocean Mist Beach Bar) in 1973 looking west toward the five cottages. Below, Carpenter's is shown around the same time. This is before the unprotected beach was washed away. (Both, courtesy of Susan Rivera Russo.)

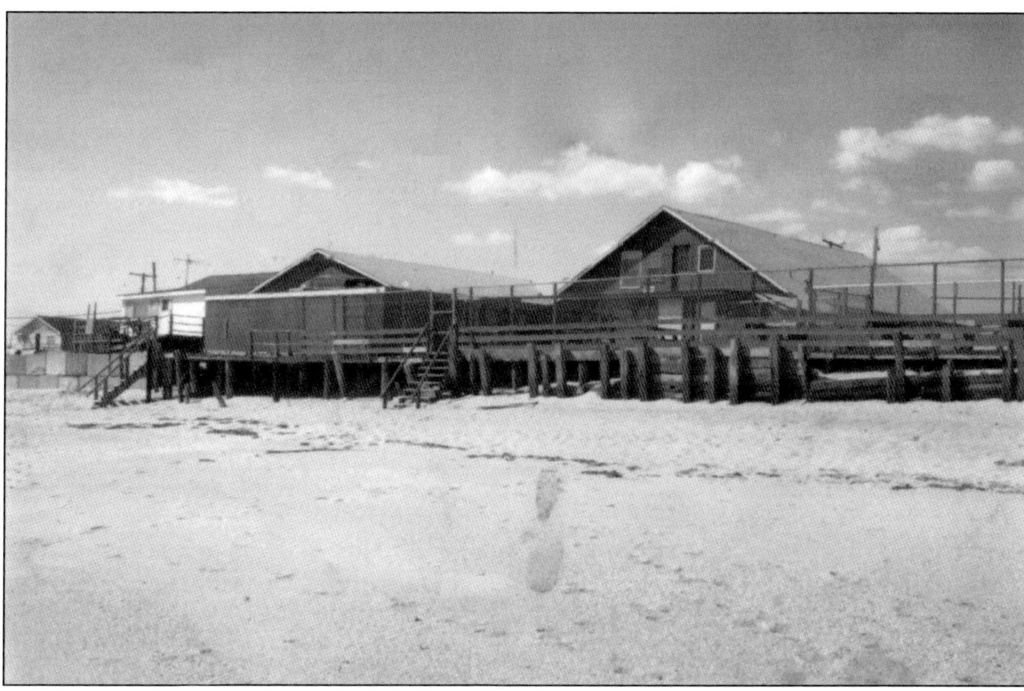

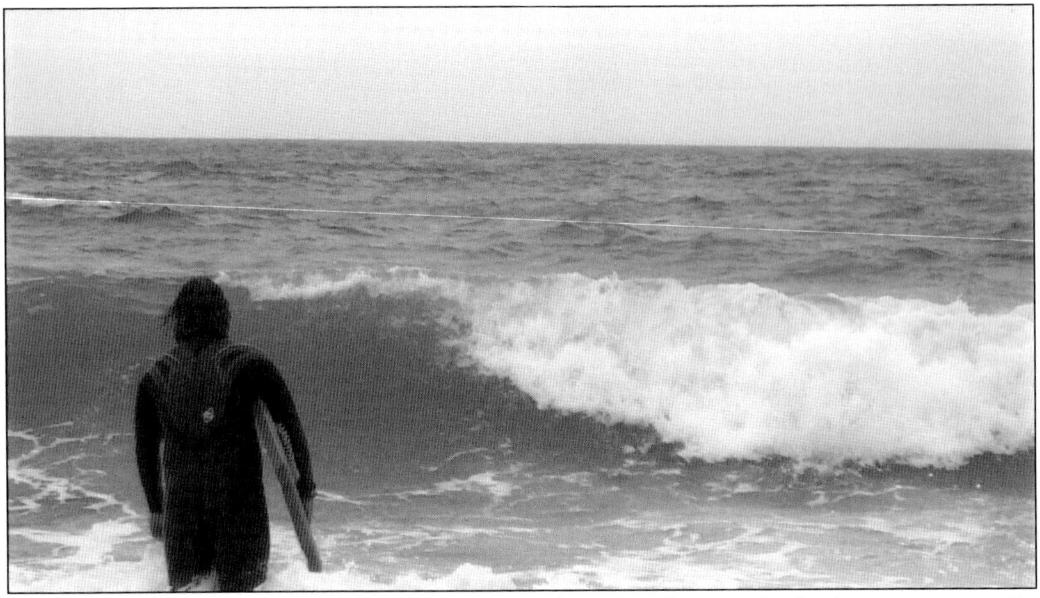

Frank W. Szymanski is about to head out into the surf. Matunuck is popular for this sport, especially in the area of Deep Hole. The village has a surf shop and the Matunuck Surfing Association, established in the 1960s. (Courtesy of Carol Szymanski.)

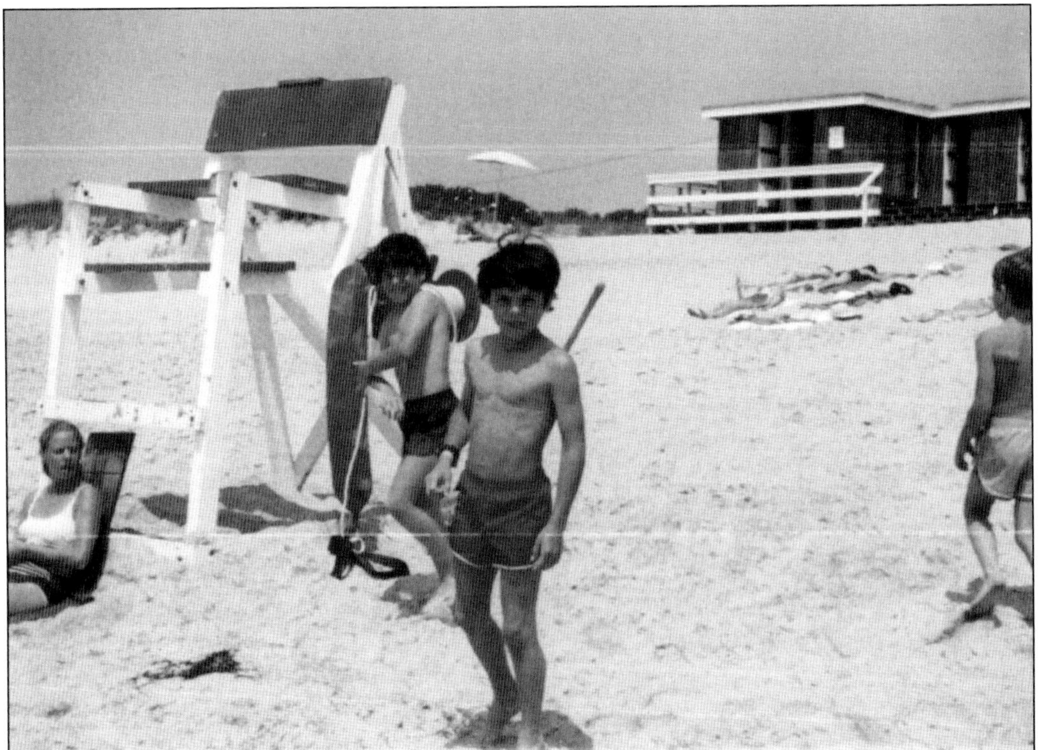

Henry Craven (center) and Josh Caswell (near chair) play at Willow Dell Beach around 1980. (Courtesy of Henry Craven.)

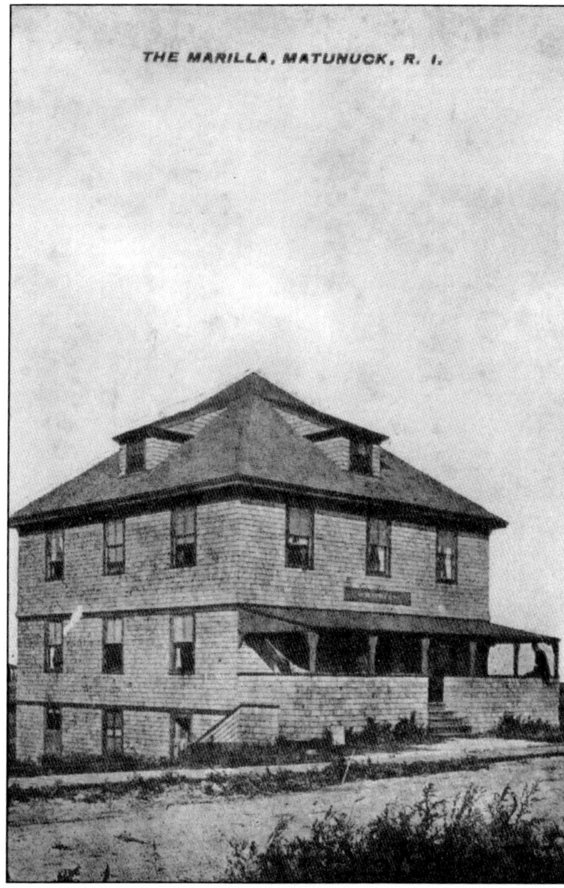

At right, the Marilla, an apartment house owned by H.O. Barney, was a two-minute walk to the beach. The apartments could be rented by two people and had two rooms. Light homemade cooking and housekeeping was available. There was a bathhouse in the same building. Below, the Matunuck Beach House was a popular hotel during the area's heyday (1898–1925), when as many as 500 visitors a day arrived at Matunuck Beach. (Both, courtesy of David Yale.)

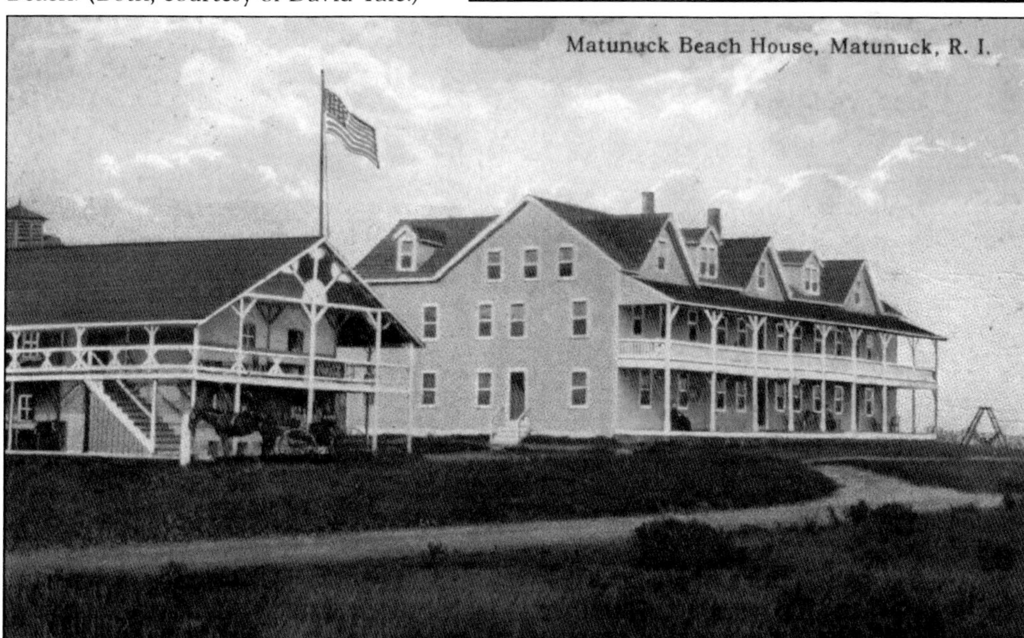

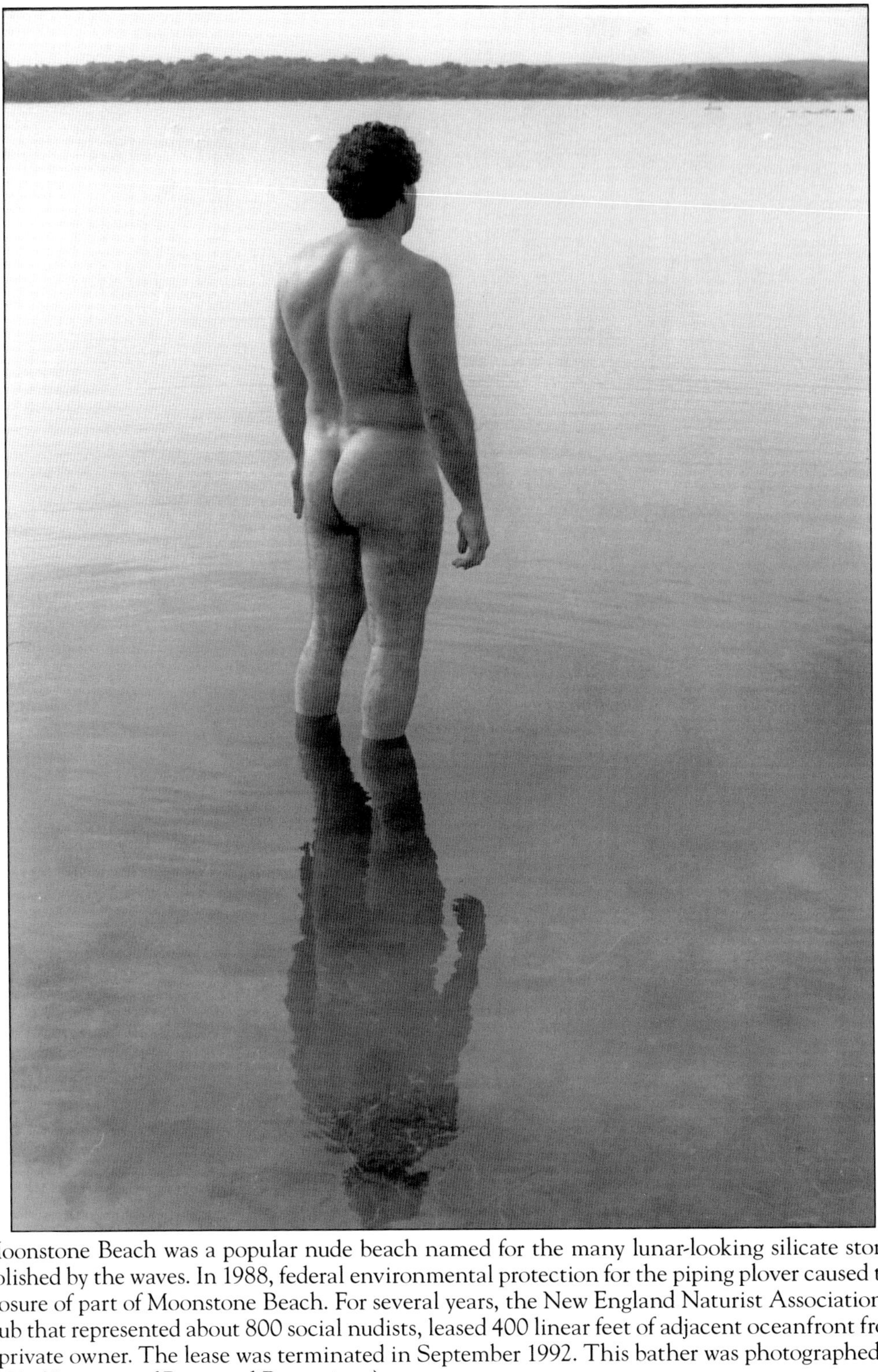

Moonstone Beach was a popular nude beach named for the many lunar-looking silicate stones polished by the waves. In 1988, federal environmental protection for the piping plover caused the closure of part of Moonstone Beach. For several years, the New England Naturist Association, a club that represented about 800 social nudists, leased 400 linear feet of adjacent oceanfront from a private owner. The lease was terminated in September 1992. This bather was photographed in 1982. (Courtesy of Raymond Beausejour.)

Robyn and Buster Rivera play on Matunuck Beach in front of what was Ma Green's, and, to the younger generation, Monahan's. (Courtesy of Susan Rivera Russo.)

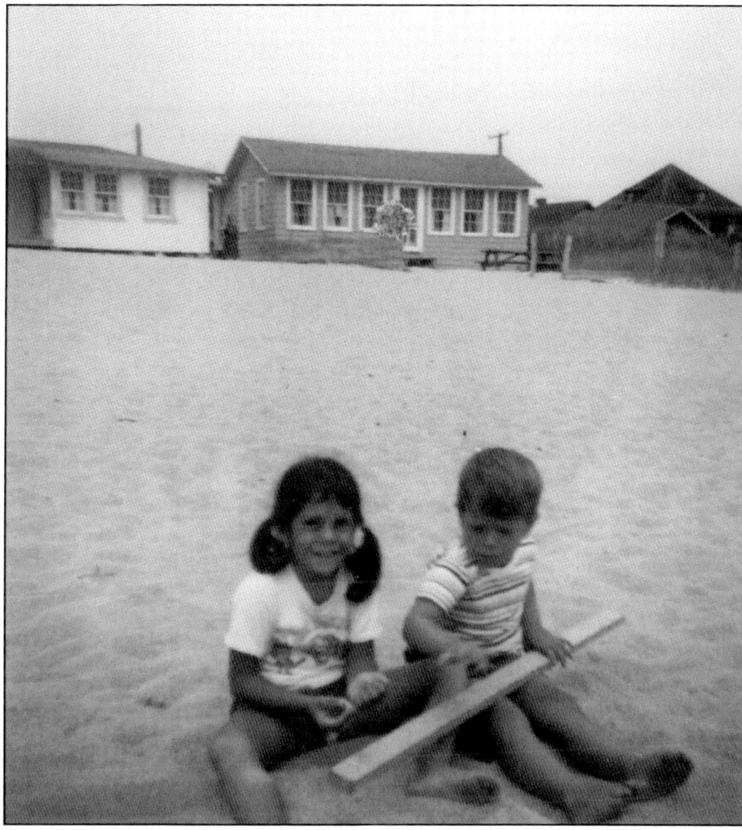

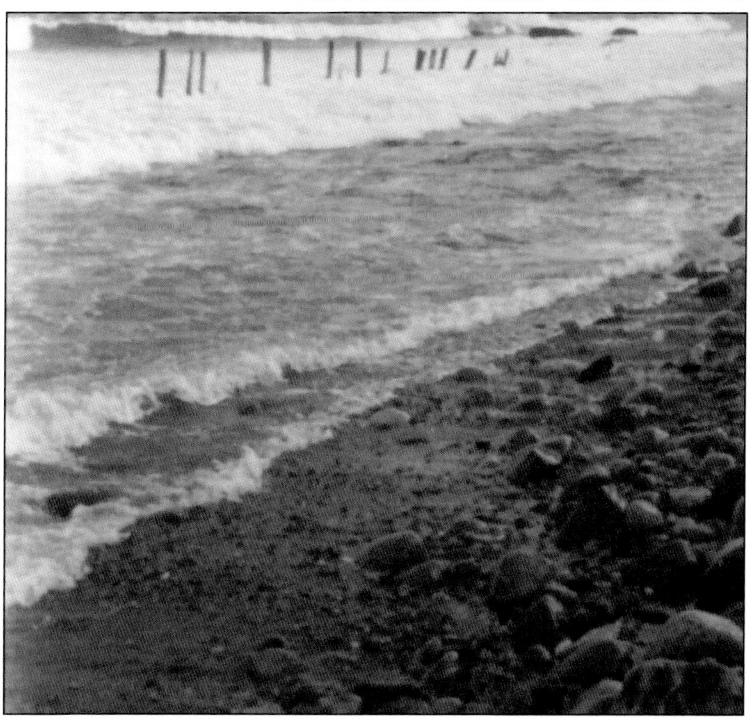

This photograph shows what were remnants of the Buena Vista Hotel on Beach Road, which was destroyed by the hurricane of 1938. These remnants no longer exist. (Courtesy of Susan Rivera Russo.)

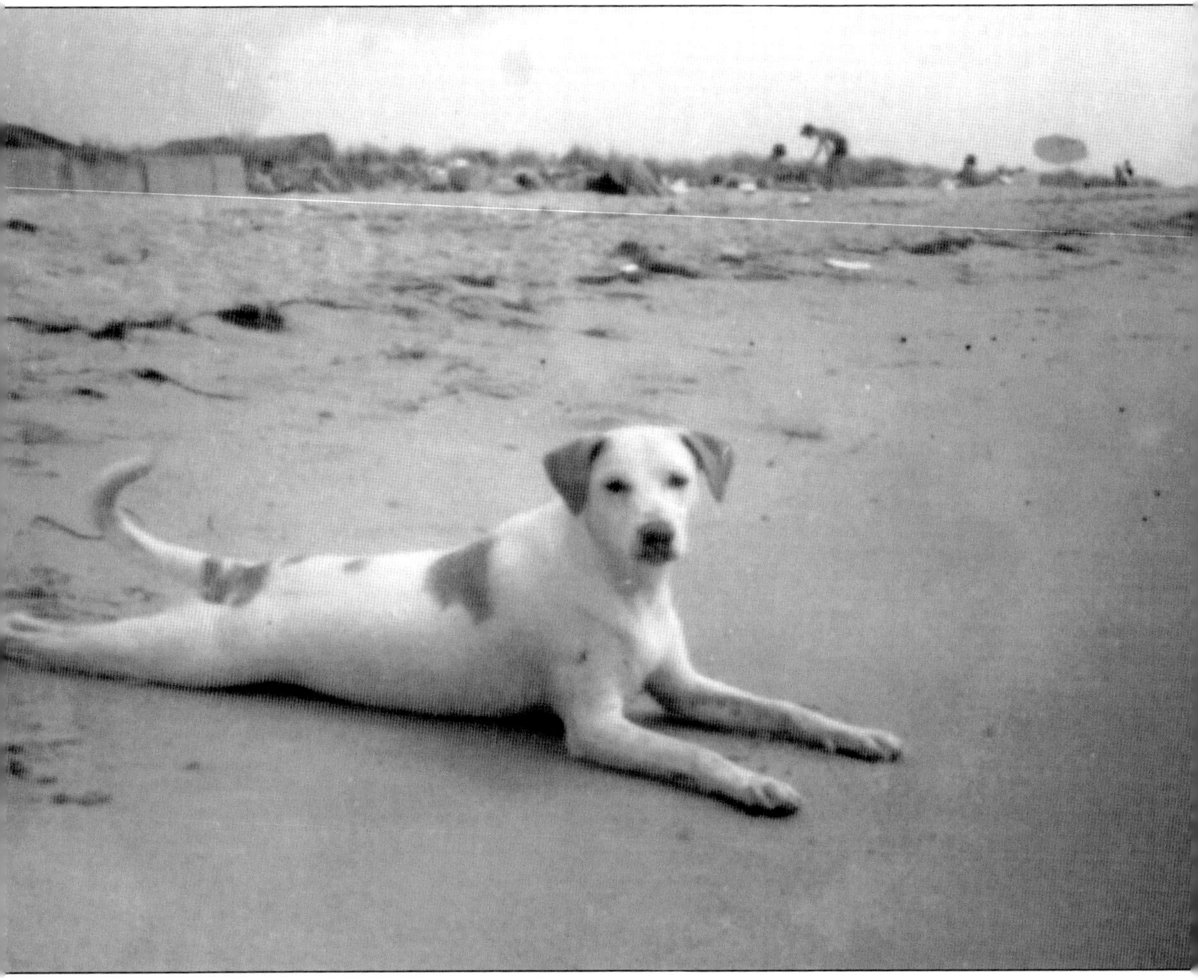

Muffin, a Rivera family dog, is in one of the better poses that she was known for during her lifetime. She was around eight years old in this photograph. (Courtesy of Susan Rivera Russo.)

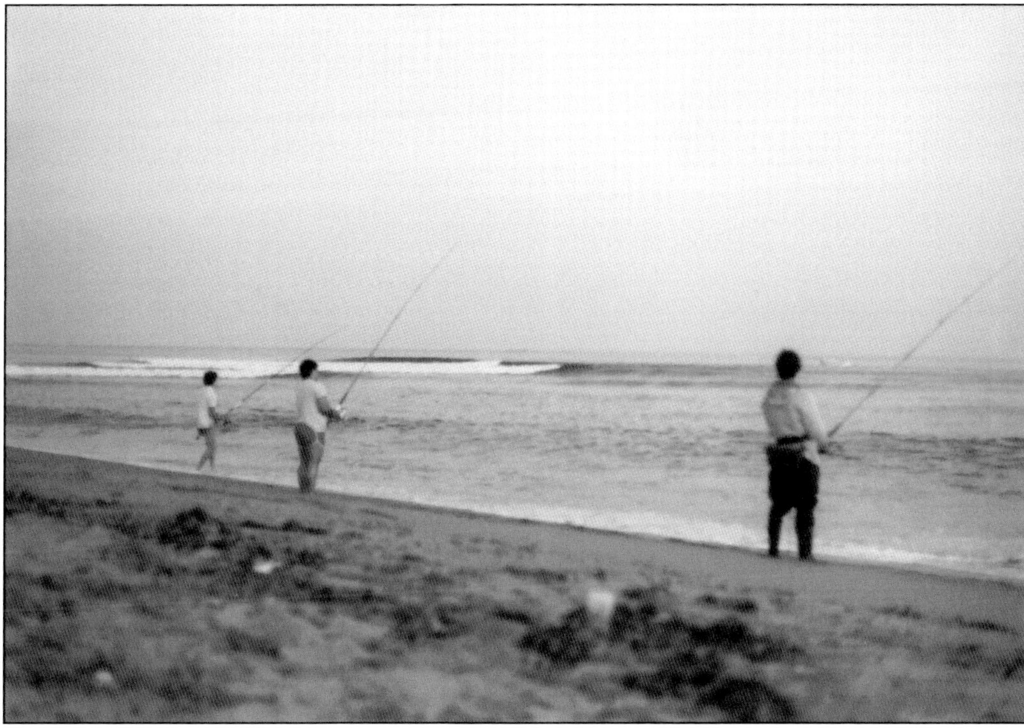

From left to right, Buster Rivera, Ray Dale, and an unidentified fisherman go after blues that often ran up the shoreline on Matunuck Beach. (Courtesy of Susan Rivera Russo.)

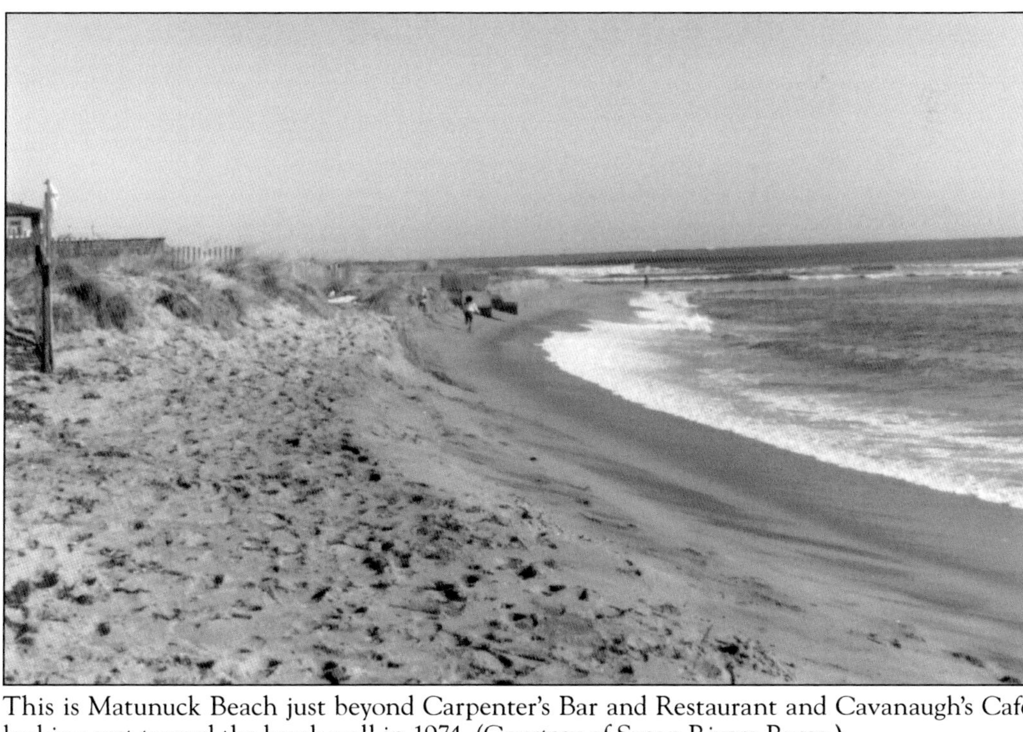

This is Matunuck Beach just beyond Carpenter's Bar and Restaurant and Cavanaugh's Café looking east toward the break wall in 1974. (Courtesy of Susan Rivera Russo.)

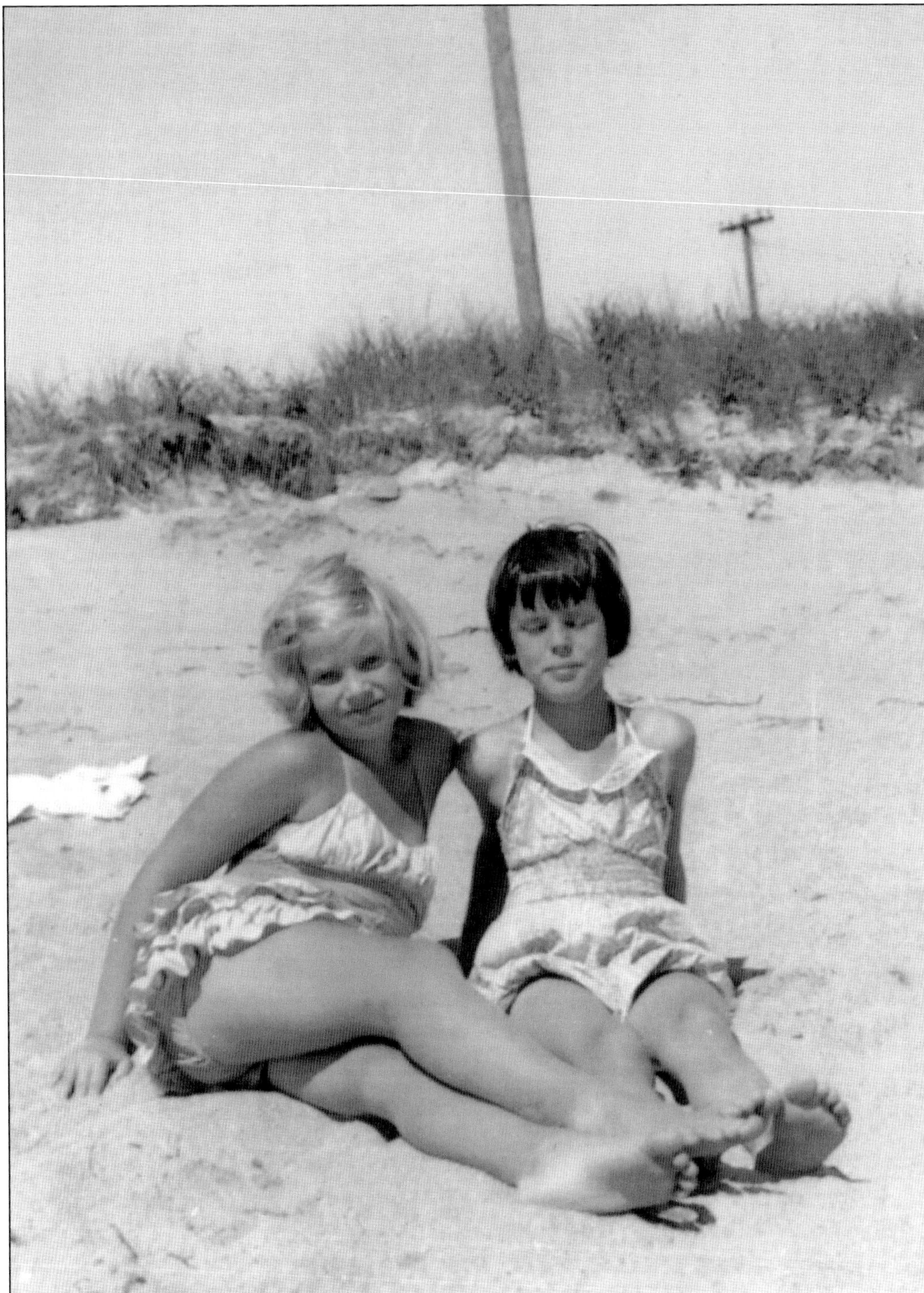

Pam McConnell Post and Lacy Cross are pictured at Willow Dell Beach around 1955. Architect Rockwell King de Moulin designed the 1938 Willow Dell Beach Club. (Courtesy of Henry Craven.)

Henry Craven and his older brother Jason Craven, sons of Lacy Cross, play at Willow Dell Beach in 1972. The boys were third-generation members of Willow Dell Beach Club. (Courtesy of Henry Craven.)

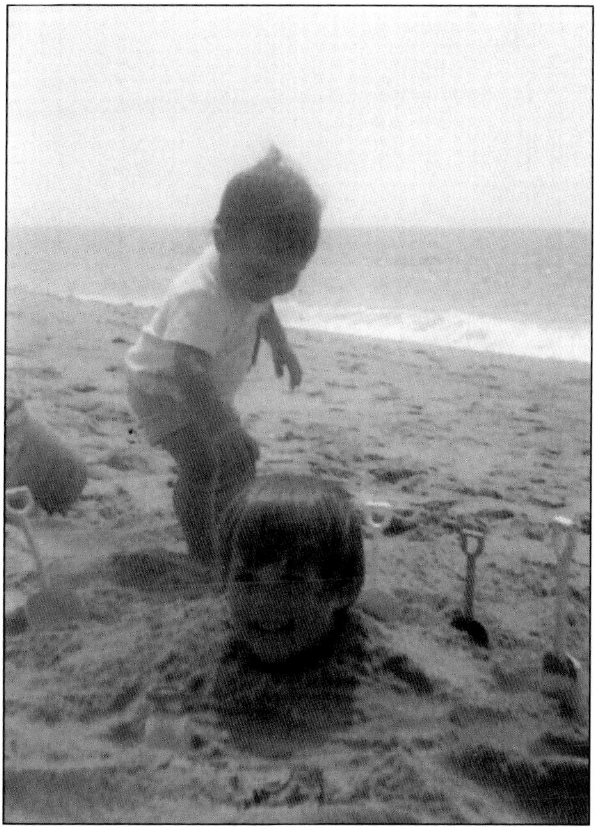

James Waterston and Henry Craven are shown at Willow Dell Beach around 1977. Today, Waterston is a film and television actor whose first role was in the 1989 film *Dead Poets Society* as Gerard Pitts. His father is actor Sam Waterston. (Courtesy of Henry Craven.)

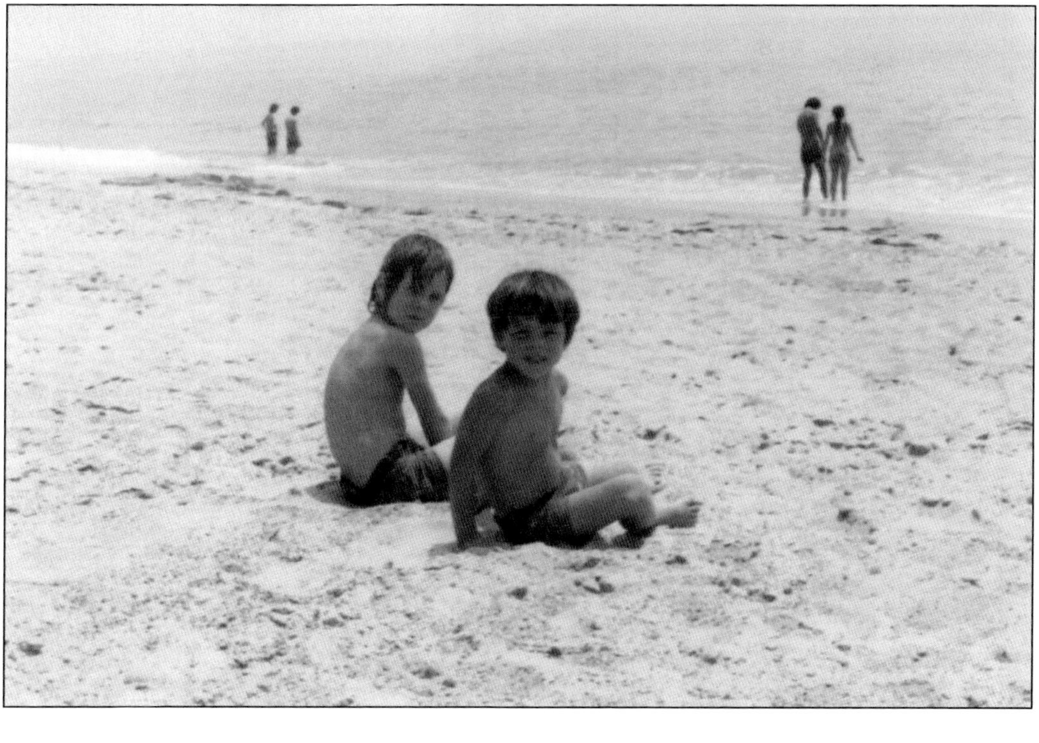

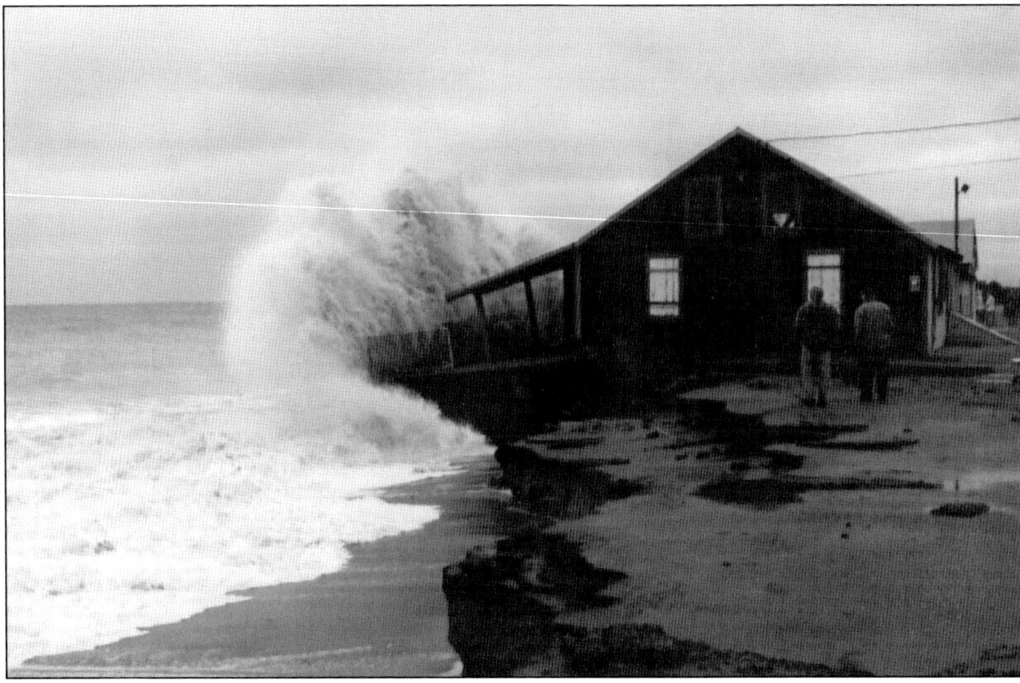

Tom McVey took this photograph at Roy Carpenter's Beach store during a nor'easter in the 2000s. (Courtesy of Tom McVey.)

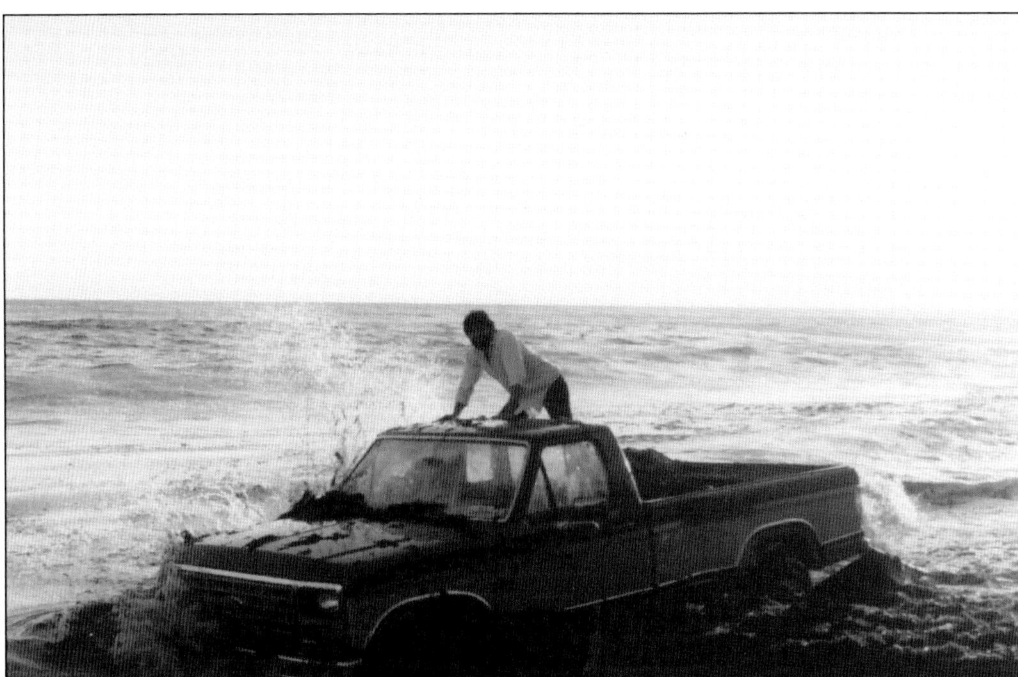

Just after Hurricane Bob in 1991, a local fisherman and his truck got caught in the ocean in front of the Ocean Mist Beach Bar. (Courtesy of Jeanne McHenry Helma.)

This building, pictured in the winter of 1972, was known as the Sea View and had many uses. There were bath houses in the lower level for people who paid to park in the lot to get to the beach. The upper level was used mostly for dances for children and teens and later for bingo. It was also a meeting hall. The Matunuck fire truck was stored in the section of the building that faced Matunuck Beach Road. (Courtesy of Jeanne McHenry Helma.)

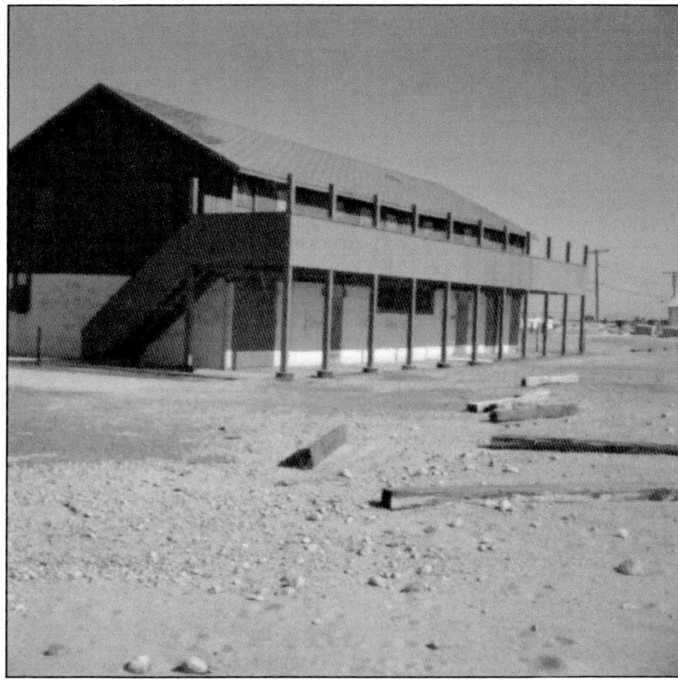

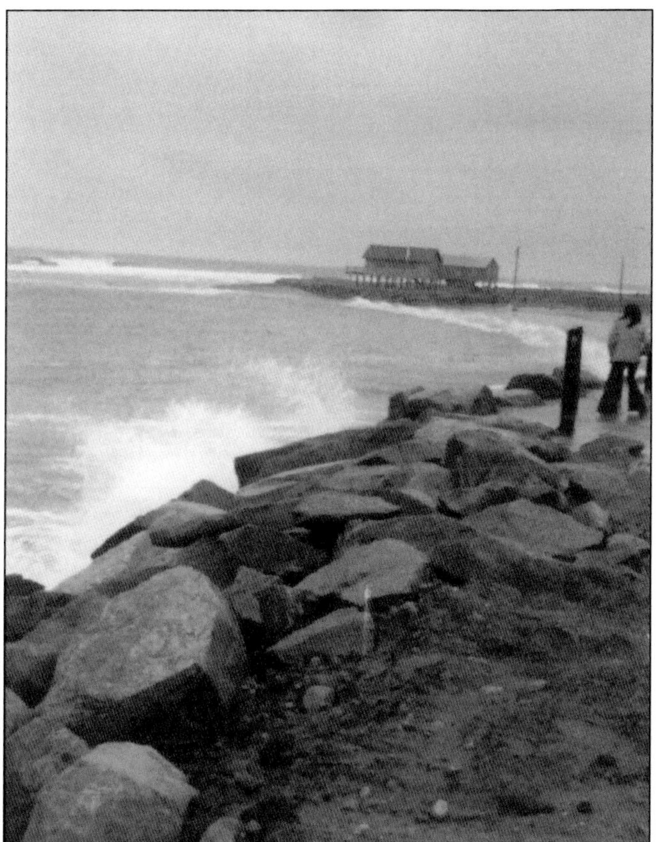

This photograph was taken from the road that leads from Matunuck Point to East Matunuck, looking toward Deep Hole. The homes that originally stood there were destroyed during the hurricane of 1938. For many years after, there were remnants of cement stairs one could sit on, depending on the tide, according to Susan Rivera Russo. After a retaining wall was put up, two houses were allowed to be built. (Courtesy of Susan Rivera Russo.)

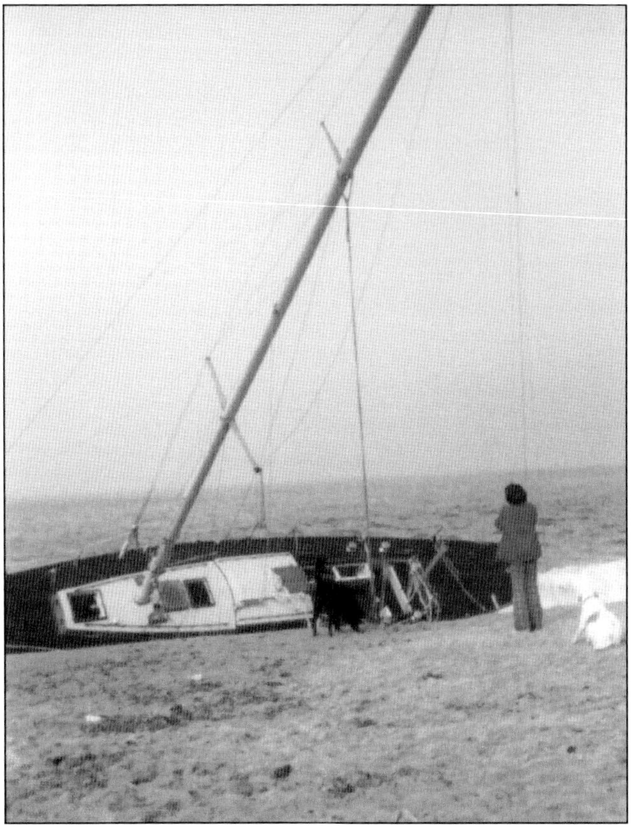

This sailboat had been on autopilot and ran aground shortly before the first set of rocks near the old Cavanaugh's Cafe. Grace Rivera and Muffin look on. (Courtesy of Susan Rivera Russo.)

Robyn Rivera and three-month-old Casey share a towel at Roy Carpenter's Beach. (Courtesy of Susan Rivera Russo.)

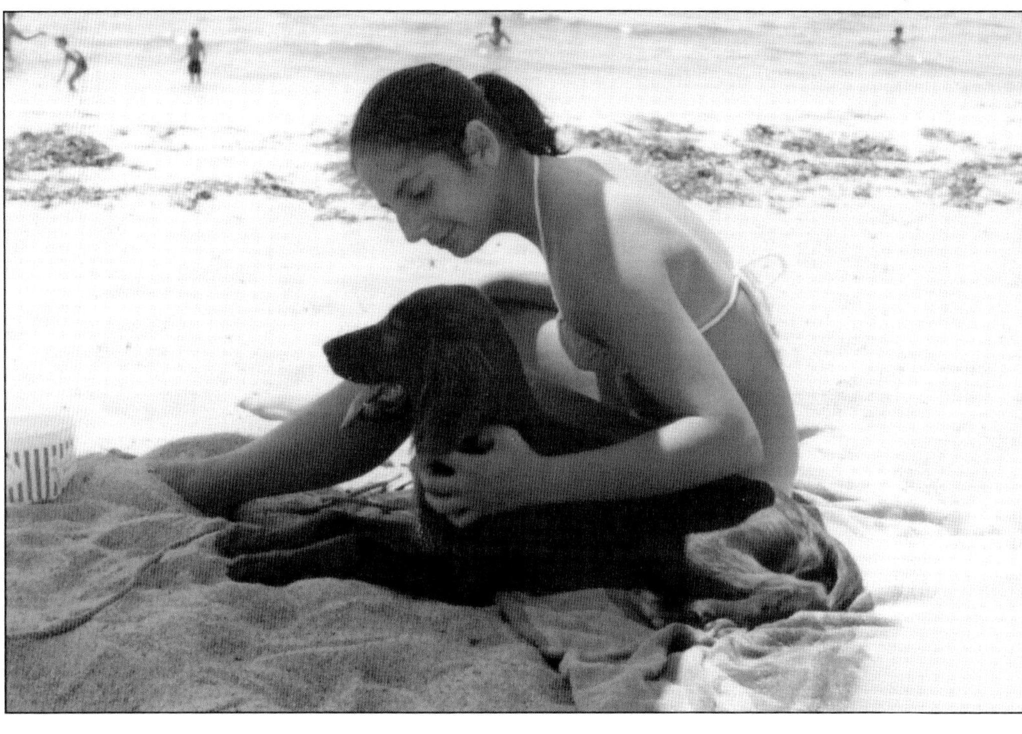

Paul Johnson finishes an afternoon of surfing at Matunuck Beach in 1970. (Courtesy of Susan Rivera Russo.)

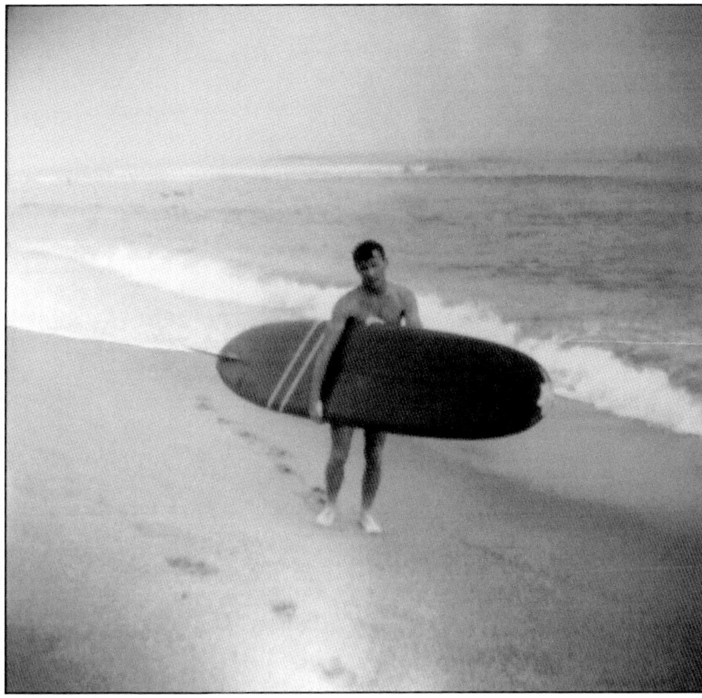

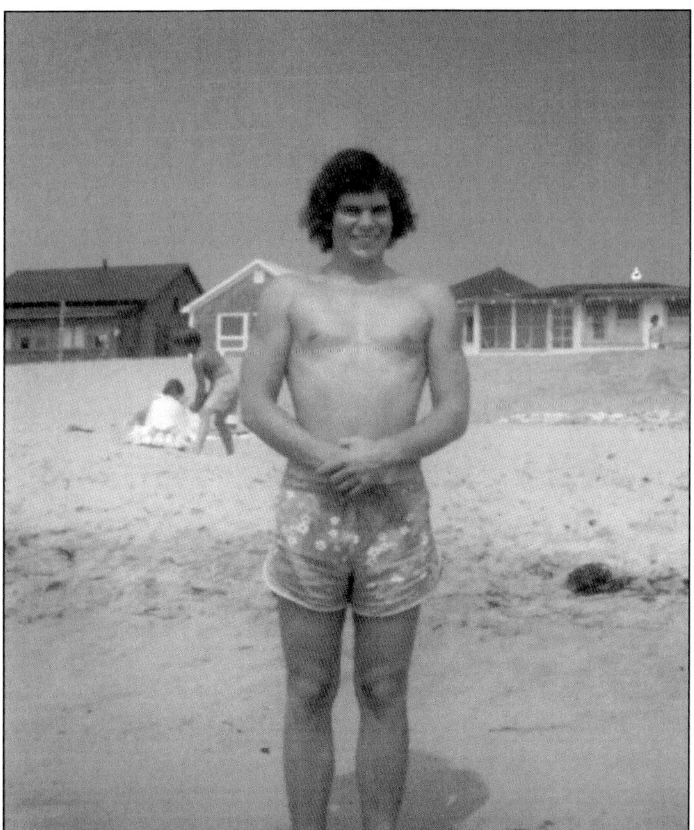

Dennis McAllister poses on the beach in 1973. He is a resident of Matunuck and the grandson of the original owners of Cavanaugh's Café (John and Bridget Gallogly Cavanaugh), now Tara's Tipperary Tavern. (Courtesy of Susan Rivera Russo.)

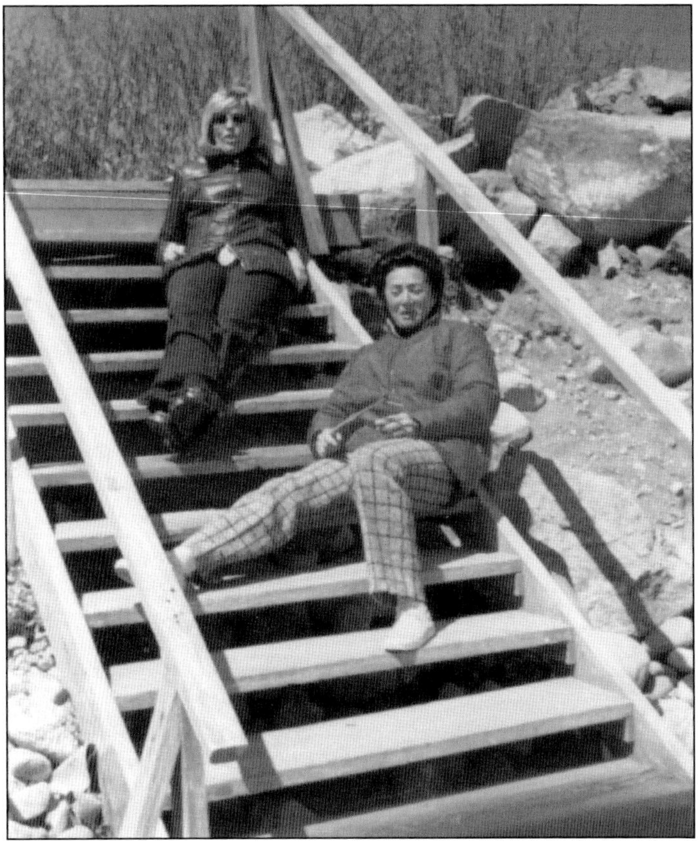

Jean Gustafson (top) and Grace Rivera are sitting on the steps at Matunuck Point Landing down to Ann's Beach in the autumn of 1972. (Courtesy of Susan Rivera Russo.)

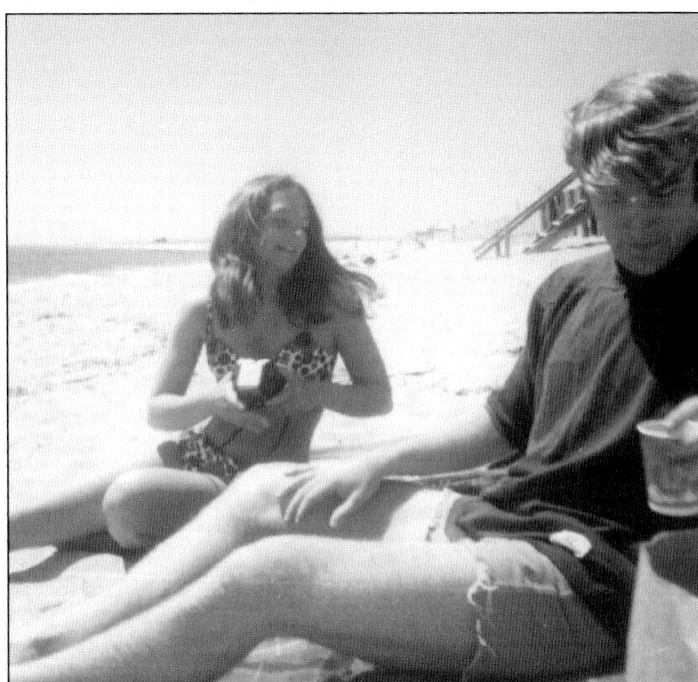

Susan Rivera Russo, with camera in hand, and Steve Bennett are on the beach in front of Carpenter's Bar and Restaurant in May 1972. Notice there are stairs leading up from the beach to the parking lot of the Sea View. (Courtesy of Susan Rivera Russo.)

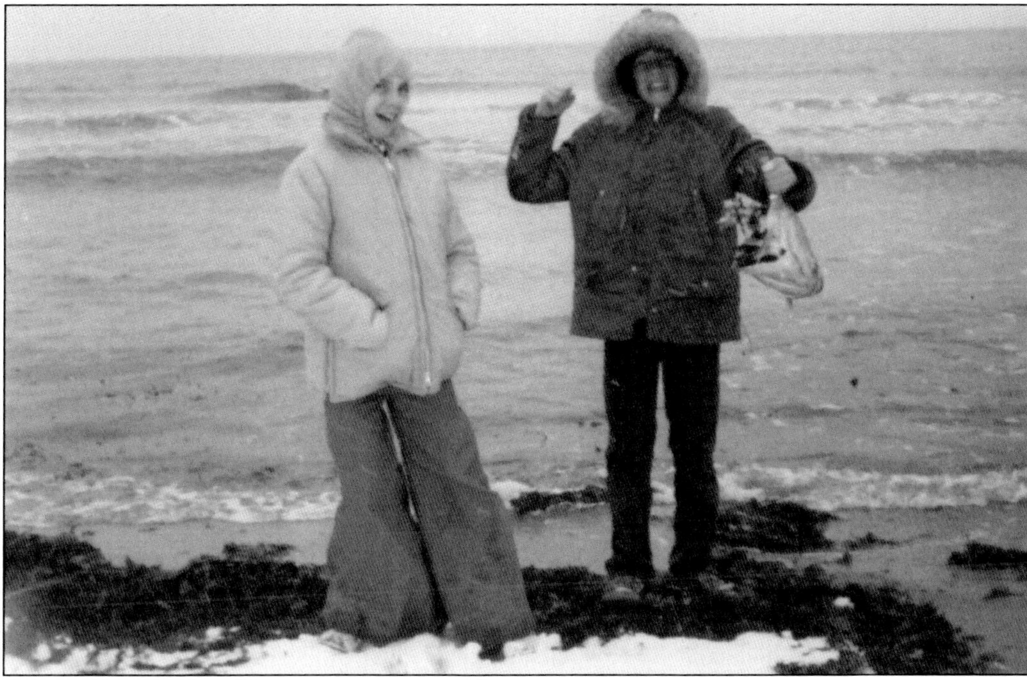

Robyn and Buster Rivera walk the beach on a wintry day in 1972. Buster was always finding something to bring home, according to his sister Susan Rivera Russo. (Courtesy of Susan Rivera Russo.)

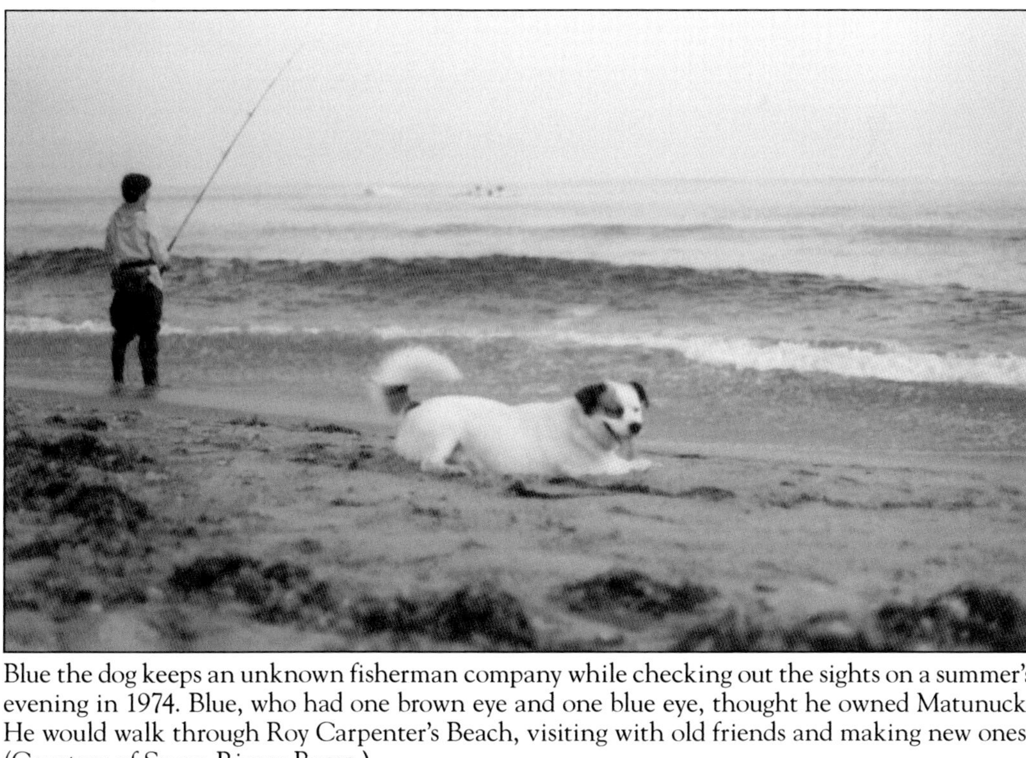

Blue the dog keeps an unknown fisherman company while checking out the sights on a summer's evening in 1974. Blue, who had one brown eye and one blue eye, thought he owned Matunuck. He would walk through Roy Carpenter's Beach, visiting with old friends and making new ones. (Courtesy of Susan Rivera Russo.)

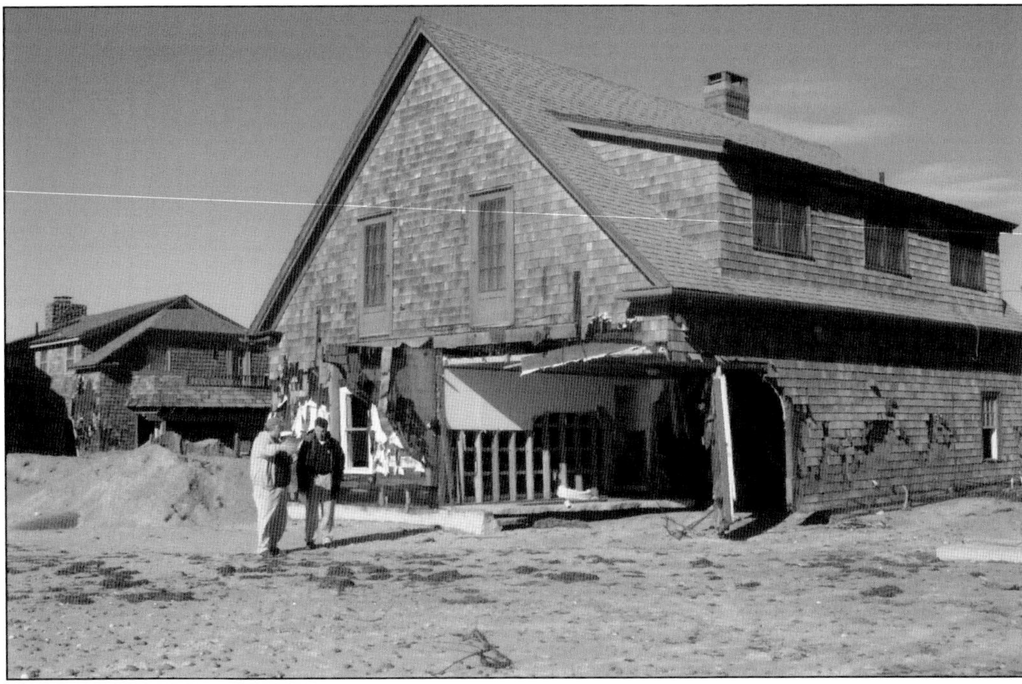

The aftermath of Hurricane Sandy is evident at this home on Browning Beach. It was one of a group of homes known as "the five cottages." In the late 1800s and early 1900s, this area along the ocean at Browning Beach was called a summer colony. There was a small cluster of seven summer homes, five of which extended in a row behind the dunes. (Courtesy of Michael McKenna.)

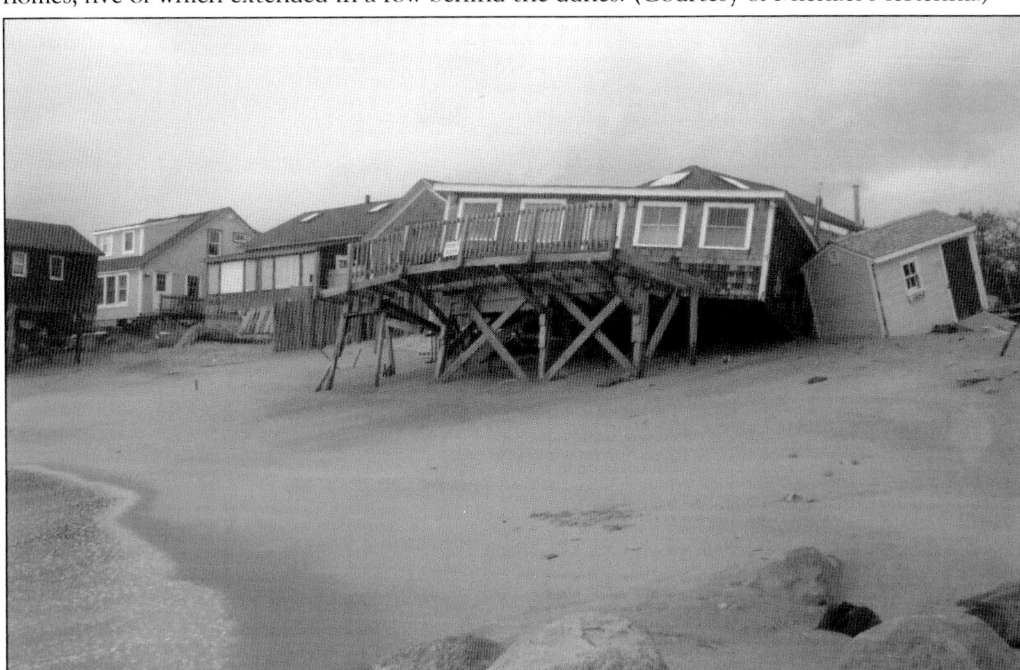

Hurricane Sandy destroyed these homes on Matunuck Beach Road beyond Tara's Tipperary Tavern. (Courtesy of Michael McKenna.)

Three

Around the Village

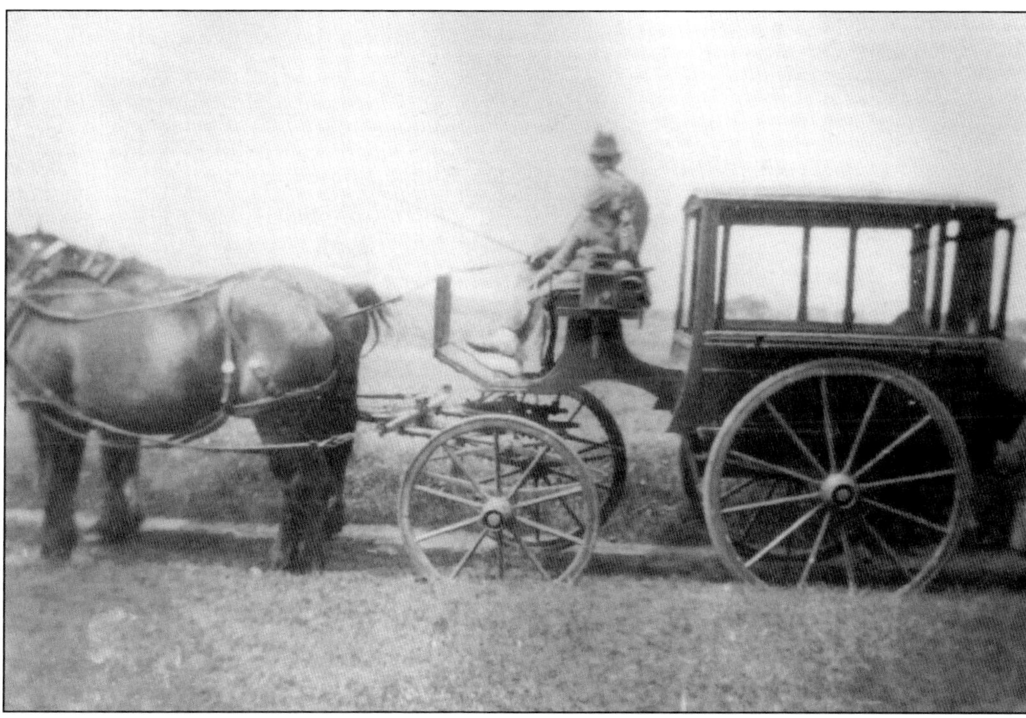

Upon close inspection, there are a man and a young girl seated in the horse and buggy. This image was in the Matunuck photo album of Virginia Broome Yale, who was born in 1909. Her parents, Charles and Esther Rebecca Weeden Broome, had their house built on Prospect Road around 1917. Virginia is quite possibly seated in the buggy. (Courtesy of David Yale.)

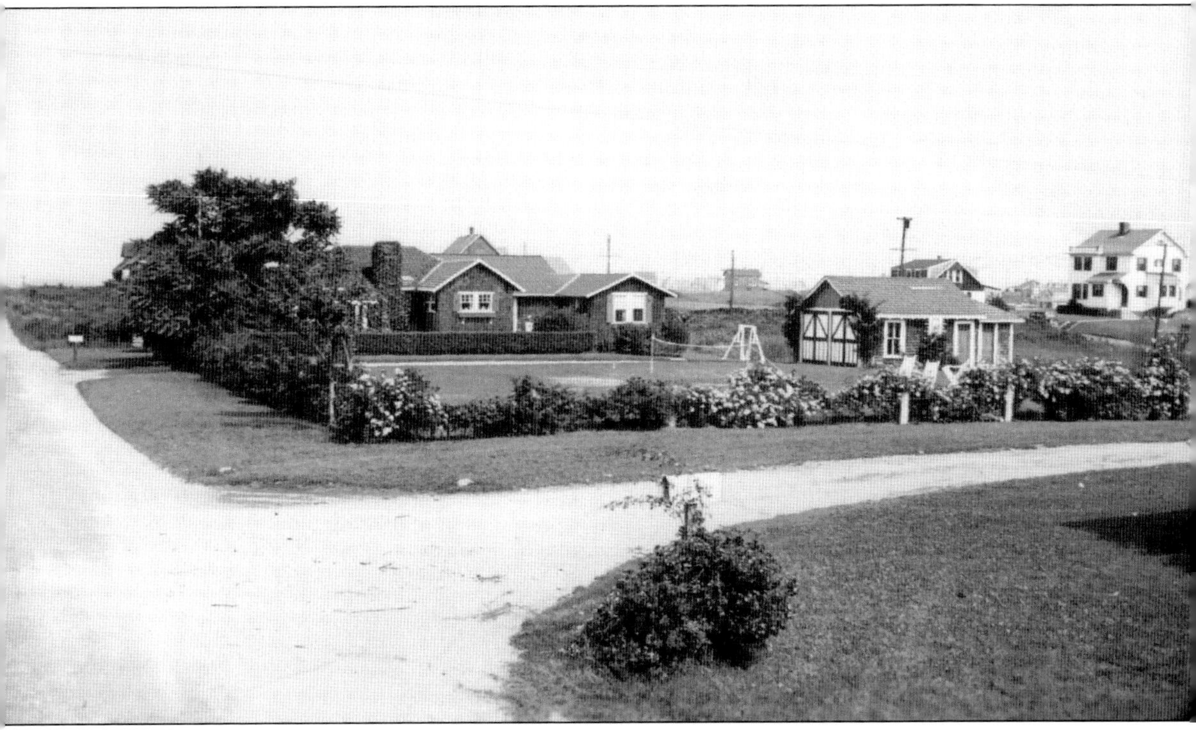

This is a view of the corner of Central Street and Park Avenue in the late 1930s. Felix F. Sr. and Margaret Harrington Gallogly bought the house pictured after the hurricane of 1938 damaged their home, the Lund Cottage. Ann Terry, the Gallogys' granddaughter, is the current owner of the house. The area of the Park, as it was called, was laid out in the 1890s, but there were few houses even in the 1930s. The large white house to the right was owned by the McKinnon family. It was demolished a couple of years ago and replaced with a new house, according to Ann Terry. (Courtesy of Ann Terry.)

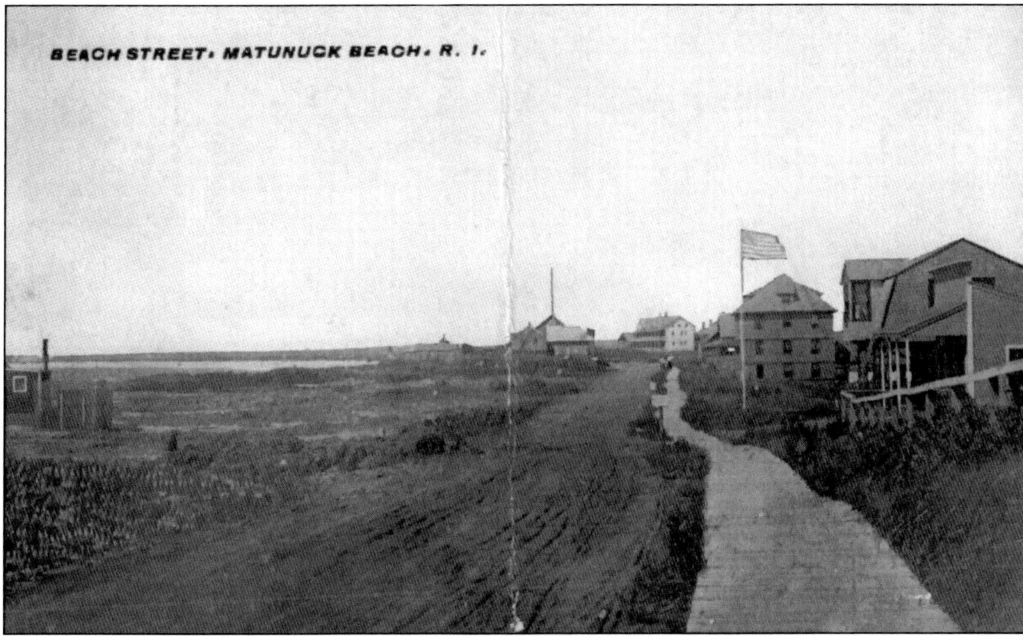

Although this postcard says Beach Street, it is actually the modern-day Matunuck Beach Road. (Courtesy of David Yale.)

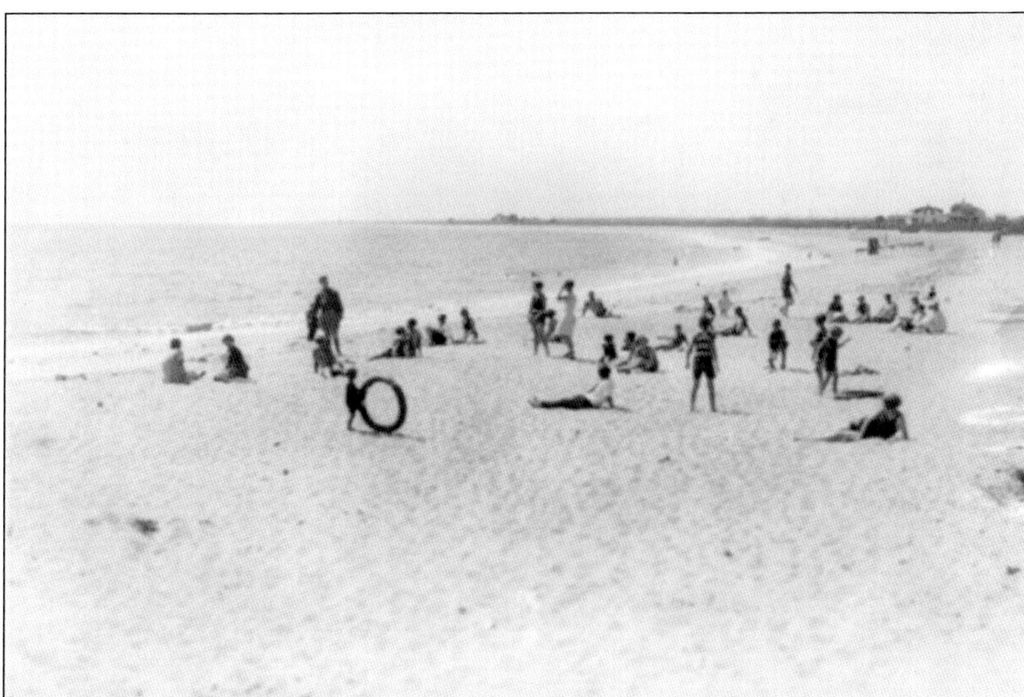

The postcard is of Old Matunuck Beach. (Courtesy of Michael McKenna.)

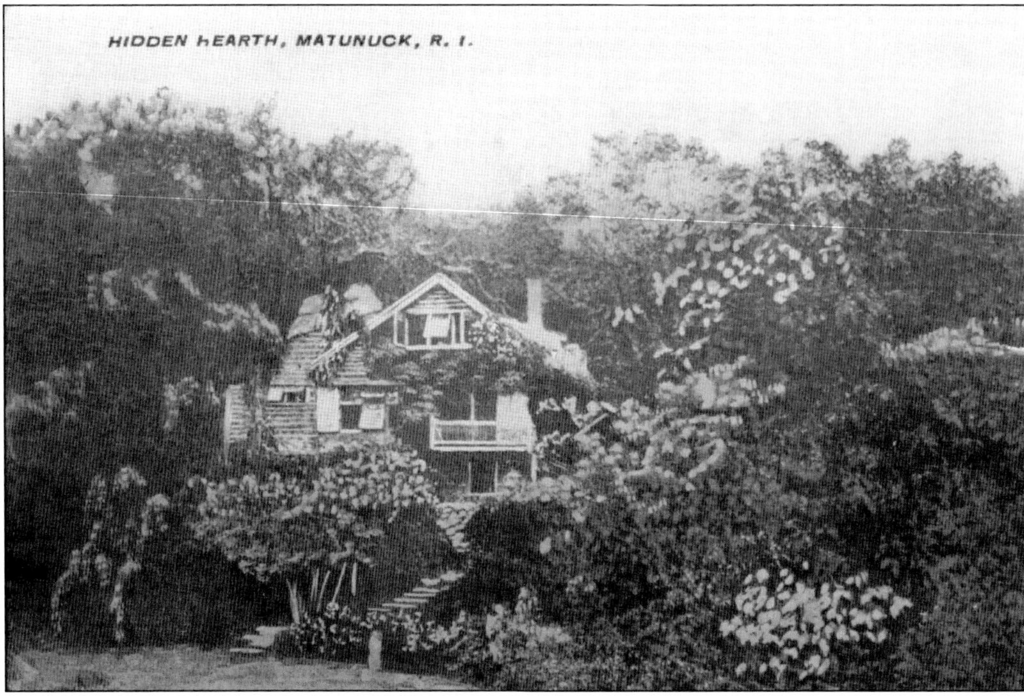

Hidden Hearth was originally a two-room stone cottage built on the side of a hill. When Boston lawyer and artist Charles Matlack purchased the home in 1885, it was in disrepair. He renovated and restored the home. (Both, courtesy of David Yale.)

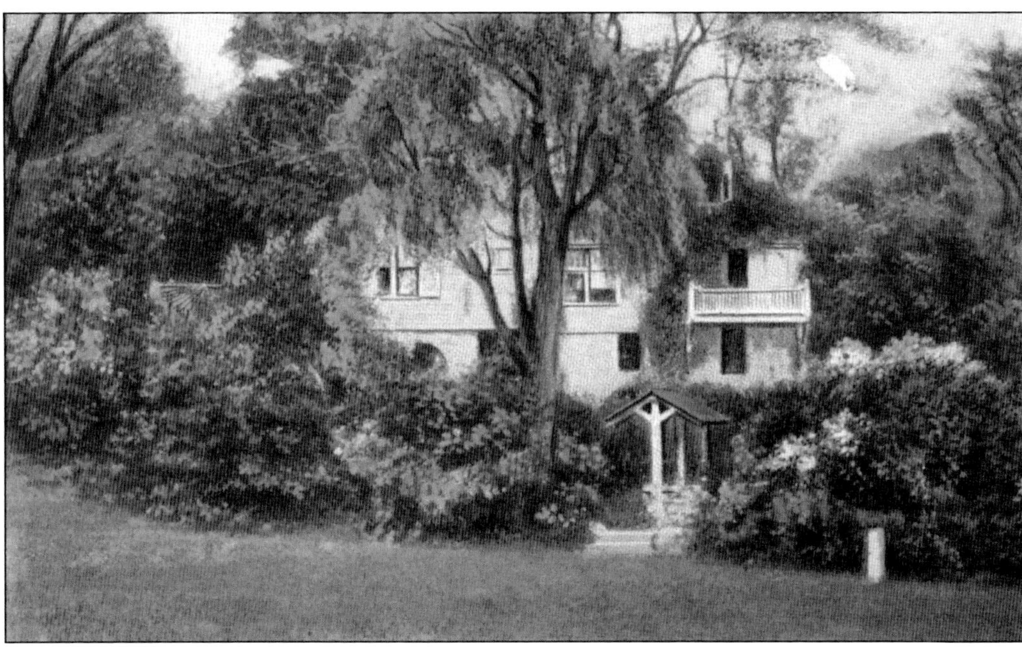

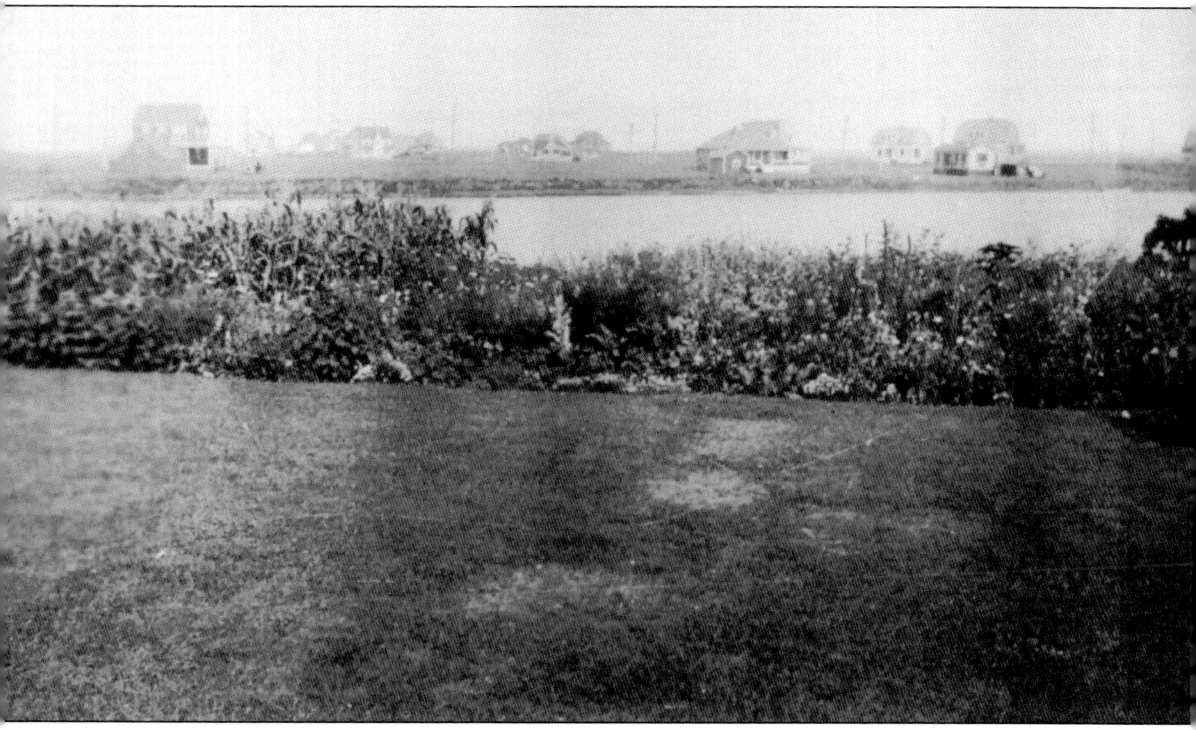

This photograph captures a scenic view of Potter's Pond. Susan Rivera Russo, who first went to Matunuck in the 1950s, said, "Another great part of growing up in Matunuck was Potter's Pond. I had a dinghy that had a three horsepower Evinrude motor on it. We used to row around the pond area near the house for fun as well as to go crabbing. We weren't allowed to go past a certain point where we could be seen from the house." Russo's family home was on Prospect Street. (Courtesy of David Yale.)

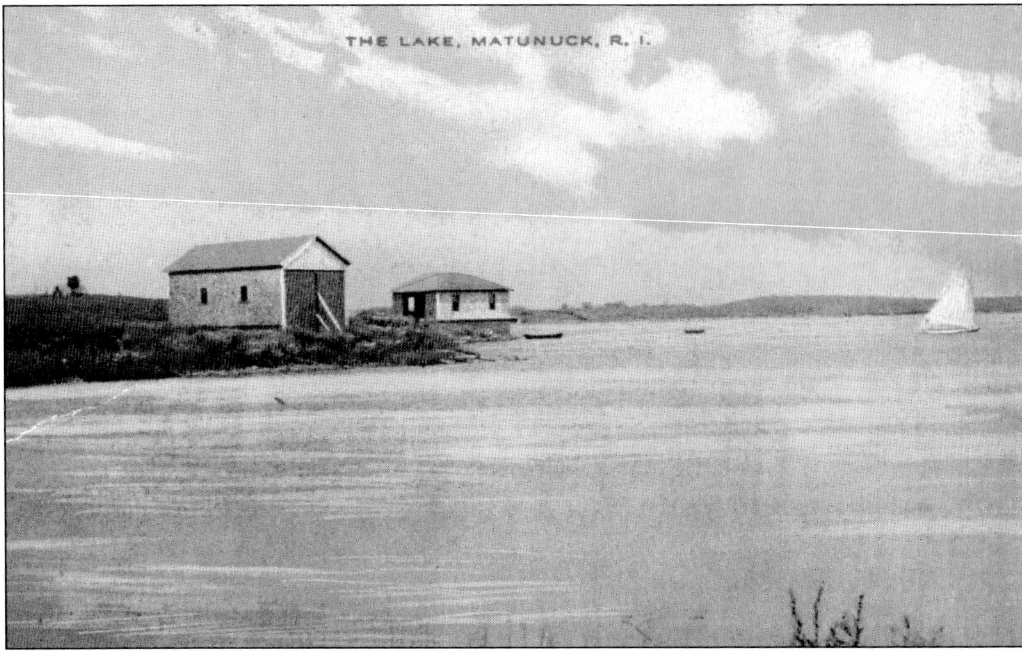

This lake is Potter's Pond. There is a section of the pond that some residents refer to as the quahog flats. At the very end of Matunuck Point, on the east side of the pond, there is an area where the water is—or was—shallow with a white sandy bottom and always crystal clear. (Above, courtesy of the Robert Beverly Hale Library; below, courtesy of David Yale.)

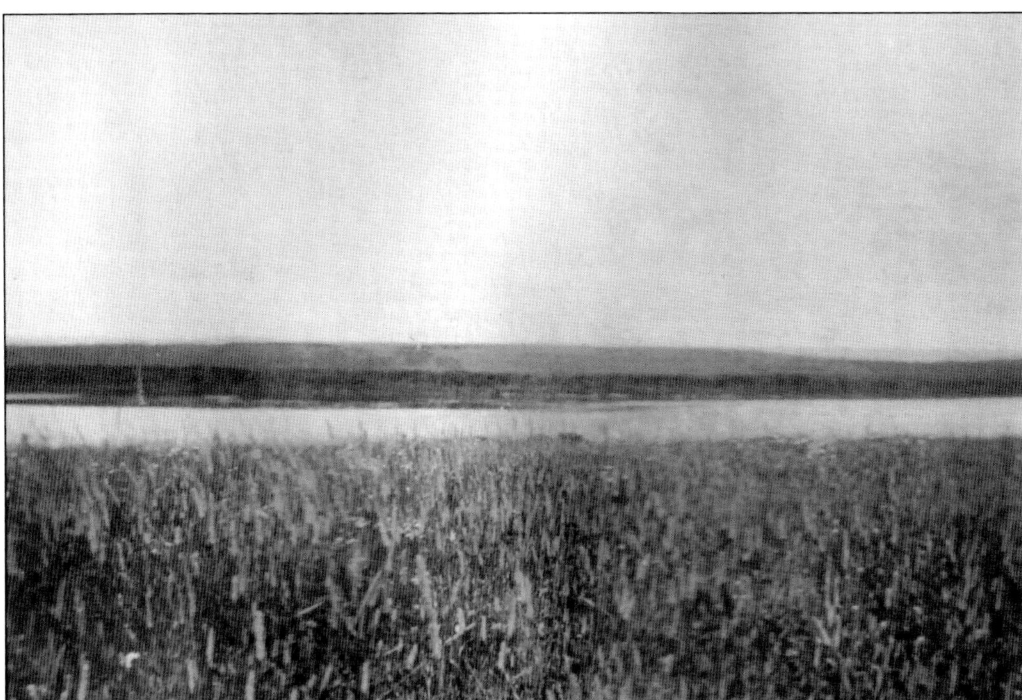

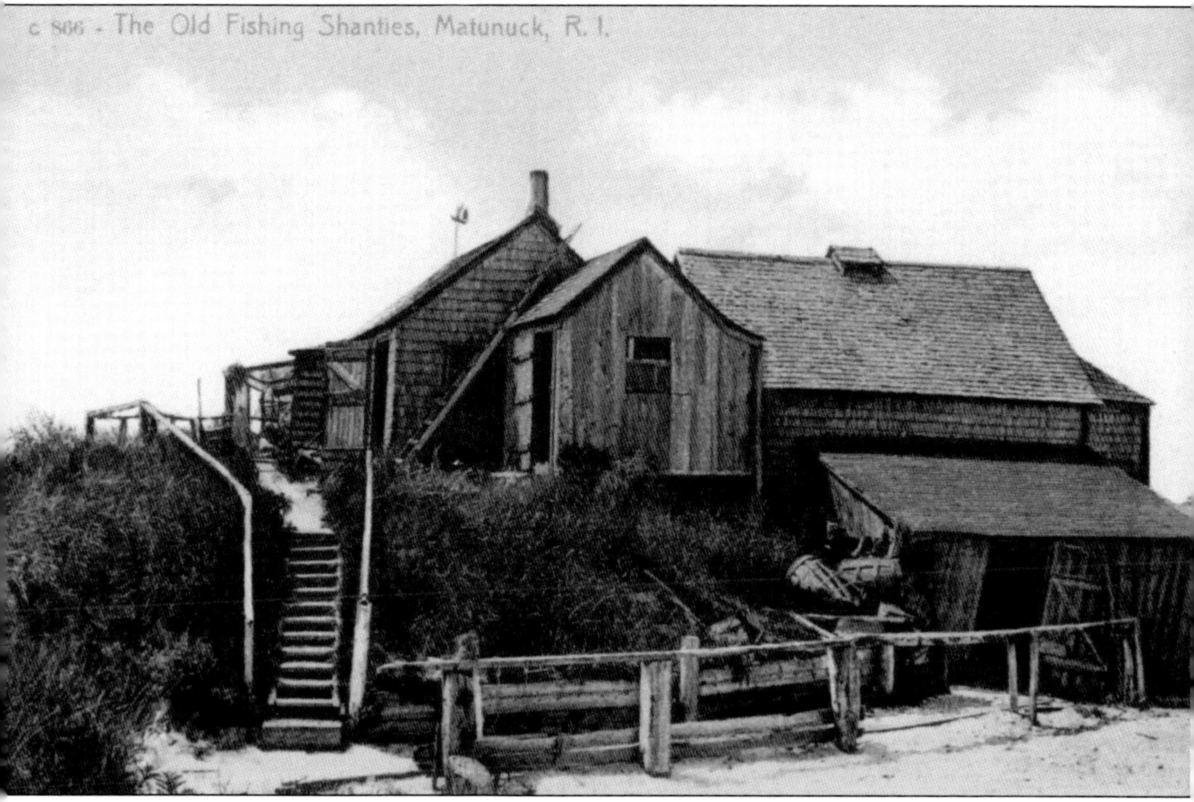

These old fishing shanties were also known as Tucker's Fish House, according to the Robert Beverly Hale Library. (Courtesy of the Robert Beverly Hale Library.)

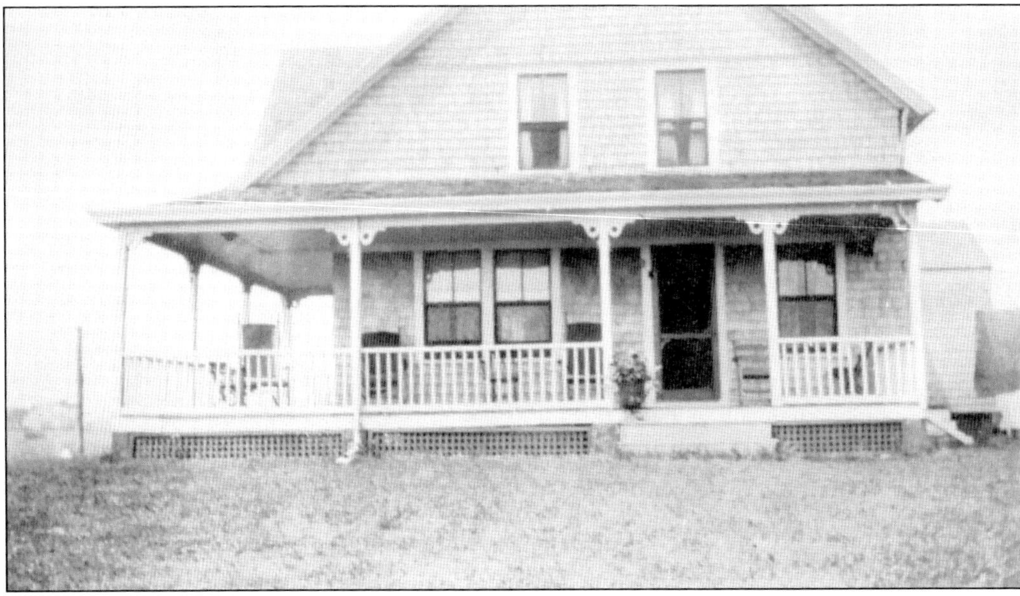

This is the home of Matthew Joseph Cummings Sr. on Atlantic Avenue in 1915. Cummings was the great-grandfather of Jeanne McHenry Helma. (Courtesy of Jeanne McHenry Helma.)

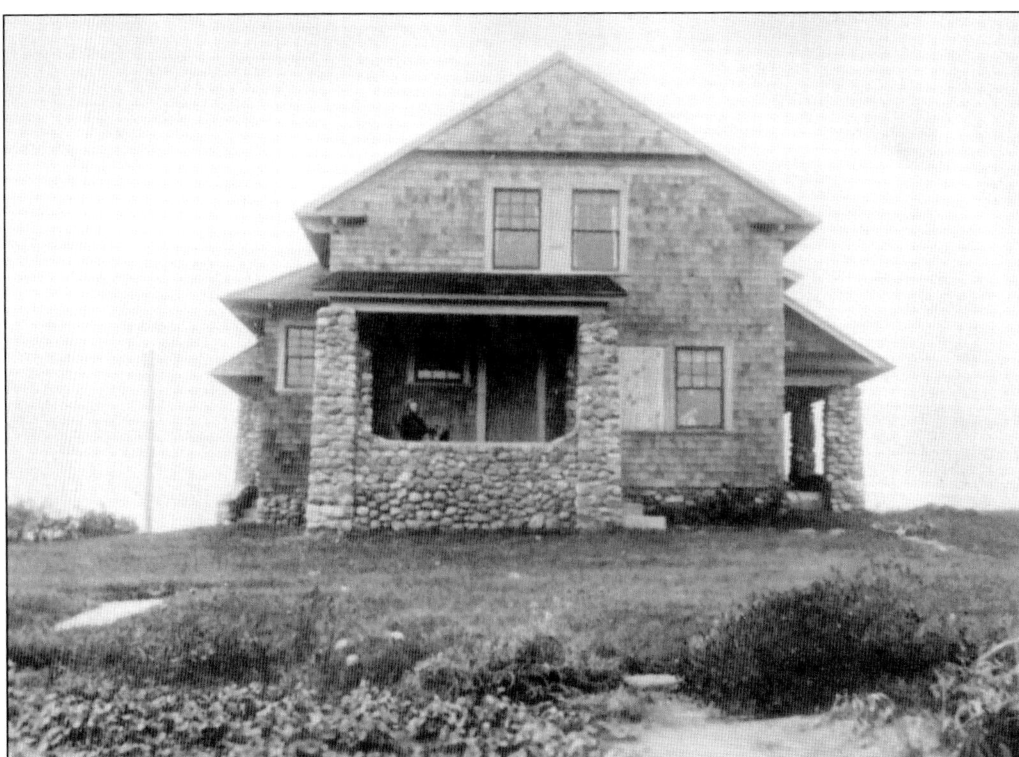

This home on Prospect Road was built for Charles and Esther Rebecca Weeden Broome in 1917. (Courtesy of David Yale.)

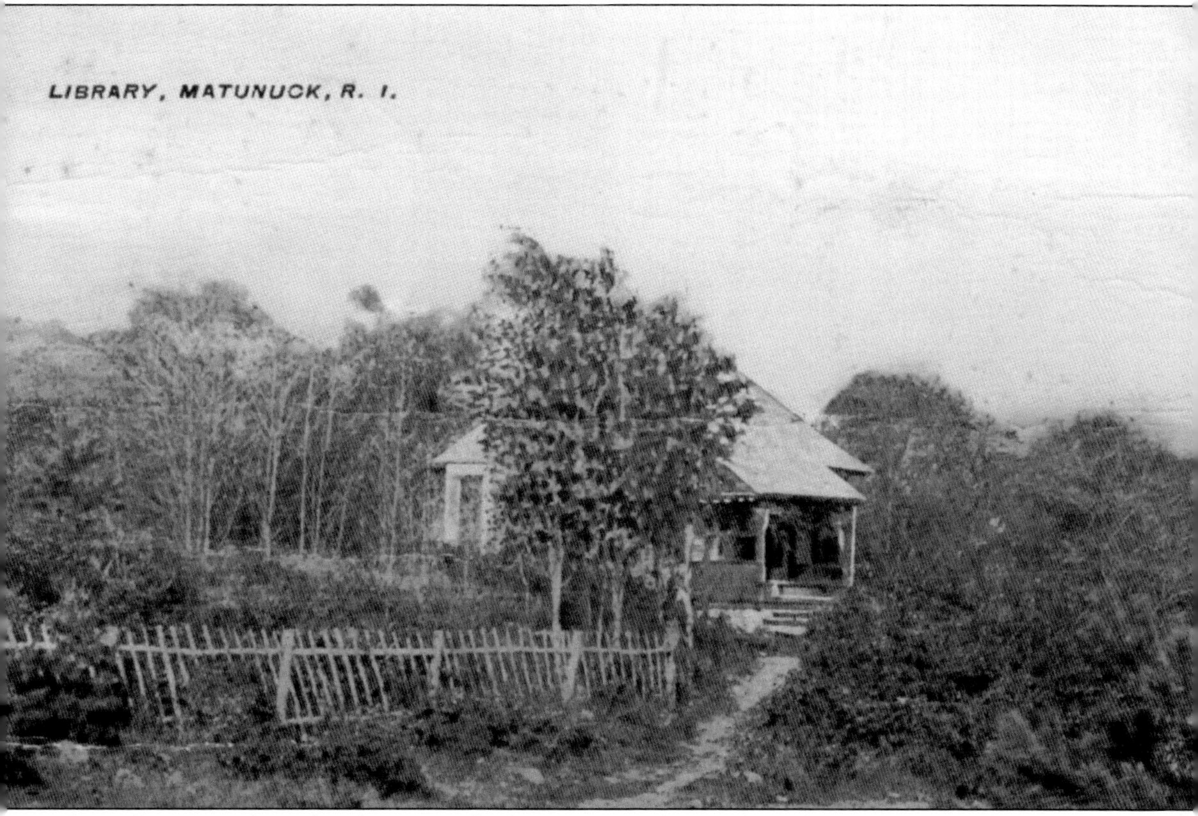

The Robert Beverly Hale Library was built in 1896 and named for the son of Edward Everett Hale, a Unitarian minister and author. The building is a one-story, clapboard-shingled structure with a stone and brick chimney and granite foundation. The main reading room has a fireplace and bay window. The Perkins Memorial Wing, the children's room, was added in 1930. Another wing was added in 1952, and an extensive renovation took place in 1991, adding a small two-story addition and storage space in the basement. (Courtesy of David Yale.)

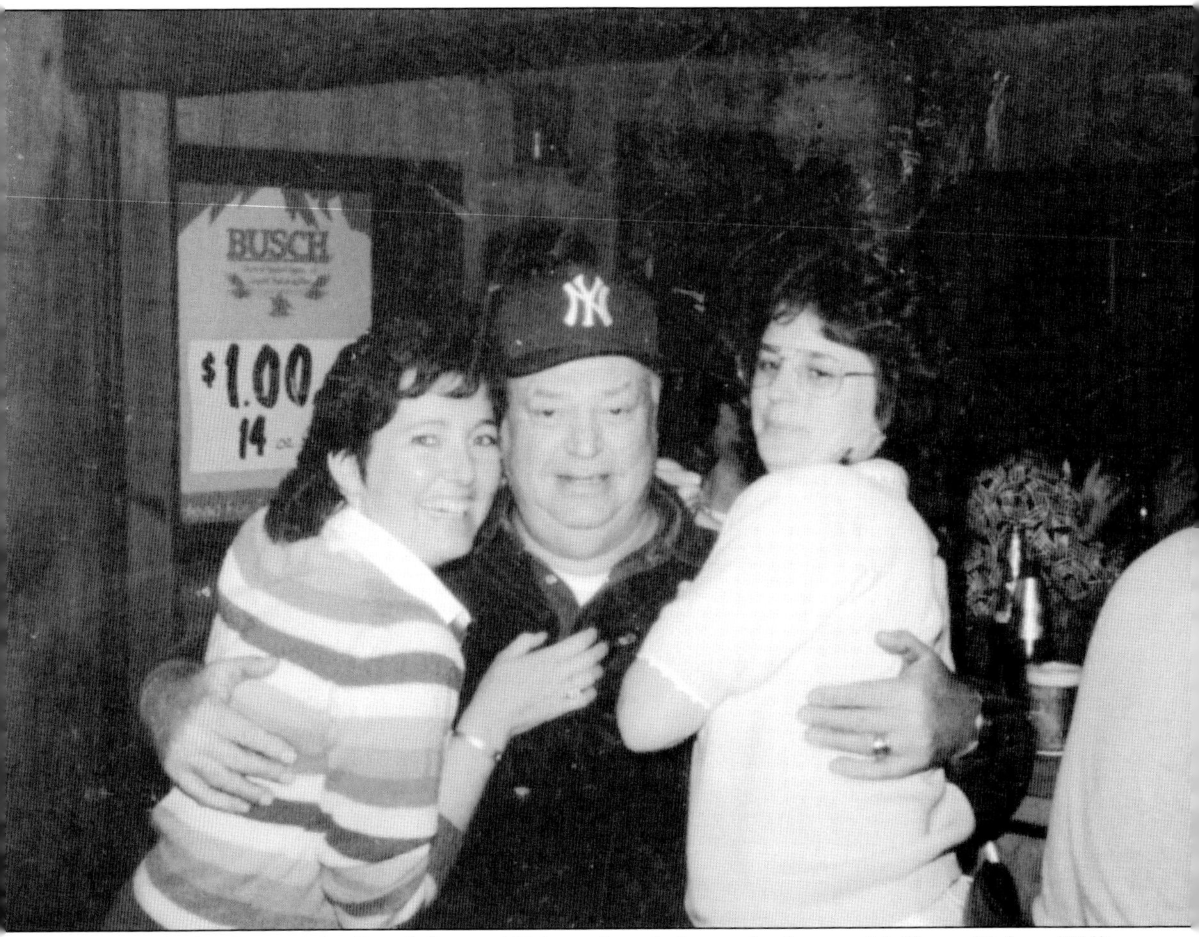

Inside the Ocean Mist Beach Bar in 1989 are, from left to right, Jeanne McHenry Helma, William "Bear" McKenna, and his daughter Carol McKenna Szymanski. The owners of the bar at the time were Steve Hearne and Dick Bagge. (Courtesy of Jeanne McHenry Helma.)

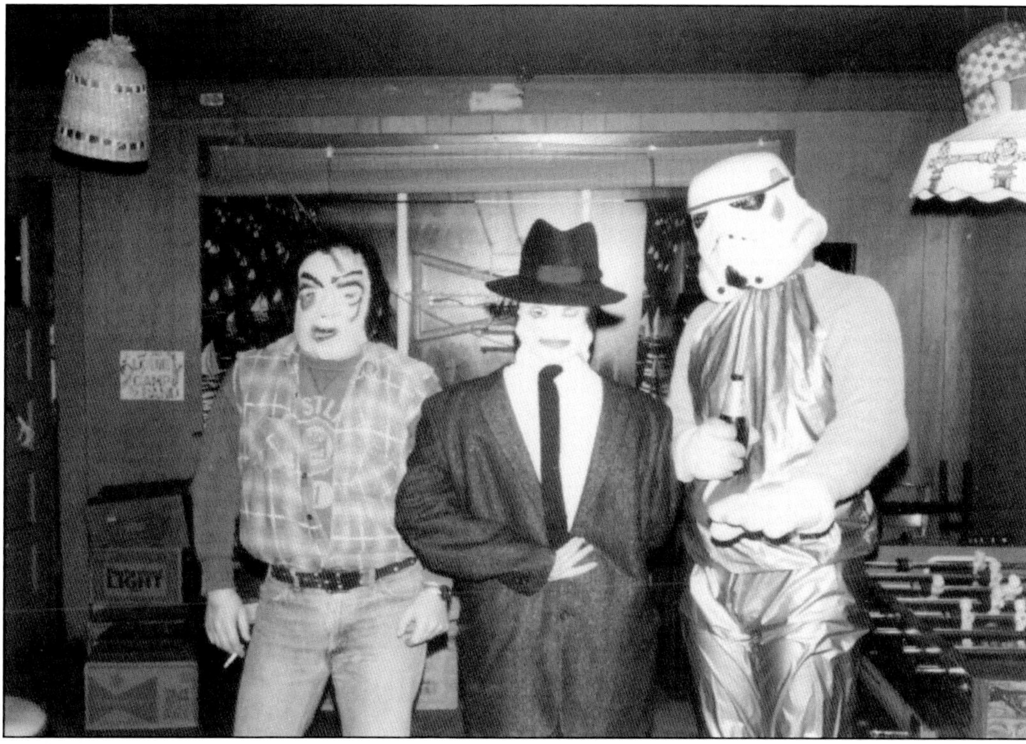

Both photographs were taken at the Ocean Mist Beach Bar on Halloween 1982. Above, Jeanne McHenry Helma (center) won third place in the costume contest. To her right is John LaCroix. Jeanne is also in the photograph below. (Both, courtesy of Jeanne McHenry Helma.)

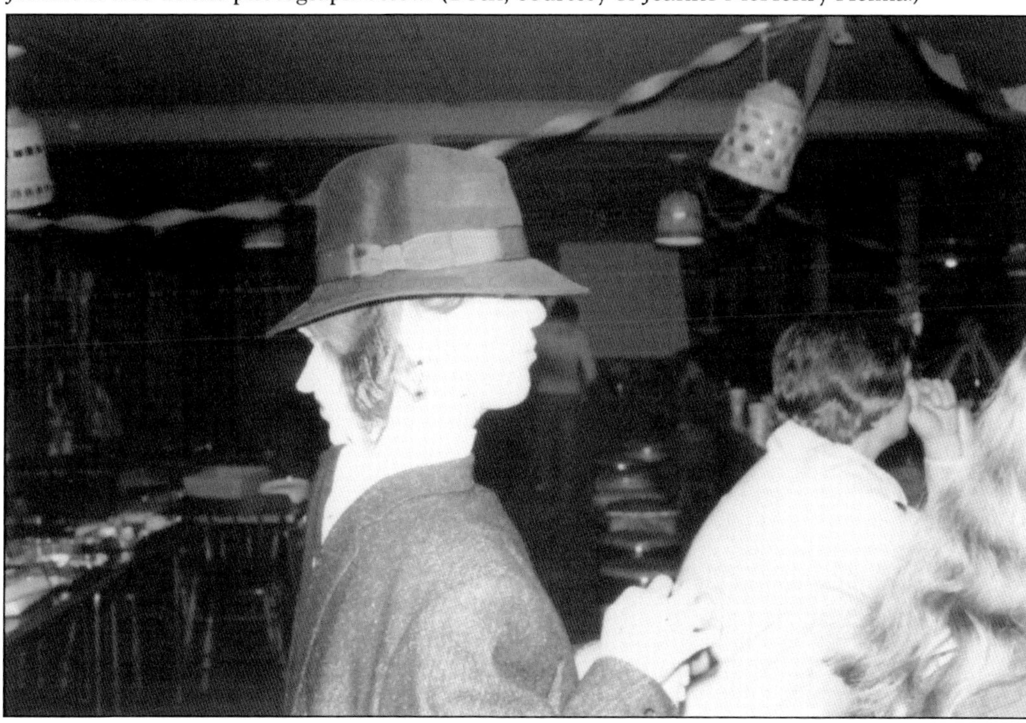

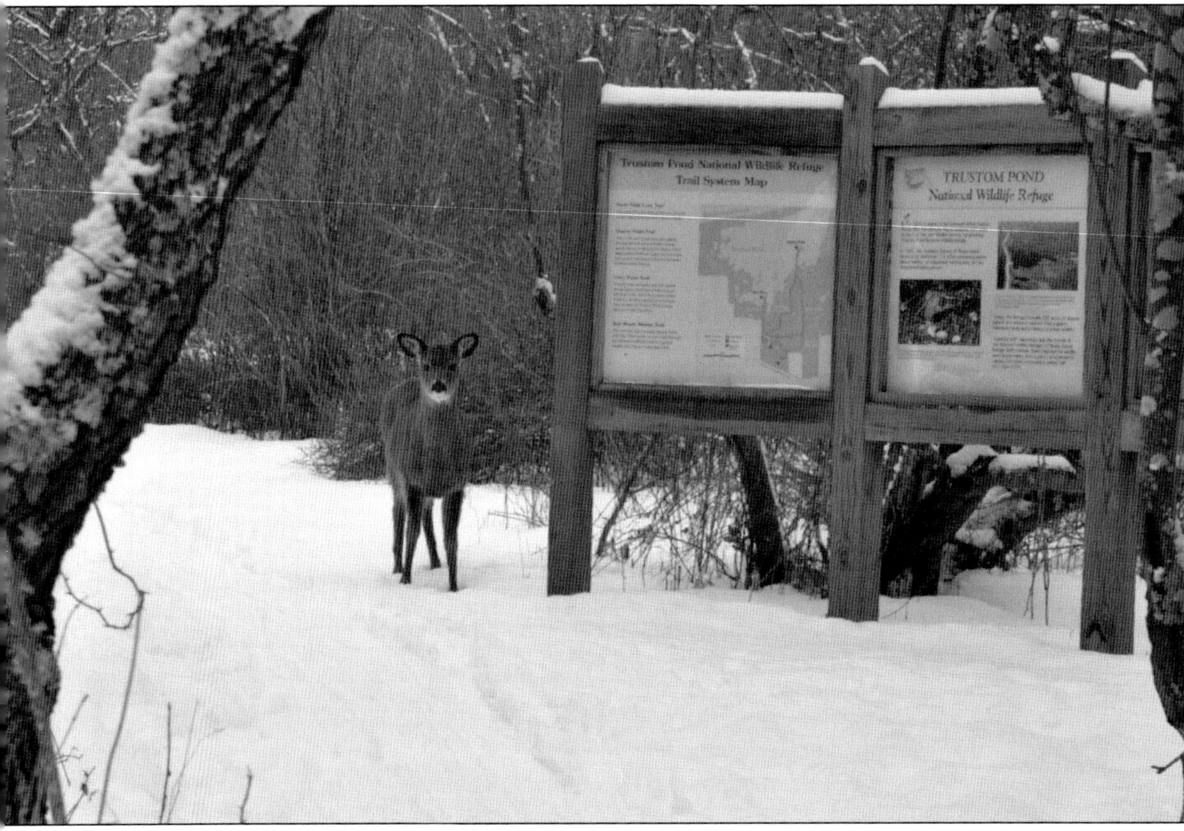

Thomas James Tetzner photographed this whitetail deer at the entrance to Trustom Pond National Wildlife Refuge on January 26, 2011. In 1974, Ann Kenyon Morse donated the first 365 acres of the refuge. In 1982, the Audubon Society of Rhode Island donated 151 acres. The refuge now includes 787 acres of various wildlife habitats, including fields, shrublands, woodlands, fresh and saltwater ponds, and sandy beaches and dunes. There are about 300 bird species, more than 40 mammal species, and 20 species of reptiles and amphibians, according to the refuge's website. (Courtesy of Thomas James Tetzner.)

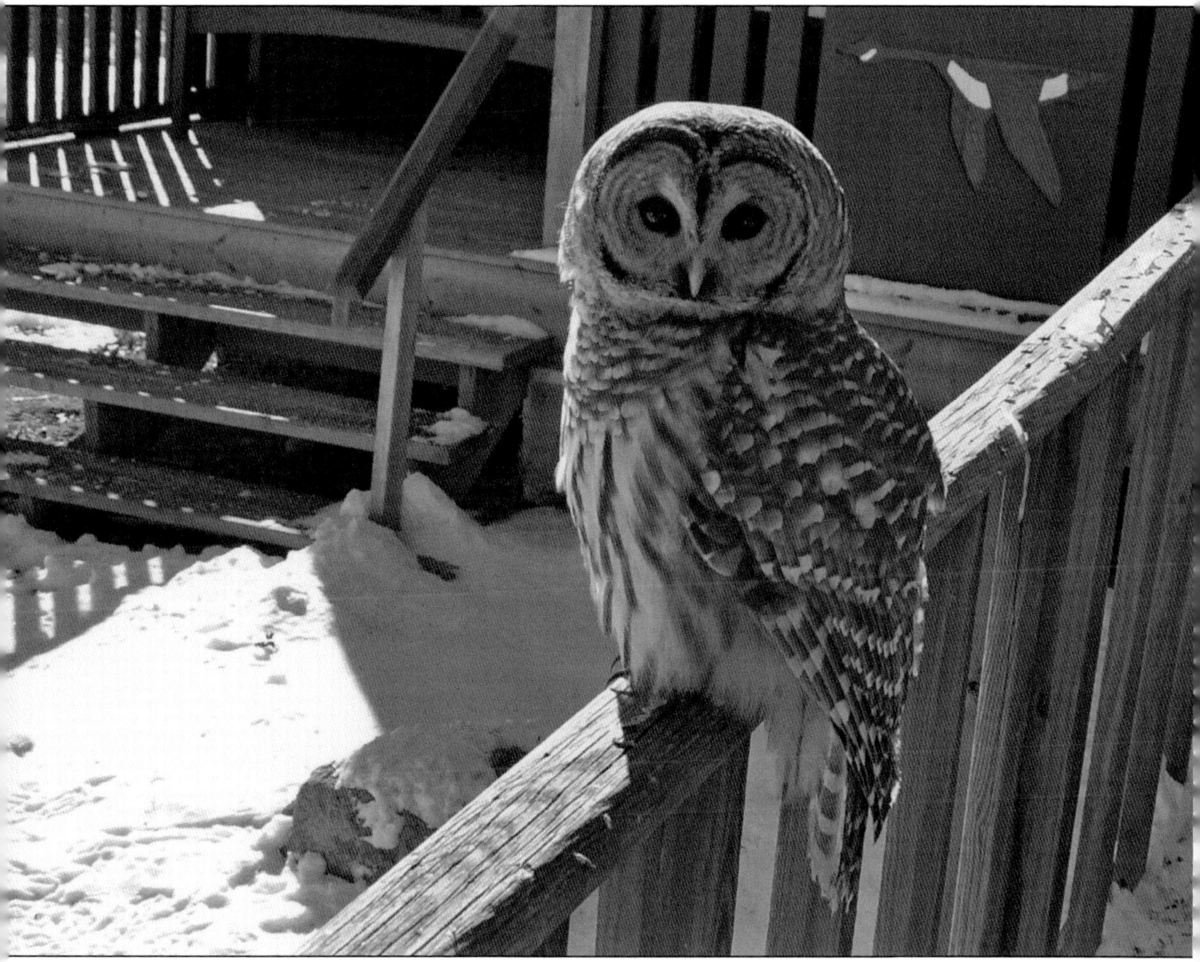

This barred owl was photographed by Thomas James Tetzner at Trustom Pond National Wildlife Refuge on January 24, 2013. Tetzner began photographing birds in 1968. "Through my photos, I hope that everyone will see the beauty in nature and recognize its value. I hope to spark an interest in people to become advocates for our environment," he said. Tetzner, a resident of Charlestown, Rhode Island, for 35 years and a wildlife photographer, began taking digital photographs in 2004. (Courtesy of Thomas James Tetzner.)

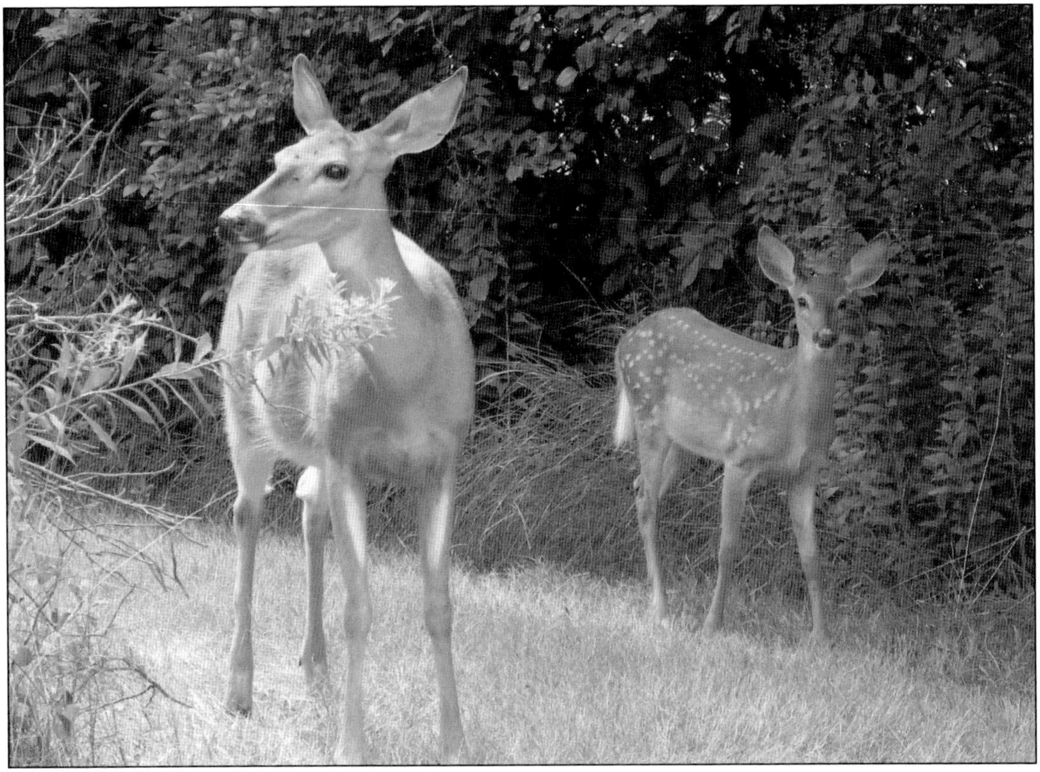

Thomas James Tetzner captured this image of two whitetail deer (above) on Otter Trail at Trustom Pond National Wildlife Refuge on August 21, 2010, and the wood duck (below) at the refuge's Farm Pond on September 28, 2014. Trustom Pond is the only undeveloped coastal salt pond in Rhode Island, making it even more valuable to wildlife. (Both, courtesy of Thomas James Tetzner.)

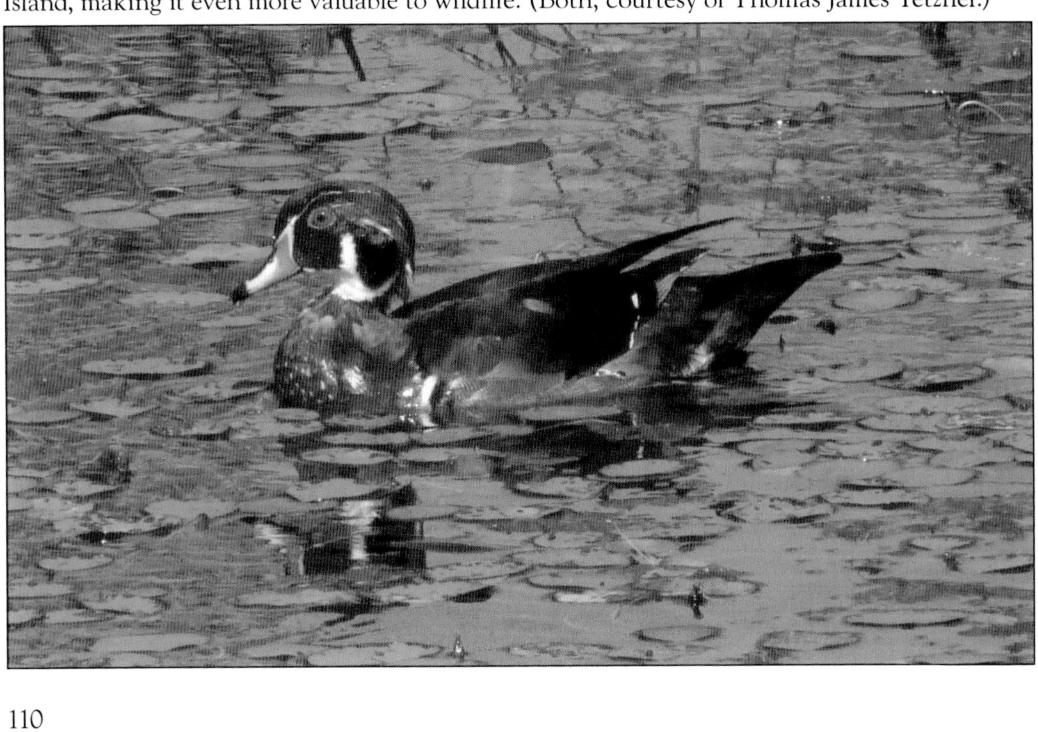

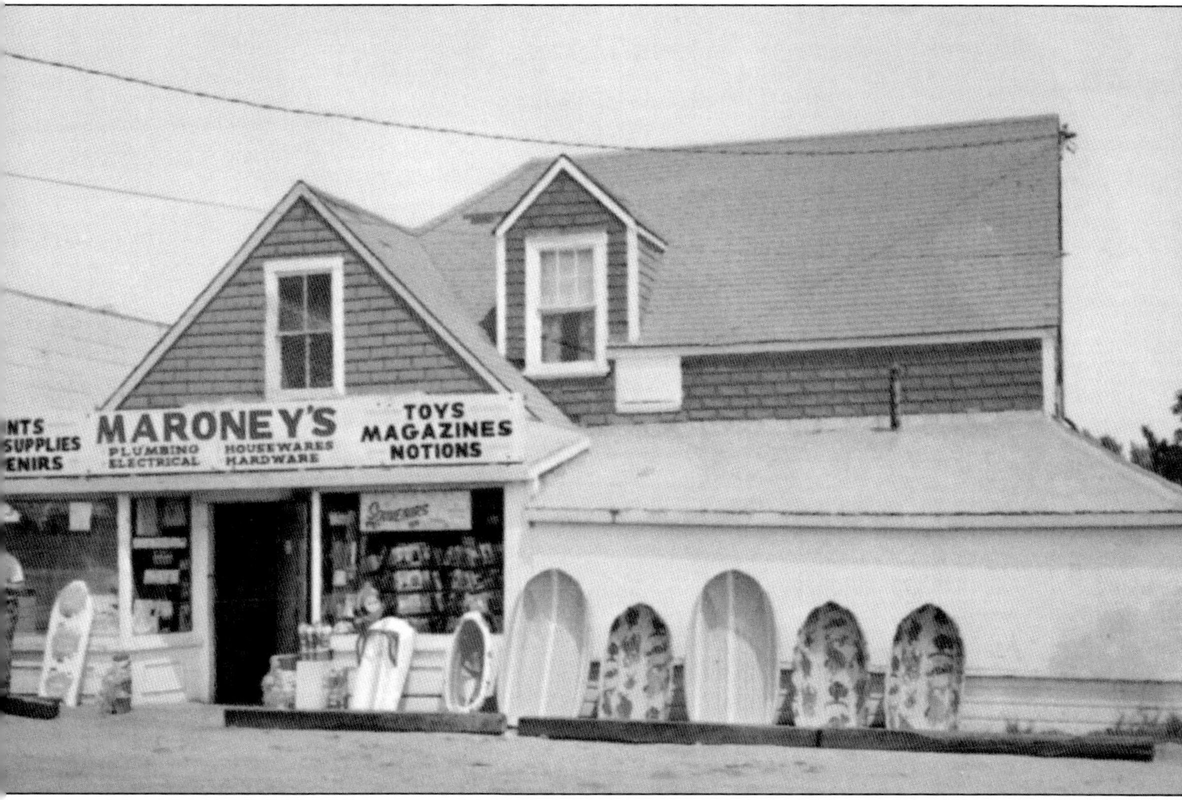

Maroney's General Store was located on Matunuck Beach Road. (Courtesy of Seaview Market.)

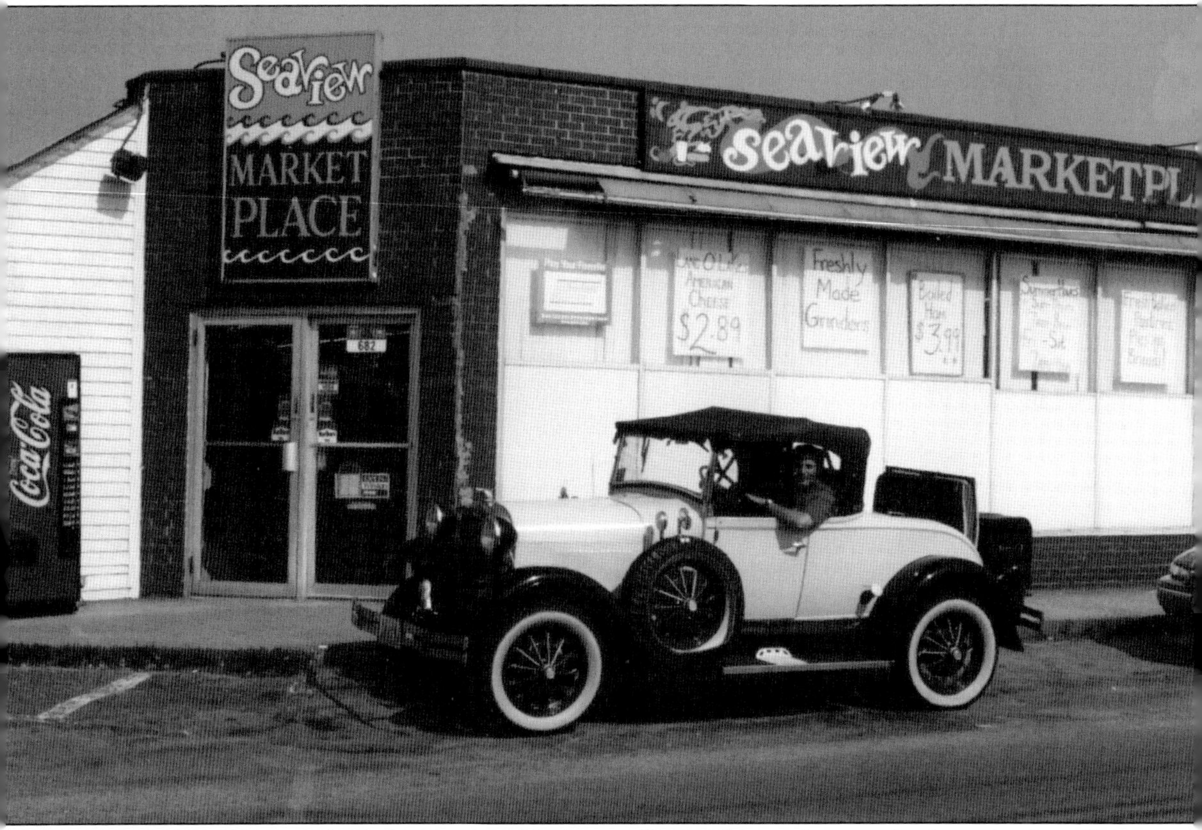

Jim Pike photographed the Seaview Market in 1998. The market was built in the late 1940s. (Courtesy of Seaview Market.)

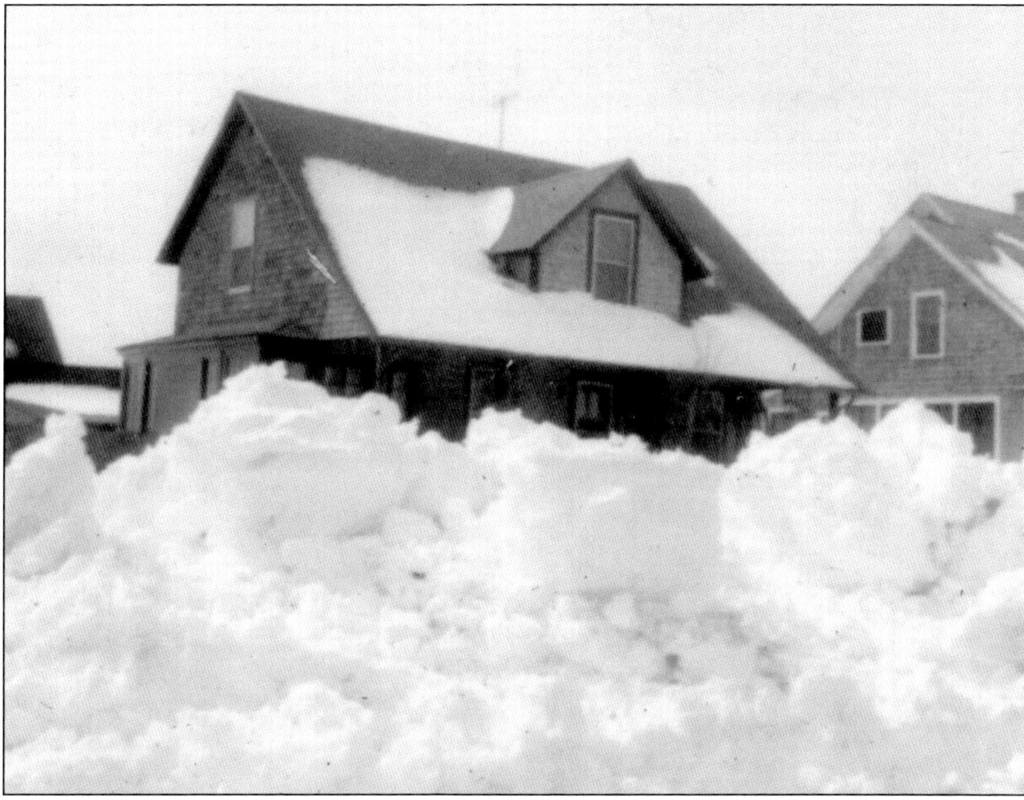

The McHenry home on Park Avenue is pictured here after a snowstorm in 1968. (Courtesy of Jean McHenry Helma.)

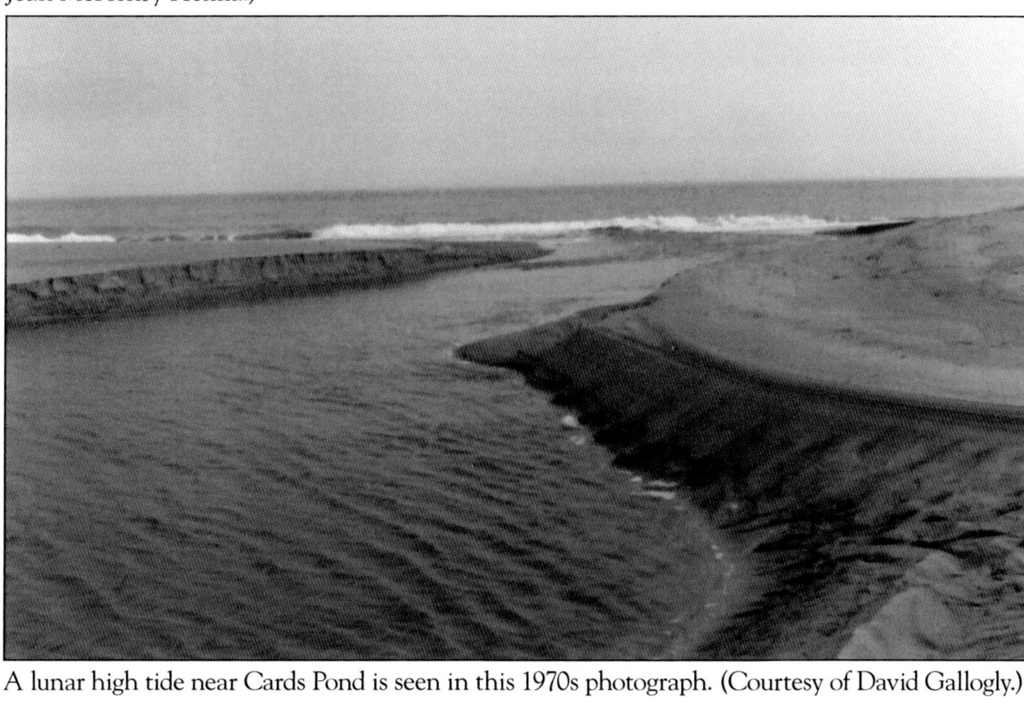

A lunar high tide near Cards Pond is seen in this 1970s photograph. (Courtesy of David Gallogly.)

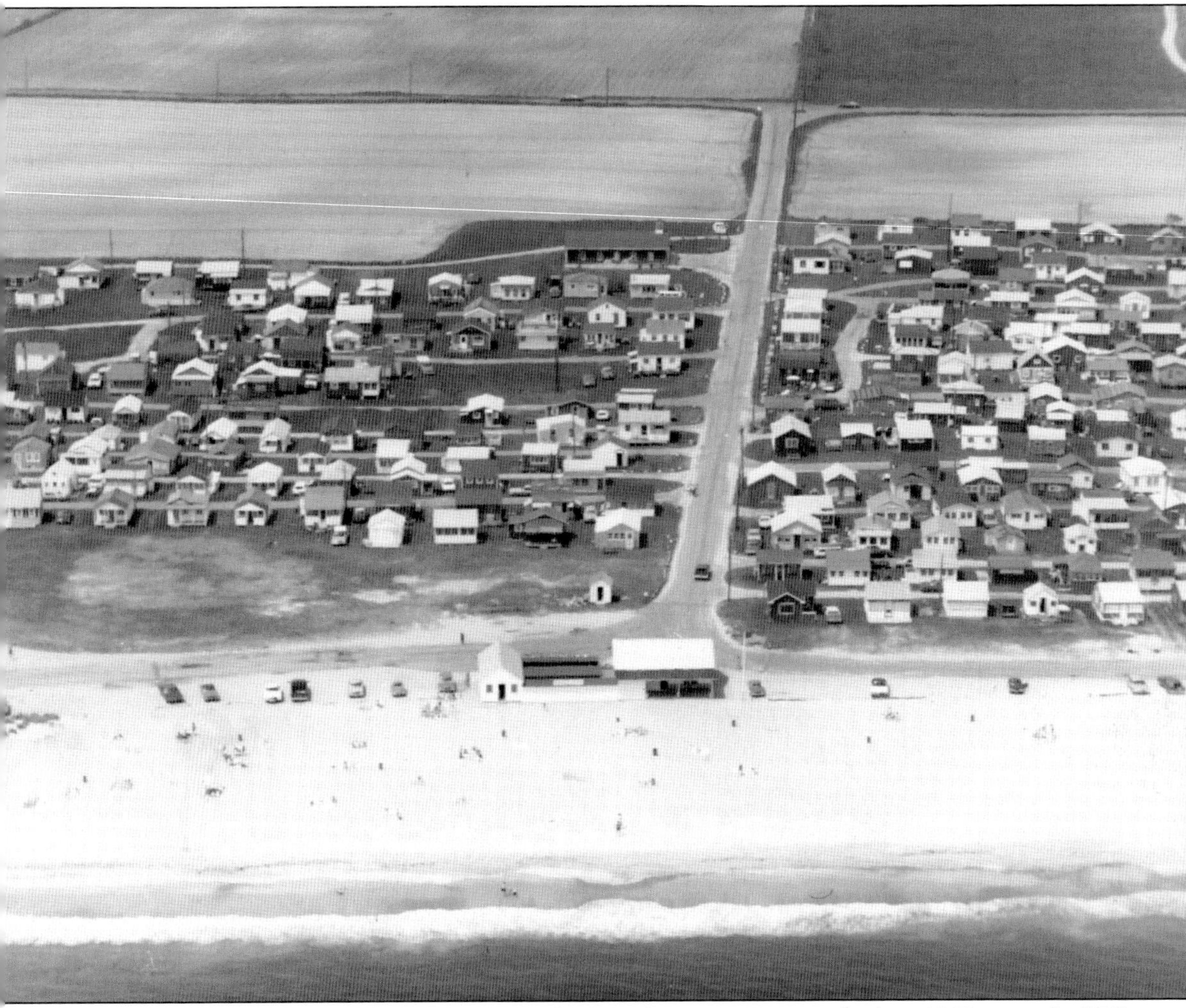

This aerial view of Roy Carpenter's Beach was taken sometime in the late 1960s or early 1970s. Most of the two rows of houses on the right no longer exist. They were either destroyed by storms, washed away, or had to be moved to rows in the back due to beach erosion. The store in the center was moved back at least 100 feet. The land is owned by the Thoresen family. Nancy Thoresen, the granddaughter of the late Roy Carpenter, along with her children, Rob and Christa, operate Matunuck Beach Properties. (Courtesy of Michael McKenna.)

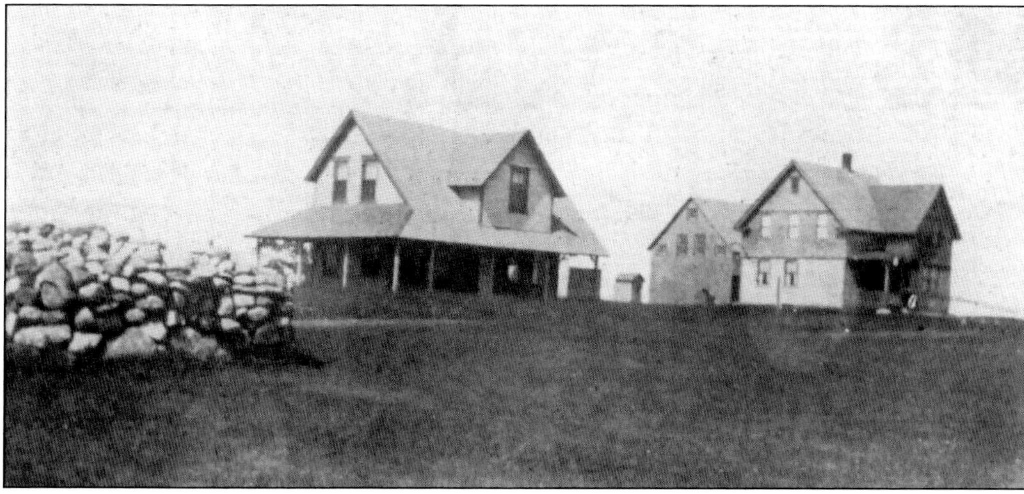

The Needham and Barney Cottages are shown in this postcard. (Courtesy of David Yale.)

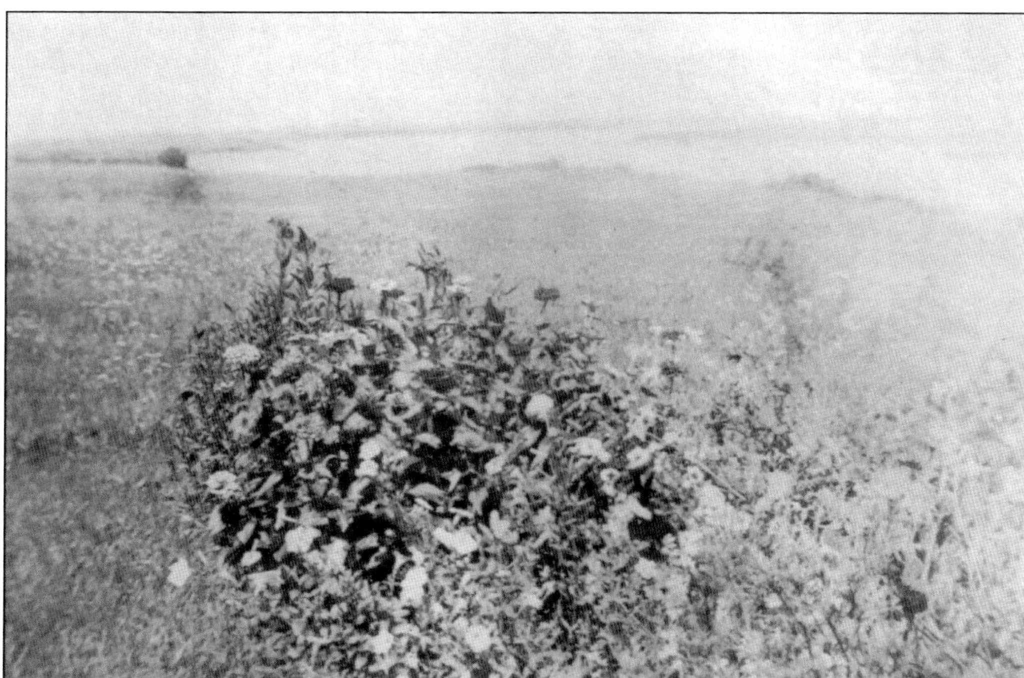

A bush blooms in the Prospect Road yard of Charles and Esther Rebecca Weeden Broome, near Potter's Pond. (Courtesy of David Yale.)

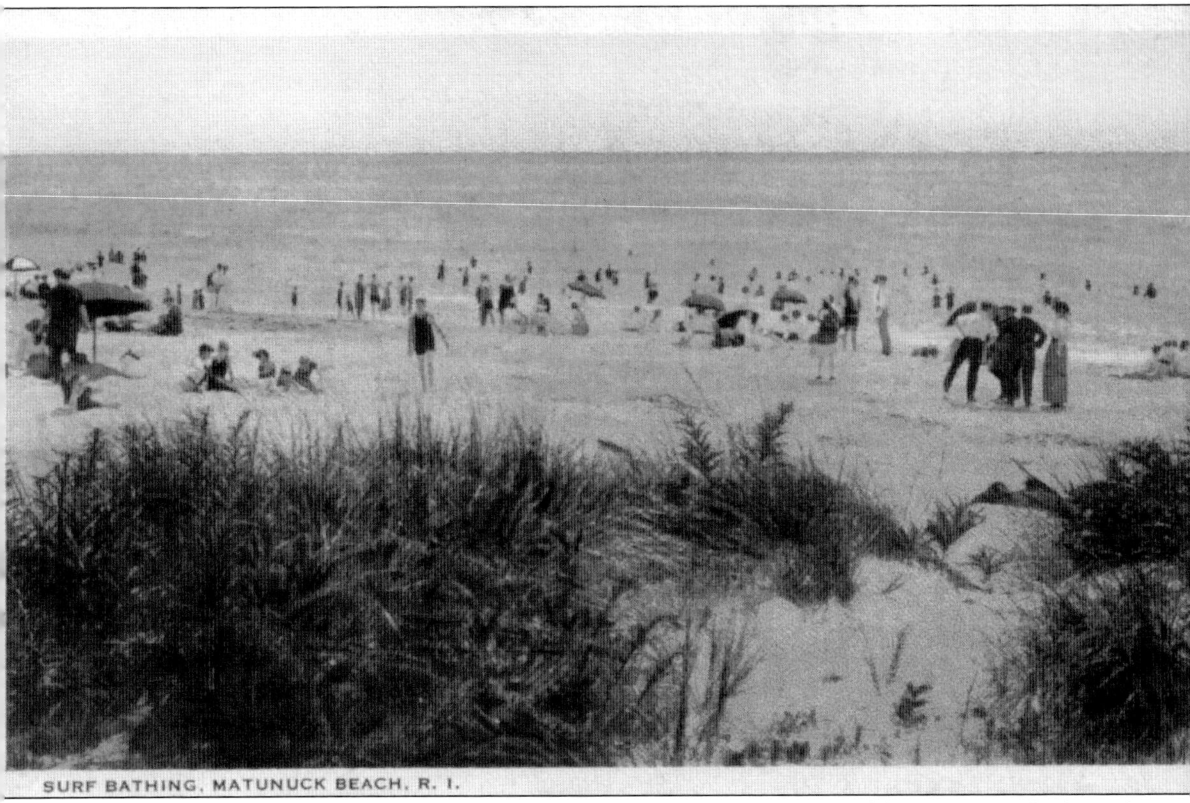

One of the earliest mentions of Matunuck Beach appeared on a map of the area in 1857. A guide book written in 1873 listed one of the first hotels at Matunuck. Two decades later, a "writer of pleasant places in Rhode Island" called Matunuck a popular place for Providence people, "more so, perhaps, than any other surf beach along the coast." (Courtesy of David Yale.)

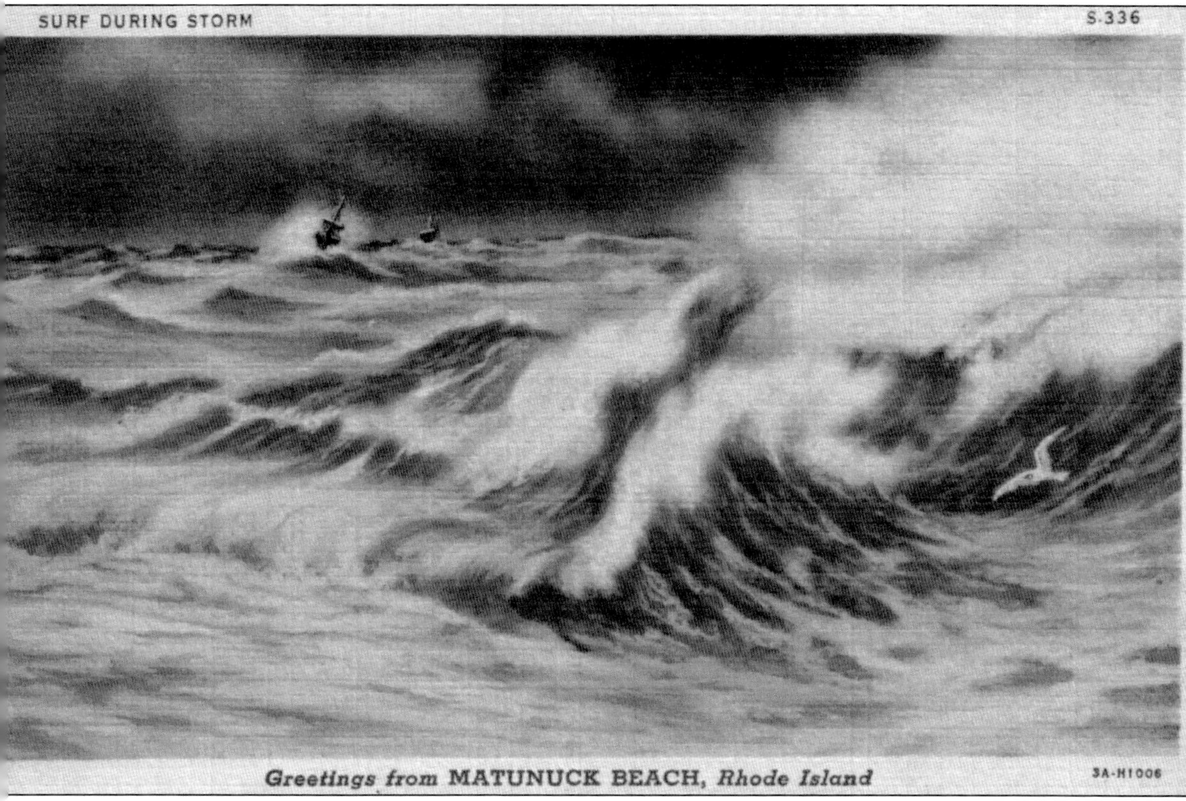

A raging gale strikes along the Matunuck coast. (Courtesy of David Yale.)

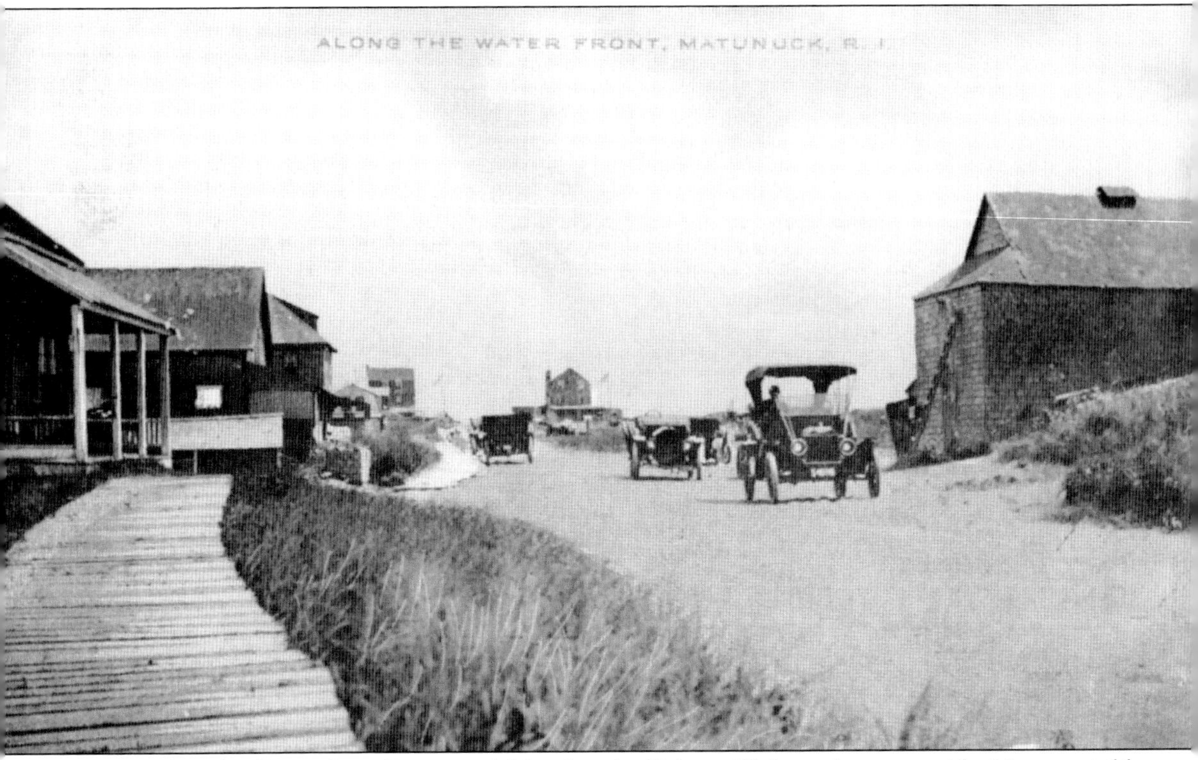

The boardwalk ran from Carpenter's Hotel to the Fishing Club on the ocean side. Houses visible on the left include Dr. Millette's, New Dawn, and the Marilla. The Buena Vista is straight ahead. (Courtesy of the Robert Beverly Hale Library.)

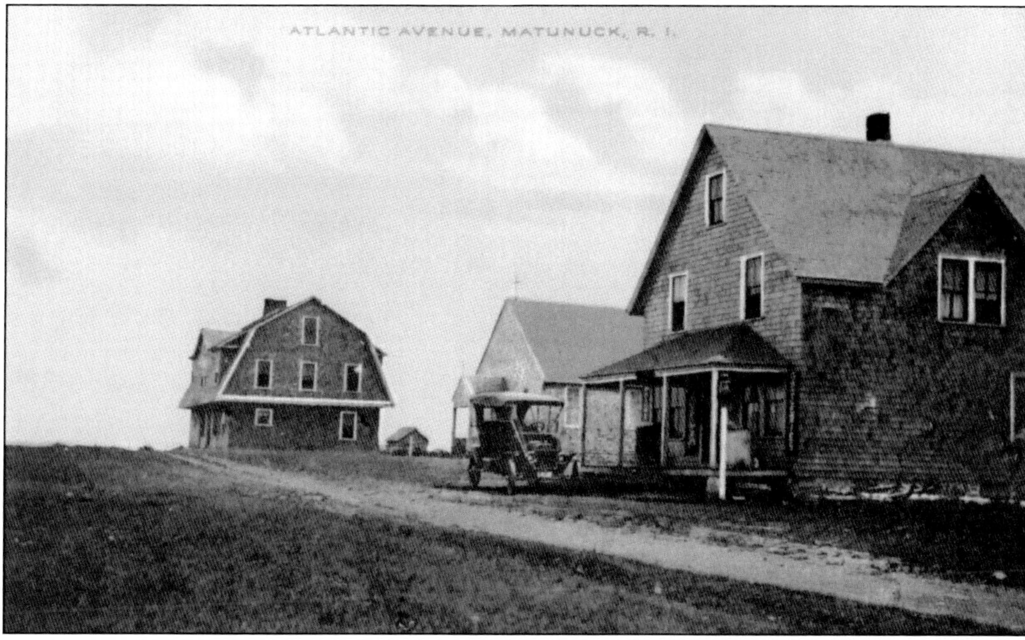

St. Romuald's Chapel is in between these two houses on Atlantic Avenue. (Courtesy of the Robert Beverly Hale Library.)

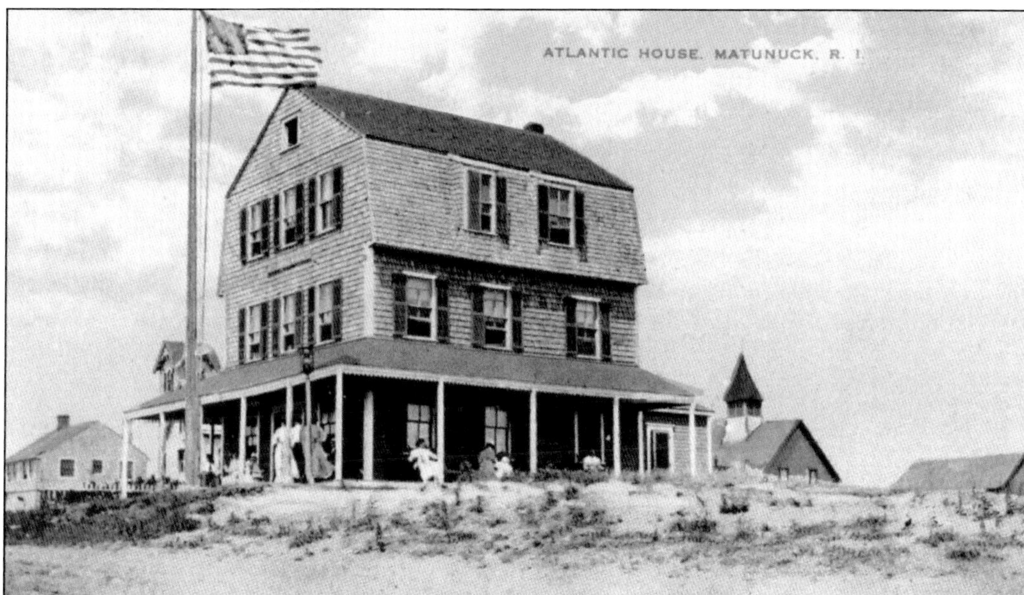

The earliest record of this property being inhabited and used for farming is 1787. The Narragansett Indians would come to trade and barter for goods with the local settlers. This house was built sometime between 1890 to 1895. At the time, the property was part of a large sheep farm known as Little Comfort Farms, according to Jim White. In 1901, the house and lots were purchased by Mary and Douglas Ahern from Francis Fleming for $900. The Aherns added two floors to the farmhouse, and turned it into the Matunuck Beach Club and Hotel. It later became the Atlantic House and was subsequently purchased by the Narragansett Salt Water Fishing Club in October 1954. The group remains there today. (Courtesy of the Robert Beverly Hale Library.)

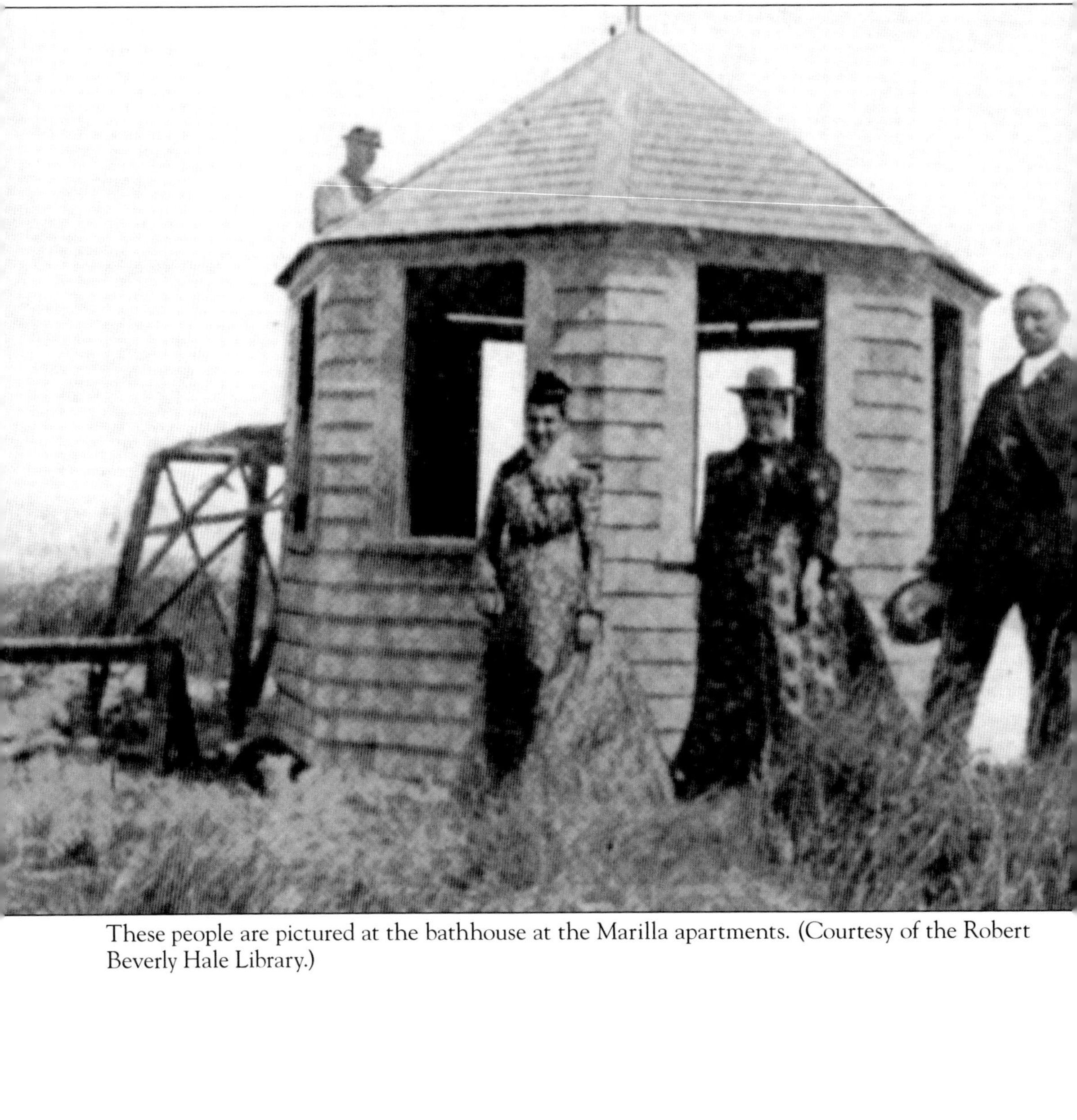

These people are pictured at the bathhouse at the Marilla apartments. (Courtesy of the Robert Beverly Hale Library.)

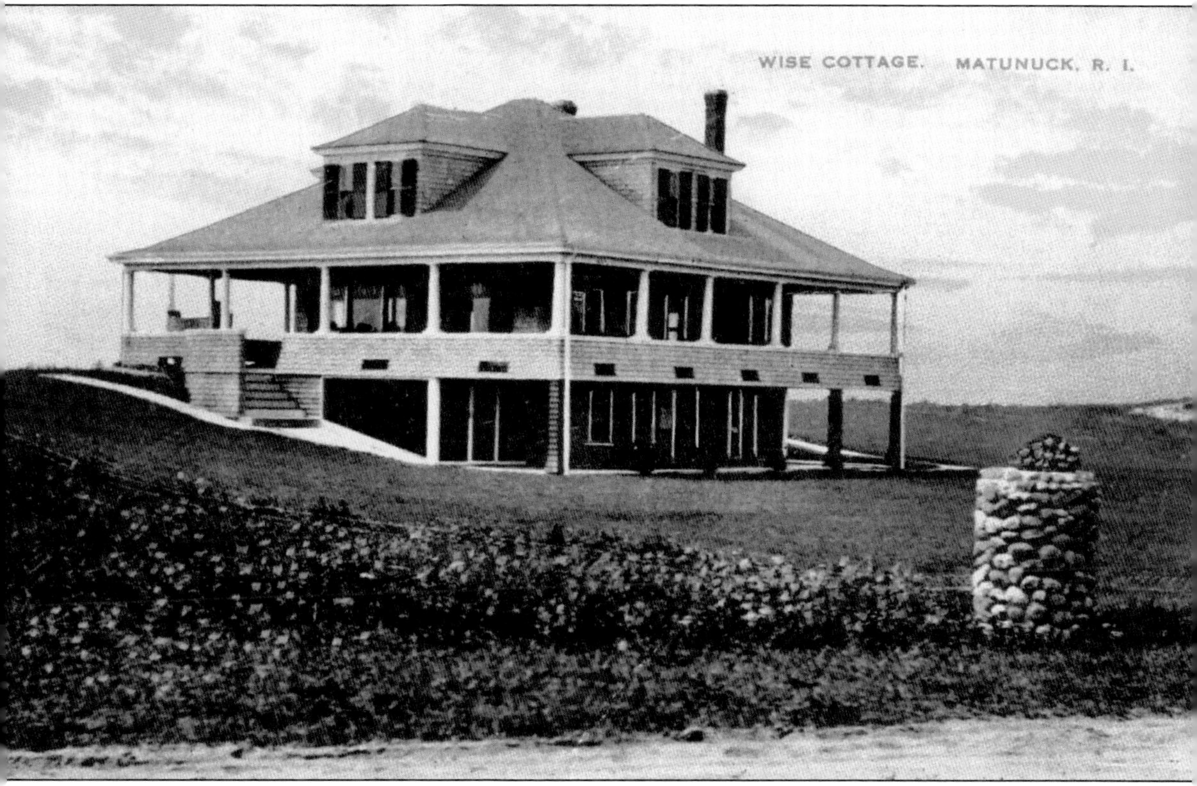

Information provided by the Robert Beverly Hale Library affirms that the Wise Cottage was located next to the Gould Cottage and later burned down. (Courtesy of the Robert Beverly Hale Library.)

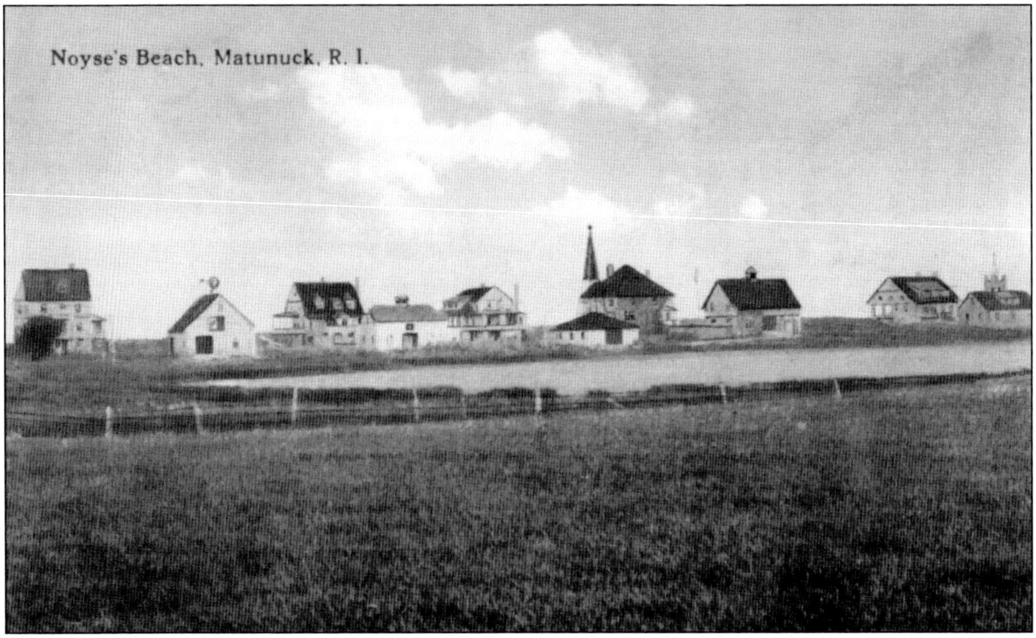

Although the spelling is slightly different, Noyse's Beach was thought to be named for Dr. Robert F. Noyes, a physician who purchased George Browning's beachfront property in 1894. Dr. Noyes and his wife, Katherine, built the Noyes-Bontecou House in 1895. (Courtesy of the Robert Beverly Hale Library.)

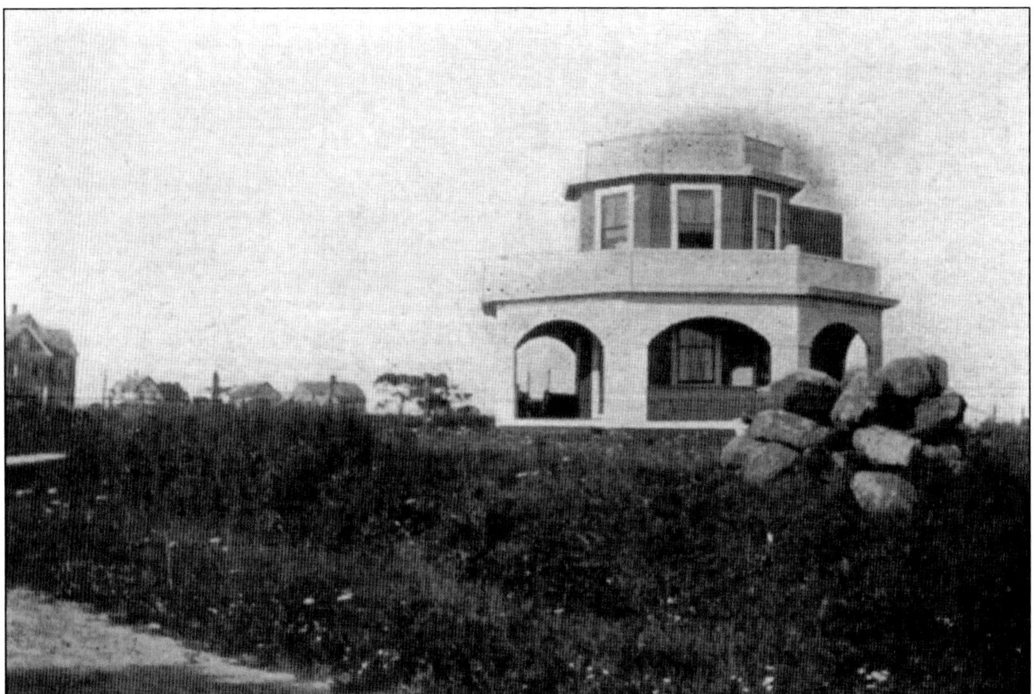

Barney's Pagoda was also known as the Allview Cottage. It was split in half and made into a house. The building belonged to the Marilla. (Courtesy of the Robert Beverly Hale Library.)

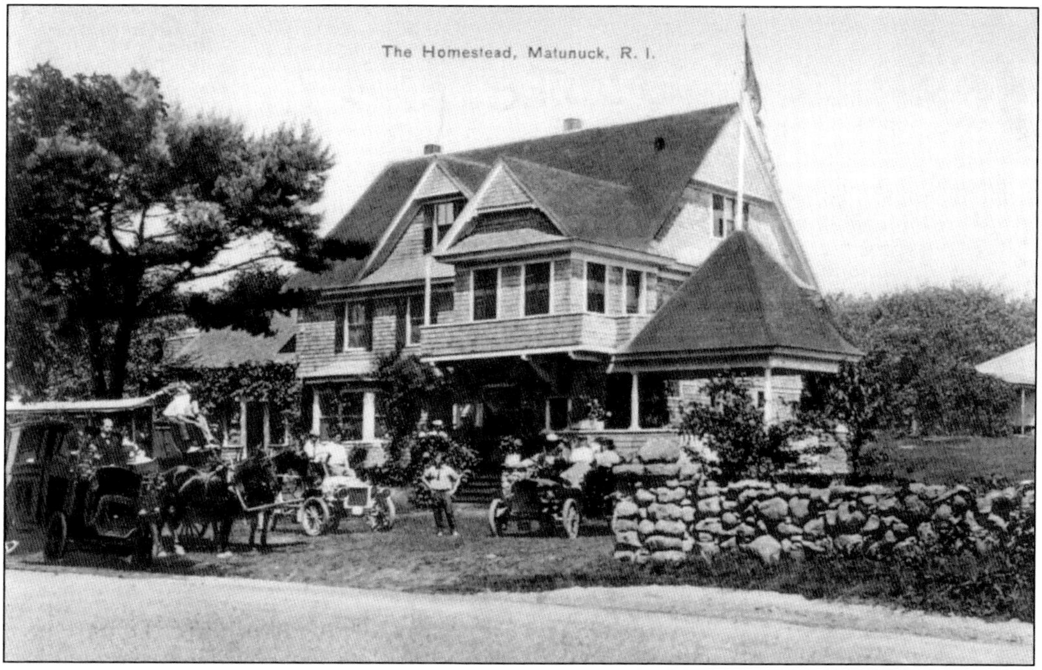

The Homestead was torn down to make way for construction of Route 1. It is shown in the early 1900s and was later known as Breezy Acres Tourist Home, according to local sources. (Courtesy of the Robert Beverly Hale Library.)

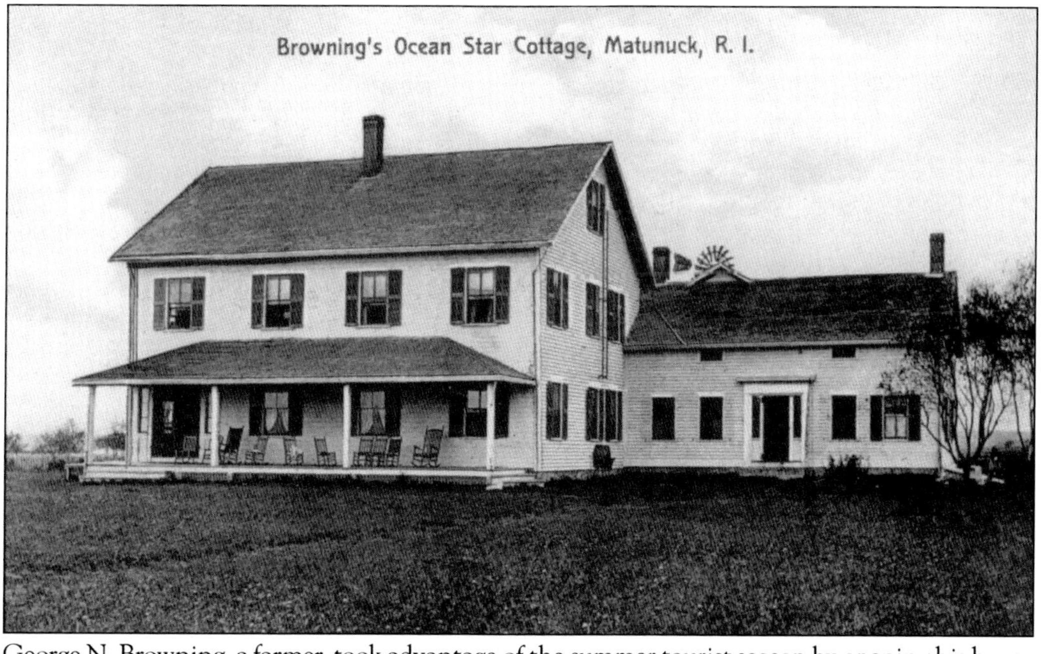

George N. Browning, a farmer, took advantage of the summer tourist season by opening his house to guests as the Ocean Star Cottage. The Browning barn would eventually become the home to the Theatre by the Sea in the 1930s. (Courtesy of the Robert Beverly Hale Library.)

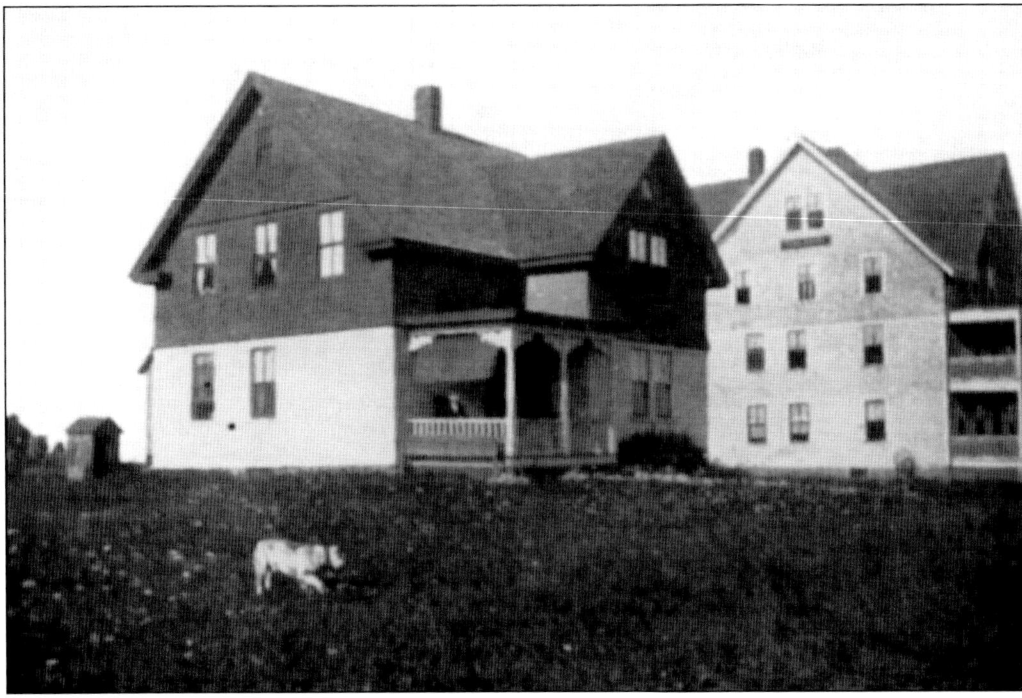

The Park House, shown in the background, is now an apartment building on Park Avenue. (Courtesy of the Robert Beverly Hale Library.)

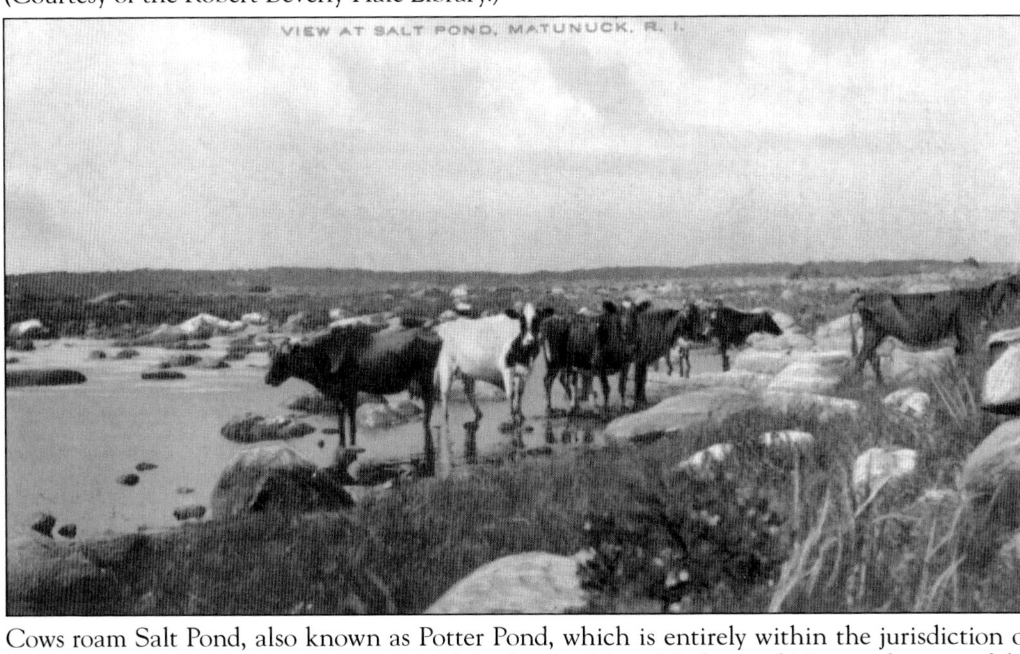

Cows roam Salt Pond, also known as Potter Pond, which is entirely within the jurisdiction of South Kingstown. With the exception of the villages of Snug Harbor and Matunuck, most of the land around Potter Pond and much of its shoreline is sparsely developed and maintains a sense of open space, according to the Salt Pond Watchers Summary Data Report 1985–1987. No rivers flow into Potter Pond. Instead, most of the freshwater flows in from underground springs seeping in around the edges of the pond. (Courtesy of David Yale.)

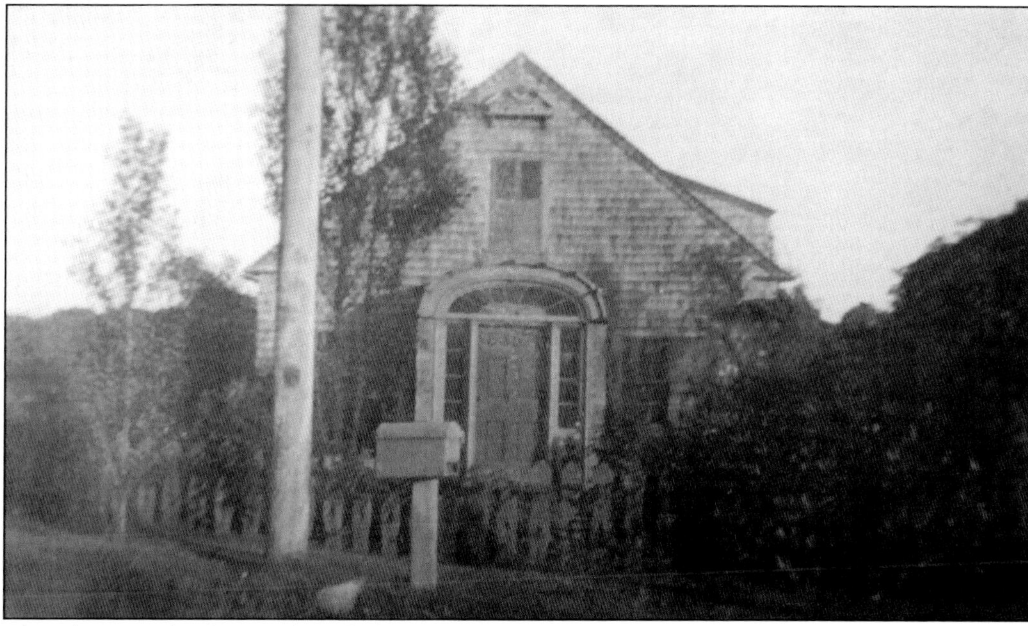

This photograph of an unidentified Matunuck home was in the photo album of Virginia Broome Yale. (Courtesy of David Yale.)

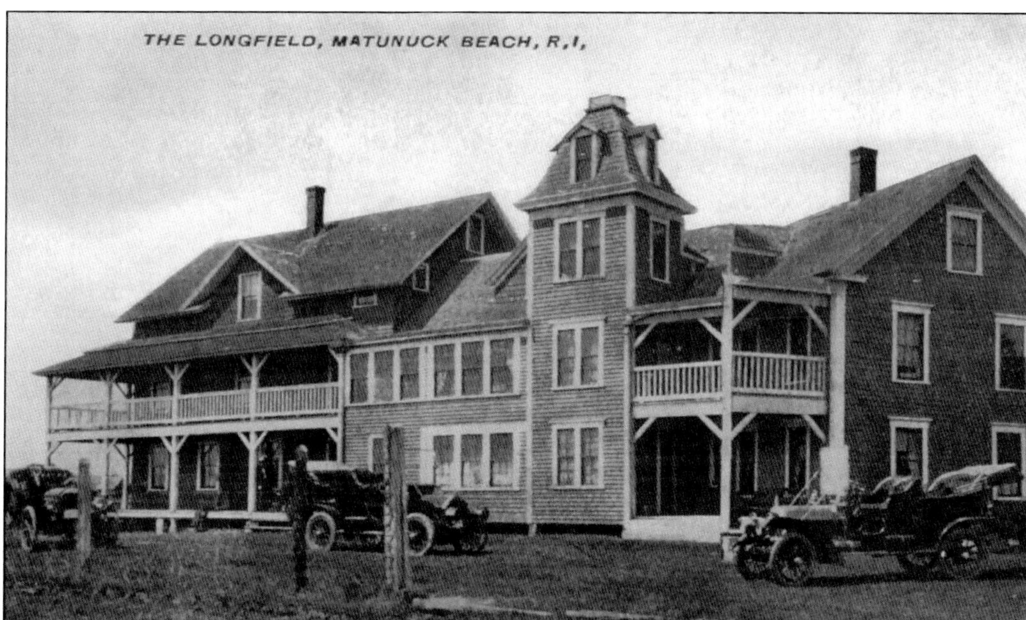

This postcard shows Longfield House, which was also listed as Longfellow House on a 1910s postcard. The hotel was located near Holden Road and Carpenter's Beach Meadow. It was abandoned but still standing in 1962. (Courtesy of Michael McKenna.)

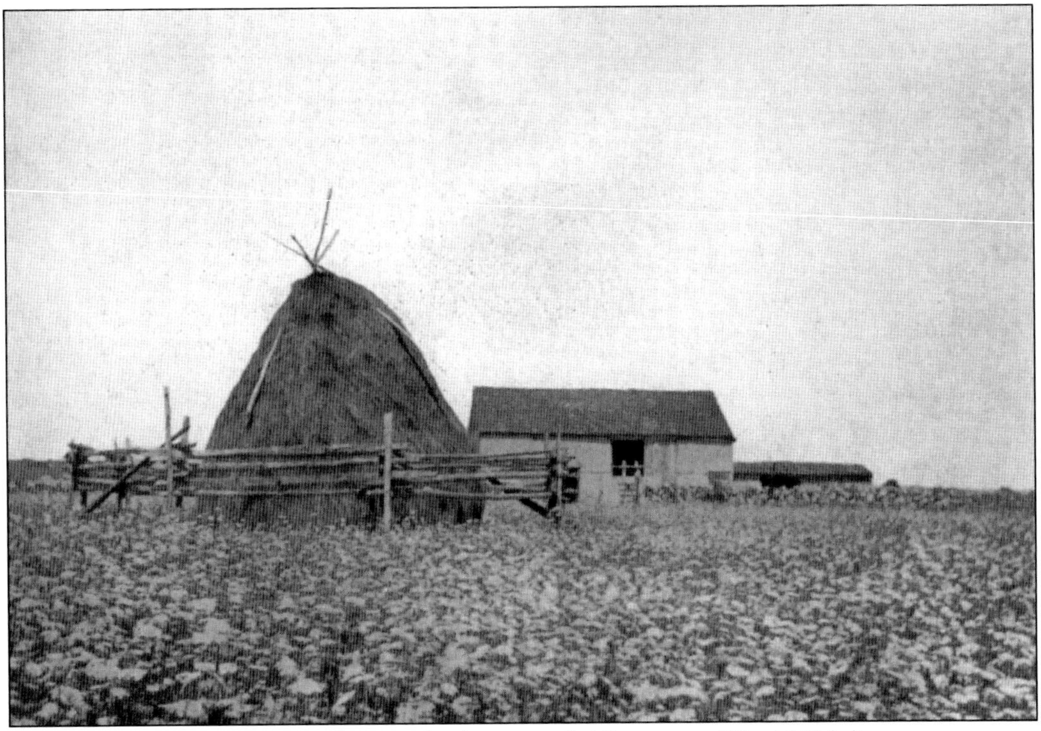

Matunuck's rural beauty is evident in this letter card. (Courtesy of David Yale.)

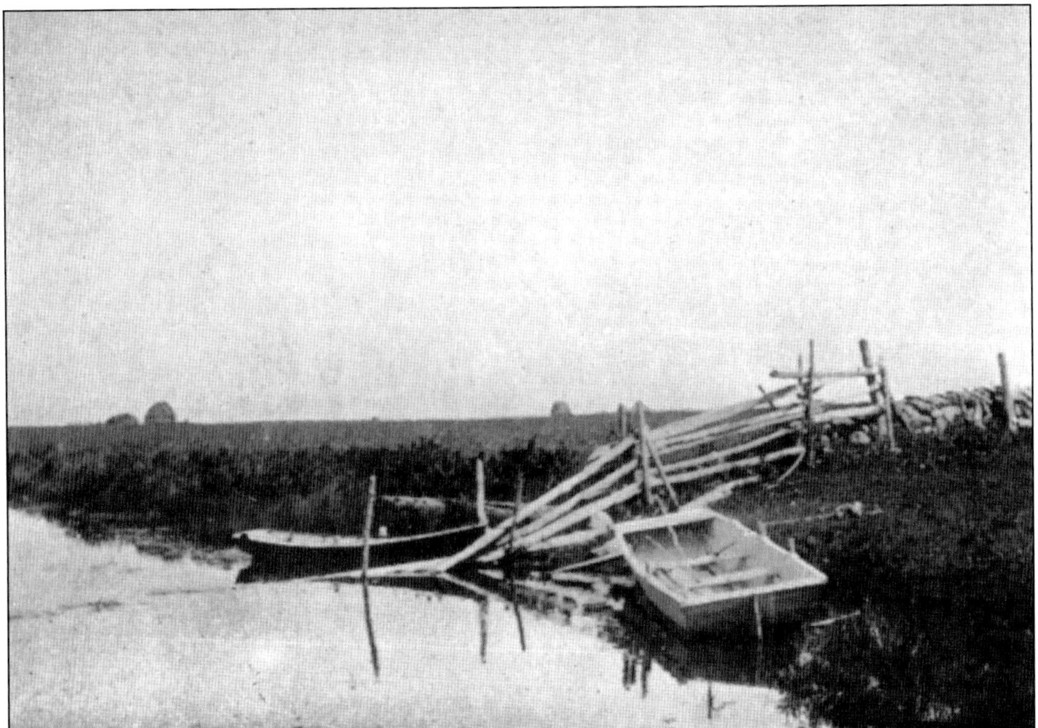

The Old Landing at Salt Pond is also known as Potter's Pond. (Courtesy of David Yale.)

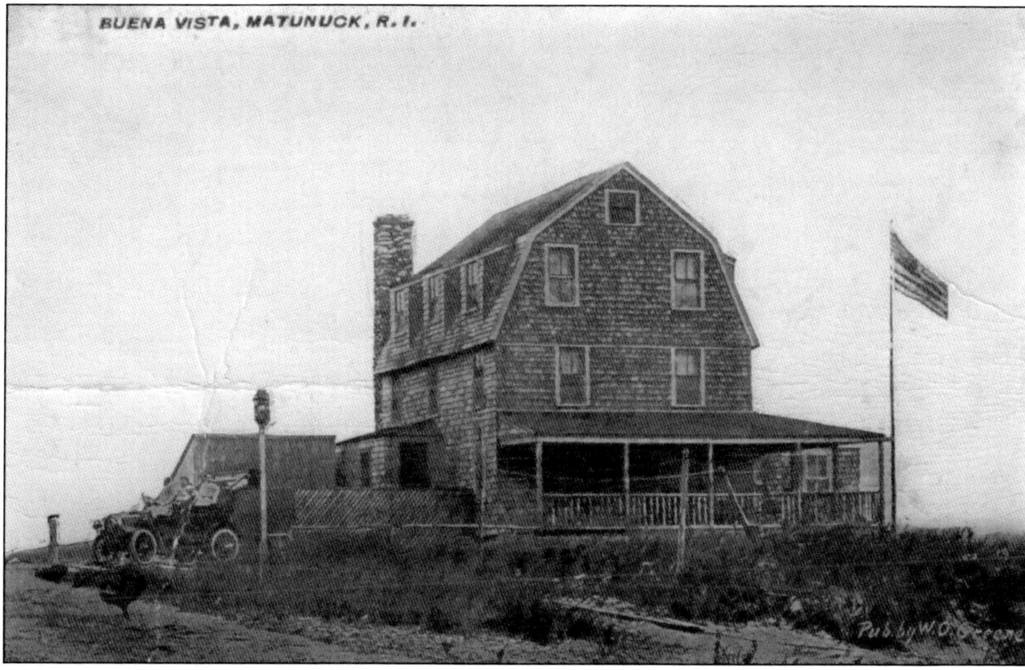

The Buena Vista, also known as the Buena Vista Cottage, was a very popular Matunuck hotel. Still, a *Journal Bulletin* reporter in the 1880s wrote that the life of Matunuck Beach's visitors was "a dull and stupid life when you compare it with the Pier folks, but it suits them and gives them rest and health." (Courtesy of David Yale.)

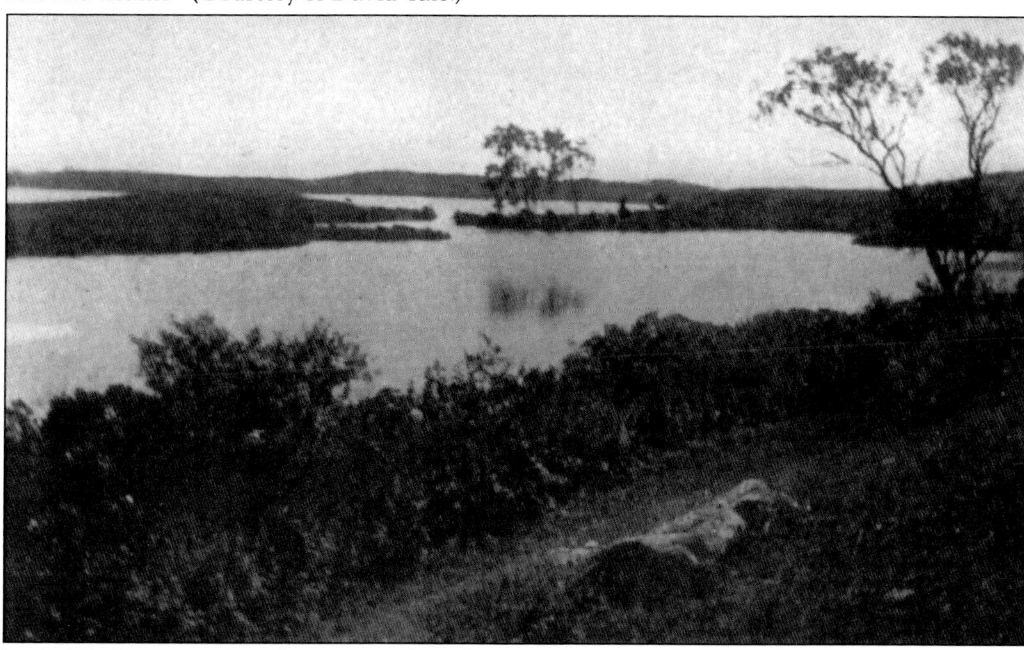

Little Wash is a pond in the Matunuck Hills area. It is part of a glacial landscape created at the end of the last ice age where the continental glacier stopped its advance and deposited a large mass of earth and rocks. This created a rough topography of knobby hills and hollows, which later became ponds. (Courtesy of David Yale.)